THE CRISIS IN SOCIOLOGY

Also by Raymond Boudon

THE PERVERSE EFFECTS OF SOCIAL ACTION

THE CRISIS IN SOCIOLOGY

Problems of Sociological Epistemology

Raymond Boudon

Translated by
Howard H. Davis

La Crise de la Sociologie
first published by Librairie Droz S.A. in Switzerland
Copyright 1971 Librairie Droz
English translation © The Macmillan Press Ltd 1980

First published 1980 by
THE MACMILLAN PRESS LTD
London and Basingstoke
Companies and representatives
throughout the world

Printed in Great Britain
by Redwood Burn Ltd
Trowbridge and Esher

British Library Cataloguing in Publication Data

Boudon, Raymond
    The crisis in sociology
    1. Sociology
    I. Title
    301   HM51

    ISBN 0–333–23528–2

Contents

Foreword

With the exception of the first, the articles that follow have appeared previously in a variety of journals. We would probably not have decided to publish them in their present form without the friendly encouragement of Giovanni Busino, Professor at the University of Lausanne.

Although they provide no more than an outline sketch of a solution, they do raise a number of general problems which in our view are important for the future of sociology. Perhaps a catalogue of these problems will prove useful.

The introductory chapter ('The Crisis in Sociology') seeks to show the implicit problematic upon which the following articles depend. The remainder of the book is divided into three sections: the sociology of sociology, epistemology and methodology. It goes without saying that the articles assembled under these headings do not pretend to exhaust the content of these disciplines. In most cases they have no aim other than to supply examples and simply specify research. One can see, however, that by their very orientation they suggest a definition of these disciplines, a definition which may be debatable but one which we believe also merits discussion.

Most of the articles brought together here were written with journals or scientific publications in mind. But we have also reproduced an article ('Sociology in the Year 2000' – chapter 2) originally written for a mass circulation monthly news magazine in a deliberately simplified and provocative style. Another ('Towards a positive epistemology' – chapter 6) was written for a journal on philosophy. Most of the chapters are reproduced in their original form, so that the reader will have no difficulty in identifying changes, repetitions and even contradictions between one article and the next. Only the titles have been altered, so as to underline the connection between each article and the implicit guiding problematic: namely, that the primary condition of sociology's progress and its very existence depend on the sociologist's critical attitude towards his own language. This is the attitude we have tried to illustrate here.

Finally, thanks are due to those editors who have kindly authorised the reproduction of the articles which follow.

1. Introduction: The Crisis in Sociology

The crisis in the universities and in society at large which has been affecting the countries of western Europe and North America for a number of years has been accompanied by a general questioning of sociology. Many sociologists have spoken and still speak publicly and privately of the 'crisis in sociology' and rightly so in our opinion.

However, it should be noted that this has little to do with the great crisis or social change which so affected sociology that it is impossible to write the history of the discipline without referring to the history of the societies in which it developed. Rather, as Georges Gurvitch has written "Sociology is a science which makes sudden jumps or at least fluctuates with every social crisis of any size."[1] Sociology, in other words, is more or less permanently characterised by a state of latent crisis.

One can look at this situation from two opposing 'ideal' points of view. The first admits that sociology's dependence on society, being constitutional, must be inescapable and therefore that it entails an irreducible epistemological specificity. In contrast, the second maintains that sociology's state of social dependency and latent crisis follows from the epistemological peculiarities and weaknesses which characterise it *hic et nunc*. In this case its susceptibility to external forces would not be constitutional but derivative, and therefore provisional. It follows from this second point of view, which we basically share, that one of the essential tasks facing contemporary sociology is what can be called an epistemological self-criticism. Of course, such a self-criticism will be without interest unless it can supply proof of its scientific effectiveness.

Almost beyond question these two ideal types we have just described occur in a more or less pure form in the sociological community. The notion of "critical sociology", which was first developed by the Frankfurt School and which has now become widespread in its various guises, is undeniably representative of the first. Here the cognitive values which govern the very idea of scientific research are actually sub-ordinated to ethical values which condemn as positivist the attempt to

1

gain objective knowledge of social phenomena.[2]

The second attitude is evidenced indirectly by the proliferation of epistemological and methodological writing in sociology in recent years. It must be said that this proliferation is associated with a trend towards autonomy and institutionalisation which sets sociology clearly apart from the other social sciences: methodology and epistemology not only form integral and distinct parts of the university curriculum: they also provide the subject matter of a growing number of specialised periodicals.[3]

We do not intend to make a sharp distinction between these two attitudes. For the moment we will simply remind the reader of a commonplace, something which demographers and economists as well as sociologists treat as a social fact. No one would deny that population phenomena, like phenomena which are relevant to the production and distribution of goods, are vitally important for society: are not overpopulation and the scarcity of resources among the most dramatic problems faced by the so-called "developing" countries?

But in spite of this, no one as far as we know proposes to replace the well-established tradition of economic or demographic research with a "critical" economics or demography. No one expects these disciplines to provide immediate solutions to the difficult problems with which they are concerned. There are other reasons for being convinced that the knowledge they provide is useful, if not indispensable. Certainly no one imagines they should limit themselves to an oppositional role.

Our hypothesis, therefore is that conceptions such as "critical sociology", far from revealing the essence of sociology or the supposed uniqueness of its object, reflect instead the epistemological uncertainties of the discipline. In the present state of sociology, these ideas represent the symptom rather than the cure. Otherwise, how would it be possible to explain the fact that some social phenomena, like those relating to population, language or the production and distribution of goods, have engendered stable research traditions which conform to the general norms of scientific induction, while others (those with which sociology deals) remain the objects of a different "genre" of knowledge, to use the language of Spinoza?

THE EPISTEMOLOGICAL UNCERTAINTIES OF SOCIOLOGY

Let us map out, in a schematic fashion, the epistemological features that are peculiar to current sociology.

The first of these special features has to do with the very object of sociology. The contrast with the majority of the other "social sciences" has been emphasised so often that it hardly needs to be repeated.

The object of economic science can be described without too much difficulty in terms of a small number of variables which have remained virtually unaltered since the work of the founding fathers, whether Ricardo, Alfred Marshall, Walras or Marx himself, until the present day. The same applies to demography, whose object can be summarised as the explanation of a small number of circumscribed phenomena: mortality, marriage rates, etc. The boundaries of a discipline such as psychology are rather more difficult to define and they are probably more flexible. But each of its branches, whether pathological psychology, the study of learning, or the psychology of child development, corresponds with an easily recognisable class of phenomena.

Sociology is quite a different case. In one way or another, all sociologists have tried to define the object of their study: which is another way of saying that no one has been successful yet. Raymond Aron writes "Sociology appears to be characterised by a constant search for itself. On one point and perhaps on only one, all sociologists are agreed: the difficulty of defining sociology." In fact, not a single definition proposed by any sociologist has won universal acceptance. Nobody at present would maintain, as Pareto once did, that sociology is the study of "non-logical action". As is well known, the Durkheimian notion of a class of supra-individual phenomena has led similarly to the almost unanimous rejection of the concept "conscience collective".

These two examples, which are both specific and yet representative, help to show incidentally that as often as not these attempts to define sociology are negative. For Pareto, "logical action" or, as we would say today, "rational behaviour" describes the economic sphere. It follows that if sociology is defined as the study of non-logical action, it must occupy the space left over by the economist. Similarly, with Durkheim, sociology is defined by what is left over from psychology.

In what follows we will try to show that the first of these difficulties is probably more apparent than real. In the light of these examples and others we shall give, we believe that it should be understood as the symptom of a temporary condition and not as an integral feature.

The second peculiarity of sociology is the way in which it wavers between description and explanation. Of course, the pioneers of sociology were keen to describe it as a nomothetic science. Unlike the essentially descriptive sciences of geography or history, its aim was, like psychology or linguistics, to discover laws. These are black and white distinctions of course whose value is completely relative to the extent to which historical analysis, even when it has to do with a specific event in space and time, must have recourse to explanatory schemas which involve general laws. The paradox is that, while history is less descriptive than some sociologists maintain, sociology itself is undoubtedly more descriptive than they would wish.[4] Many current sociological or sociopsychological investigations are more valuable for the information they provide about social situations here and now than for their contribution to the understanding of general social laws. Consider for example the studies done, mainly in the United States, on the recent university crises: they aimed to further the explanation of the crisis phenomenon as such. In actual fact, theirs is essentially a sociographic contribution to the understanding of the milieu in question.[5]

This observation leads to another: whereas the objects of linguistics, economics or demography are generally abstract constructs, as often as not those in sociology are directly encountered in reality. This point was emphasised recently by Pierre Bourdieu so we need give no more than a brief summary.[6]

One of the fundamental concepts of linguistics, the phoneme, is a typical example of the constructed object. There is general agreement among linguists that, properly speaking, the phonemes of a language do not exist but are actually primary units which are identified by complex mental constructions rather than by descriptive procedures. It is significant that the great scientific revolution inaugurated by Saussure occurred at the very time when linguists stopped thinking that their object was defined by natural languages in their concrete complexity and when they began to isolate a limited and abstract problem, that of identifying the smallest meaningful units of language. This problem was to give rise to what is currently one of the most advanced sections of modern linguistics: phonology. When the time came to tackle the problem of syntax, it was no longer seen in terms of description, as in traditional grammar, but in analytical terms: a question of constructing formal models which could generate the structural properties of natural languages.[7]

In economics, an analogous revolution occurred when economists isolated certain abstract problems and ceased to claim the concrete totality of economic phenomena as their object of study. It is instructive here to compare the image of economics still held by authors like Dupont de Nemours and especially Adam Smith with the one held by the modern pioneers like Say or Ricardo. In *An Inquiry into the Nature and Causes of the Wealth of Nations*, economic phenomena were still viewed in their concrete complexity. Now, economics is defined in terms of a number of abstract problems which prepare the ground for the formulation of analytical theories: the theory of rational decision-making, the theory of utility, of economic cycles, of equilibrium, etc.

In sociology, the situation is nothing like as clear-cut. From a logical point of view, some parts of the discipline can be equated with phonology or the theory of business cycles. This is particularly true of those parts which deal with social interaction or circulation. Thus a notion like social mobility is more a constructed object than a directly visible one. It can lead not only to descriptive research but to an analytical theory able to account for the causes and consequences of mobility as well as its variation or lack of variation in space and time. It is clear that a theory of this kind will only have a chance of success if the sociologist abandons the perspective of the "total social phenomenon" (in the mistaken sense of the term) in order to identify a small number of factors which he regards as pertinent to the explanation of mobility phenomena.[8]

The same goes for the notion of conflict. Of course it is possible to make this or that particular conflict the object of a descriptive study. But the very idea of conflict can help to generate analytical research as, for example, the theory of games or recent attempts to construct a theory of international relations illustrate.[9]

However, it is rare for sociological topics to be defined in this way. A flick through the pages of almost any textbook of sociology is enough to show this. Alongside sections which deal with "abstract" problems one almost inevitably finds chapters defined by concrete objects or "areas", as sociologists call them: sociology of the family, rural sociology, etc.

To avoid misunderstanding, we must emphasise straight away that we are not assuming that all sociological studies under these headings are necessarily descriptive. Neither, it must be said, do we mean to suggest that descriptive studies are valueless. All that we wish to point out is that the presence of these sub-divisions in sociology shows that this discipline, contrary to sociologists' own wishes, has an orientation which is often more descriptive than nomothetic. Drawing the analogy with linguistics, it could be said that contemporary sociological studies are far more reminiscent of the grammatical studies of Vaugelas than the modern theory of grammar. The fact that these studies are sometimes packed with figures and even complex mathematical models does little to alter this impression.

The consequences of this "sociographic" orientation in sociology are numerous, but there is one in particular which deserves attention. Namely, that even when sociology directs its attention towards constructed objects, it frequently remains preoccupied with description, which subsequently leads to theoretical research of a more speculative than analytical kind. The case of social mobility is significant in this respect. As we have said, it is not difficult to imagine sociological research in this area imitating the logical models of phonology or economic theory. For example, the theory of economic cycles, as it is called, consists of a number of models by which the economist seeks to understand business fluctuations in terms of the relationships governing a set of variables (investment, consumption, etc.). Of course it is possible to envisage studies of a descriptive nature in the same context. For instance, one could ask whether economic fluctuations are tending to diminish or whether they seem to be more important in one country than another. But no economist would be likely to limit himself to these aspects. In fact, he would almost certainly see these descriptive questions as a transitional stage to be left behind.

Turning now to the case of social mobility, it is easy to imagine a theory of mobility which, for example, would be an attempt to explain the intergenerational mobility tables which have gained such a reputation. It would put forward hypotheses about the relationships governing a small number of variables which are clearly responsible for the observed mobility (class differences in fertility, social inequalities prior to education, the relation between educational achievement and social rank, changes in the occupational structure, changes in the educational structure, etc.). In practice it is rare for the sociologists involved in collecting the data needed to construct mobility tables to have considered analysing the underlying processes. The tables are mostly used for purely descriptive purposes to provide answers to questions such as: is there more social mobility in one country than another? Is it tending to increase or decrease? This is why a large part of the methodological literature devoted to these problems deals with the construction of indices of mobility.[10] There are correspondingly few attempts to formalise the generative mechanisms of social mobility (or immobility).[11]

As we shall see later, this situation can be explained, to some extent at least, by the action of diffuse social factors. But these factors would probably be powerless to create a situation as different logically from that found in the neighbouring disciplines were current sociology not so completely characterised by a descriptive perspective.

If we now turn to the "theories" that relate to mobility and to social stratification in general, we find frequently that they are either constructions of a speculative kind or systems of tautological propositions. Thus, one fashionable theory which seeks to explain the persistence of social inequalities in spite of education, deduces this phenomenon from the axiom that an education system of whatever kind can only reproduce social distinctions which originate in the family. Another theory puts forward the principle that if social mobility is weaker than might be desired, this is because excessive rates of mobility generate dysfunctions which are incompatible with the harmonious organisation of the social system. Despite its apparent simplicity, the first theory is mistaken in supposing an intergenerational stability in the social system and a preestablished harmony between the school system and the social system, which the evidence fails to uphold; as for the second, if not tautological, then it has the drawback of being so general that it is impossible to see how it could be translated into analytical models open to verification.[12]

These two examples may have special features, but this typically follows from the relatively hazy epistemological status of the notion of "theory" in sociology. Our hypothesis is that this other "epistemological uncertainty" is partly attributable to the descriptive orientation of a large proportion of current sociological research.

One can find indirect support for this proposition in the fact that the earliest sociologists, like Pitirim Sorokin, did sketch the outlines of "theories" about the problems of social mobility which took the concept way beyond its normal usage.[13] Several chapters in *Social Mobility* actually contain systems of logically interrelated propositions expressed in such a way that they could be made the object, if not of verification in the strict sense, then at least of an attempt at verification. One therefore cannot help wondering why the interaction between theory and "empirical" data which can be seen here has apparently been interrupted in most recent studies of social mobility. These observations, which admittedly rest on a particular though not isolated example, pose an interesting general problem in the sociology of sociology which can now be formulated. The problem is that of the way in which sociologists' implicit epistemological and logical frameworks have been conditioned by "empirical" sociology's broad movement, especially since the Second World War, in the direction of microsociology.

Difficulty in defining its object, vacillation between sociographic description and sociological analysis, elasticity in the notion of theory: these are some of the epistemological characteristics of current sociology. Or, to put it another way, sociology is marked by a higher degree of polymorphism than the other sciences. Depending on the circumstances, the work of a sociologist may take the form of a brilliant essay, a survey which will be descriptive but from which he will try to remove the element of subjectivity by resorting to standardised procedures of data collection, an empirical theory which in principle is open to verification, or a speculative theory which gives rise to interesting interpretations and orientations without providing a basis for detailed research.

Let there be no misunderstanding. We are not concerned with introducing polemical distinctions nor apportioning blame. We simply wish to specify the epistemological differences which are so patently obvious when sociology is compared with the other social sciences, although these differences are not sharply defined. For example, we would willingly admit that an essay may approximate to a theory in the proper sense of the term, provided its author is sufficiently gifted. Alexis de Tocqueville is a significant case in point. In some cases, *Democracy* calls forth travelogues in the eighteenth century manner. In others, and especially in a book like *L'Ancien Régime*, it describes a theory of the relationship between forms of government and various aspects of the functioning of social systems.[14] It is also true that speculative systems in essay form may suggest interesting directions for research or may play a positive critical role. This proposition is not just applicable to sociology. Indeed, the inadequacies of the logical models which a discipline applies to certain problems are often signalled or first thrown into relief by a theory which is speculative in nature. Thus it could be that the "vitalist" critique which highlighted the inadequacies of mechanistic models in biology helped somewhat confusedly to prepare the way for the introduction of more sophisticated paradigms such as cybernetics. Once again, therefore, we would say that it is not a question of denying the importance of description in scientific matters. For instance, no one would disagree that the largely descriptive discipline of palaeontology played a crucial role in the genesis of evolutionary theory.

It is not the fact that it is both descriptive and nomothetic which sets sociology apart. Rather, it is because in the first place description and explanation are very often confused and secondly, the interaction between these two aspects of research is usually weak and certainly unsystematic. A final point which cannot fail to surprise the observer is that these peculiarities, instead of diminishing in importance, are probably more pronounced today than they were in the time of Durkheim or Sorokin.

In our view, neither is it the case that sociology's polymorphism, as we have called it, is a result simply of its faltering between sociography and sociology in the true sense. Institutional and epistemological factors also play their role. In fact the objects and the problems with which the sociologist has to deal sometimes place him in a position which is much less favourable than the economist's or the linguist's, for example. The situation of the linguist often approximates to the experimental conditions which are typical of certain natural sciences: for instance, he can create a formal model of grammar, test it against a sample of utterances, reformulate it if it seems to be at variance with certain utterances, apply the new model to further utterances, etc.[15] Meanwhile the economist can prevail upon national "observatories" to provide him with regular information about the variables that he uses to construct his models. As far as the sociologist is concerned, he rarely encounters an experimental situation in the strict sense. And it often happens that the information which he relies on or hopes to use is very inadequate in relation to the questions which he is asking. This is sometimes because of institutional constraints but it may even be for logical reasons.[16] We could give numerous examples to support this proposition, but one of which will suffice.

Suppose that we consider the question: does an extension of the period during which a cohort of pupils belongs to the same un-differentiated group help to enhance the democratisation of education? That is, does it undermine the processes which ensure that the social composition of the upper levels of education is an almost perfect reflection of the social composition of groups of the same age. A sociologist wanting to test this hypothesis should in principle make a spatial or temporal comparison. In both cases he will come up against a tricky logical problem: being sure that the *ceteris paribus* clause applies. In the first case, he will need to collect a considerable amount of international information. In the second, because his work takes place in real time, he will certainly have to wait too long for his results to be of interest to society. The problem would obviously be solved if there were a suitably finite and accessible system of social accounting for educational phenomena. No such system exists at present. The sociologist is therefore compelled to adopt a compromise solution and the risk that his results will be tarnished with subjectivity increases accordingly.

CRISIS OR CONTINUITY

In our view, the epistemological uncertainties which we have been attempting to describe are largely responsible for two important features of the discipline of sociology: firstly its peculiar susceptibility to the influence of what, to use a Parsonian qualifier, can be called *diffuse* social factors and secondly, the related fact that it frequently experiences change by way of crisis rather than continuity.

It is obvious that these diffuse factors (described thus in opposition to specific factors of an institutional kind) play an important part in the selection of those themes which periodically attract the attention of sociologists in various countries. Without what Philip Coombs calls the "world educational crisis", it is unlikely that the sociology of education would have experienced the vogue which it currently enjoys.[17] It is also apparent that the growth of studies in what is known as urban sociology is associated with the explosion of traditional cities. Similarly, the sociology of decision-making corresponds with the spread of the mechanisms of social planning. To take a final example, the fact that sociological studies of youth are associated with a much older tradition in the German-speaking countries than in most other European countries is clearly a consequence of the *Jugendbewegung* which emerged in Wilhelmine Germany at the end of the last century and persisted in a variety of forms until Hitler reached power.[18]

But diffuse social factors do not only act upon the dominant themes of sociology. They can also influence its orientations, its methods and, more generally, its language. The example of American sociology is significant in this respect. Until the end of the Second World War it was mainly oriented towards microsociological problems. This resulted from the fact that the first social problems which sociologists believed were capable of being solved were problems of interpersonal relationships within the firm or within the city. In contrast, the macrosociological tradition which was highly developed in Europe, did not really take hold in the United States until quite recently. One could hypothesise that this change is a result of the recent universalisation of interest in economic development among sociologists. With decolonisation, development became a problem for every country. For some, this is because they themselves are what is called "developing"; for the others it is because the game of international relations gives them "responsibilities" towards the first group. The United States occupies a key position in this game between the nations and this doubtless helped to awaken for the first time among American sociologists an interest in the classical problems of the European macrosociological tradition.[19]

This hypothesis in the sociology of sociology could be verified without great difficulty: one would almost certainly notice that the studies which have appeared recently in the United States with a macrosociological orientation are quite closely dependent on economic studies in the field of development. This is true, for example, of Amitai Etzioni's book *The Active Society* which evidently received a warm welcome from the American sociological community: the most important chapters of this book rely on the work of specialists in development such as Hirschman and Lindblom.[20]

In the European countries the situation is rather different. Of course the sociology of development tradition is well represented. But it is generally regarded as a "specialism" and does not seem to have incurred the same "band-wagon" effects as in the United States. This can possibly be explained by a strange reversal whereby "empirical" sociology in Europe has acquired a general orientation towards microsociological problems whilst in the United States there has developed a general trend towards research with both a quantitative and a macrosociological orientation.[21]

These examples show the way in which diffuse social factors can affect the general orientation of sociology and consequently its language. Another example which throws light on the same problem is that of the recent university crises. In practically every case, the "traditional" methods of sociology have been called into question at the same time. In particular, sociologists became aware of the inadequacy of question-naire surveys in situations of social crisis. In fact no logical artifice can bridge the gap between a survey of attitudes or behaviour, which is necessarily situated at the microsociological level, and explanation of a phenomenon of social crisis situated at a macrosociological level. This is why the method of historical, comparison, which has been rather neglected since Max Weber, is currently experiencing a revival of interest, witnessed for example in the recent work of Seymour M. Lipset or the rediscovery of S. N. Eisenstadt's book *From Generation to Generation*, which first appeared a decade earlier.[22]

The influence of diffuse social factors may therefore be felt at every level of sociological language from the most elevated, that of general orientations, to the lowest, that of techniques. In this connection we can again quote the example of social mobility studies. In Europe, they developed with particular rapidity and intensity in the "welfare states" of northern Europe, as can be seen in the by now classic works of Natalie Rogoff, Kaare Svalastoga, Gösta Carlsson or David Glass.[23] As this interest clearly followed more or less directly from the prevailing political ideology, the questions, as we have seen, dealt especially with the problem of comparing mobility rates in different countries and at different times. Perhaps certain sociologists secretly wished to reveal a growth in mobility rates over time. Perhaps they also wanted to demonstrate the superiority of the welfare states in this respect. The fact that these hopes were evidently somewhat misplaced is a fascinating sociological problem in itself. But it is not of direct interest to us here. What is important is that the very nature of the questions these sociologists were asking led them to use national surveys or even several surveys grouped within an international framework, when the majority of sociologists were doing local survey research.[24]

It can also happen that the pressure of diffuse social factors does not meet with the expected response because of the inertia of institutional factors. This situation is characterised by a system of "contradictory pressures" and poses equally interesting problems of epistemology and the sociology of sociology. The sociology of education, which we have already had occasion to refer to, is a significant case in point. A great many of those questions which are prompted by the action of diffuse social factors are macrosociological (for example: how does this or that system of schooling affect the democratisation of education?). On the other hand, it often happens that sociologists lack the institutional facilities to make observations at an appropriate scale in relation to the problem in hand. The result is that debate commonly takes a more rhetorical than scientific turn.

In summary, the hypothetical model which we are trying to present by way of these remarks is as follows:

(a) Sociology has a susceptibility, which for reasons of space we will call "natural", to diffuse social factors;
(b) The epistemological uncertainties of sociology tend to accentuate this natural susceptibility;
(c) The combined action of these first two causes means that change within this discipline tends to proceed by way of crises rather than via a linear process;
(d) It is all the more true that the operation of diffuse social factors makes itself felt at the level of form (language) as well as at the level of content (themes).

One particularly obvious symptom of the latent crisis which characterises sociology is the part played by epistemological and methodological disputes in this discipline. This part is undoubtedly much greater than in any other social science. In normal scientific practice, when a method, an orientation, a theory or a model have proved their scientific usefulness but are inadequate for handling a new problem, the response is to identify the reasons for the failure, to perfect the method and to generalise the model in question. Of course discontinuities may appear: one may be forced to replace the outdated instrument with another. Thus, when the mechanistic paradigm was discovered to be incapable of understanding finite systems, it was replaced by the more powerful cybernetic paradigm. Subsequently, certain authors, such as Ludwig von Bertalanffy, in introducing the notion of general systems theory, had to stress the need to develop paradigms capable of understanding systems with a capacity for learning as well as finite systems.[25] However, the important thing is that these discontinuities did not take the form of crises: nobody dreamt of denouncing the mechanistic paradigm as useless.

In sociology, on the other hand, one often finds that the critical phase is omitted and that the passage from one methodology to another, from one perspective to another, has the form of a rupture or crisis.

It is not hard to find examples of these phenomena of rupture. Earlier we recalled the effect of the recent university crises: they caused some sociologists to reject established survey techniques and orientate themselves towards historical comparison, for example. Others began to see participant observation as the panacea for the methodological difficulties they were encountering: whereas the standardised survey had the disadvantage of relying on pre-established frameworks, participant observation seemed to them to enable a direct grasp of reality. Clearly it does not require much thought to be convinced that this is illusory: how indeed could there be such a thing as direct observation of macrosociological phenomena? These responses are nonetheless interesting. It was predictable that the emergence of social crisis should cause sociologists to pose the general problem of the methodology of observation and the sociological explanation of crisis phenomena. If such an analysis had been carried out it would have led quite clearly to the conclusion that microsociological surveys, although insufficient in themselves, do provide useful information which has to be integrated within more general system of observation. Instead of which we witnessed a phenomenon of rupture.

Another interesting example is that of the movement backwards and forwards in sociology between microsociology and macrosociology. We noted above that the operation of diffuse or specific social factors was partly responsible for these oscillations, which are not necessarily synchronous between one country and another. The important feature is that microsociology and macrosociology appear to be antagonistic rather than complementary. Caricaturing slightly, one could say that these two aspects of contemporary sociology are not only distinguished by their logical level. They are also opposed to one another stylistically. Research in the one case is essentially concerned to develop highly detailed methods of observation, to introduce a rigorous language and to produce proofs. In the other case the dominant style is still that of the essay. However, it is difficult to see why macrosociological phenomena could not also become the object of a similar concern for rigour.

The application of statistical methods to sociology is a further highly revealing example of these phenomena of rupture. It is all the more interesting because statistics, by virtue of its interdisciplinary character, plays an essential role in the majority of social sciences, whether in economics, demography or sociology itself. But while a brief examination of the history of sociology since the end of the nineteenth century would show that statistical methods have regularly been the object of general condemnation this has not been the case in economics or demography for several decades at least. It is interesting to analyse in some detail this recurring process which seems to have developed each time according to a remarkably stable pattern.

Around 1930, Edwin Sutherland, in his *Principles of Criminology* set out to assess the methods and the findings of the sociology of crime.[26] When he came to examine statistical methods he issued a harsh verdict. In effect his claim was that these methods allow one to obtain interesting results from the descriptive point of view but they have nothing to say about the explanation of the phenomena which they help to display. He gave a very precise example in support of this thesis: statistics show that delinquent children are more likely to have parents who are alcoholic than non-delinquents. But they provide no means of comprehending this phenomenon. In fact, Sutherland continues, the observed correlation can be explained in several different ways among which statistics cannot choose: parental alcoholism can lead to a disintegration of moral norms in the child, a neglect of children's education, degradation of the father's image, etc. "Statistics" in short do not help one to decide among different "intervening variables" as we would call them today. In the end Sutherland concluded that, if one wishes to explain a fact of this kind, the "clinical" method is greatly to be preferred to the statistical method.

As every sociologist now knows, this alleged refutation of statistics actually results from the way in which Sutherland and many other authors with him assimilated the notion of statistics to one very particular type of statistical model, namely a model with a single equation consisting of only two variables. Within this category of model, the problem posed by Sutherland is actually insoluble. But it is possible to make use of more complex models which make a solution feasible. In fact the model which would answer Sutherland's question would be a multiple equation model with the form:

$$y = f(u)$$
$$u = g(x)$$

where y represents the variable "delinquency/non-deliquency of children", x the variable "alcoholism/non-alcoholism of parents" and u any intervening variables explicitly introduced by Sutherland himself as part of the hypothesis. In contrast, there is no solution to the problem within the framework of single equation models with the form

$$y = f(x)$$

to which Sutherland implicitly reduces the notion of "statistics".

Today one can still see "refutations" of the statistical method by sociologists. In every case, the process is identical in form to the one we have just described. It consists of:

(a) Assimilating statistics to a particular category of statistical model;
(b) Giving examples to show that this or that problem cannot be handled by statistics defined in this way;
(c) Proposing an alternative methodology, usually defined in a rather confused way and relying on intuition, which is said to guarantee a return to the concrete in place of the aberrations of statistics.

Lately, certain sociologists have for example noticed that a worker employed in a small-scale traditional enterprise and a worker belonging to a large-scale modern enterprise are in fact two distinct sociological entities and have concluded that it is hardly "relevant" to use a variable in sociology such as "socio-economic status". In such cases, they argue, it is necessary to construct a kind of super-variable which takes into account the work situation as well as occupation. Taking this argument a stage further they end up by denouncing the artificial character of the notion of the variable itself and rejecting statistical methods as a whole.

As in the case of Sutherland, it is clear that the argument actually refers to a particular category of statistical model. In this instance, statistics is implicitly assimilated to the category of *linear* models. We would not of course deny that linear models have a tendency to be misused because of their simplicity. But there is nothing to prevent the construction of non-linear models in which the relation between occupational classification and any dependent variable would be a function of the work context.

In principle it could be shown that the majority of recently published critiques of statistical method are the product of reductionist approaches, whether this reduction is to:

(a) Models of a linear form, when there exist non-linear models;
(b) "Atomistic" models (models which consist only of variables defined in individual terms), when it is possible to build "contextual" models (models which include both variables defined in individual terms and in terms of groups of individuals);
(c) Synchronic models (models in which all the variables are observed at the same point in time) when by means of an appropriate observational design it is possible to construct diachronic models.

It is certainly not our intention in these observations to show that statistical methods are always usable or always appropriate in sociology. There are cases where they cannot be used because of the simple fact that the universe of objects involved only contains a small number of elements. There are also cases where although usable these methods seem to be rather unsuitable. A genuine *critique* of statistical methods, in the Kantian sense of the term, would involve an inquiry into the forms which induction could take in those cases where this methodology is patently inapplicable. It would further involve precise analysis of the reasons why, even where it is applicable, it might be preferable to use another kind of method. Instead, as we have just shown, criticism often takes a negative turn: like the baby, statistics is thrown out with the bath water and has to make way for a new methodological creed which, because it relies more on a series of prohibitions than on positive rules, has a good chance of being rapidly overtaken by another "fad or foible".

WHAT IS TO BE DONE?

In our view it is not going too far to say that few sociologists have remained unaware of the problems that we have just described. As for the solutions which they have attempted to put forward, they can be conveniently divided into four categories. However, we should make it clear that these are to be regarded as ideal categories, to the extent that they are neither mutually exclusive nor is it likely that any one sociologist could be assigned to any single one of them.

For the purposes of this account, the first solution will be described as "active". Broadly speaking, it consists of an attempt to describe a general theoretical or conceptual framework with the aim of providing a focus, or if you prefer, a point of convergence for the varieties of sociological work. In combination with other solutions, this one is found among the classical authors, Durkheim or Pareto for instance. But it can also be found among a number of contemporary sociologists. For example, functionalism as defined by Robert Merton is an attempt to provide sociology with what could be called a general paradigm, that is to say a formal framework which describes the vocabulary and the syntax of sociology independently of any particular content.[27] Yet it is interesting to find that in spite of his efforts and the remarkable clarity of his arguments, Merton has failed to convince his colleagues that functionalism is only a formal paradigm and nothing more. Instead, many see in it a general theory of society and place it alongside others – Marxism for example. One could also say that the fundamental inspiration behind the work of Talcott Parsons is the wish to provide a general framework for sociology. Depending on the stages of his career, Parsons saw this framework either in terms of a conceptual system (the famous "pattern–variables"), in terms of a formal paradigm related to but distinct from that of Merton (structural–functionalism) or in terms of what can be called a theoretical paradigm, notably in his recent attempts to present a theory of the distribution and circulation of power analogous to the economic theory of the distribution and circulation of goods.[28] In this connection it is interesting to note that in one of his first presentations of structural–functionalism, Parsons attributed it with a role in sociology analogous to that which differential calculus seems to have had in the development of economic theory.[29] This statement clearly shows that Parsons conceived of structural–functionalism as a language rather than a theory. However, whilst nobody has ever identified a particular economic theory in differential calculus, Parsons has had no more success than Merton in convincing people of the formal character of structural–functionalism. Many sociologists continue to identify it with a particular sociological theory, whilst the harshest critics see nothing more than an abstract representation of a single society: American society. Of course our purpose here is not to choose between these different interpretations, but simply to stress that this ambiguity is probably a sign that the Parsonian paradigm has still some way to go before reaching its objective.

Today, the widespread interest in structuralism, cybernetics or general systems theory shown by a large number of sociologists is further witness to the impulse to unify sociology with the help of a general paradigm.[30]

It is undeniable that these general paradigms have played and still play a fundamental role in the development of sociology. In supplying a logical framework which serves as a guide to observation, they can have a heuristic function. They also have a theoretical function to the extent that they enable apparently unconnected facts to be reconciled within a single explanatory system. They can also have a methodological function and define new methods of proof to improve on the more traditional procedures like statistical induction.[31] Of course it is impossible for us to enter here upon a full discussion of the logical functions of these paradigms.

But there is a fact which one cannot escape noticing: not one of these paradigms has so far succeeded in asserting itself with sufficiently convincing evidence to initiate an independent research tradition. *A fortiori* not one has risen to a commanding position in sociology. On this point, the comparison with neighbouring disciplines such as linguistics or economics is once again enlightening. In the pre-modern stage in their development, these two disciplines covered very large fields. Like current sociology, they were characterised by a high degree of polymorphism. In this modern form, they are dominated by a small number of logical paradigms which are evidently rich enough to support an apparently unlimited quantity of research. One could say for example that the greater part of modern linguistics is dominated by research with hypothetico–deductive models which make it possible to reproduce the structural properties of natural languages. These models certainly have different forms according to whether the linguist is tackling the simpler or more complex levels of linguistic phenomena: formalisation is more developed in the realm of syntax than in that of stylistics or semantics. But whatever the different modalities, one always find the fundamental paradigm to which linguists themselves have given a name: structuralism, which in this case has a clearly defined meaning. In economics, the paradigm of *homo oeconomicus*, though very old and with origins that can be traced back at least as far as philosophical utilitarianism, dominates a large part of economic theory.

These observations pose a complex question which cannot be fully answered in the present context. We can do little more than provide the elements needed in a reflection upon it without attempting to answer it explicitly. The question is this: why is it that sociology, as opposed to other disciplines, cannot accept a small number of paradigms sufficiently rich for them to be used as a basis for organising its activities?

Why did linguistics and economics move rather suddenly from a state of marked polymorphism to a tradition of linear research? Perhaps this situation is partly a result of the fact that the paradigm used by Auguste Comte, the official founder of sociology, that of the study of historical laws, was never very likely to become an object of general assent. But as it happens, Comte was writing at a time when industrialisation was making social problems particularly visible and was providing the impetus for a science of society orientated towards the problem of global social changes. It has also taken a while to rediscover that Montesquieu, in his comparative analysis of political regimes, Condorcet, in his theory of collective decision-making, or Quételet, in his social physics, proposed equally useful paradigms for a science of society.[32]

But perhaps sociology's polymorphism can also be explained by the fact that the social sciences have had to include a residual and therefore anomalous discipline, especially since some of them began to specialise and abandon part of their original sphere of activity.

This hypothesis leads us directly to the second solution to the epistemological problems of sociology which sociologists have put forward. We will call it the "resigned" solution. It is essentially the view which admits that sociology's fragmentated state is a fact to be faced and explained rather than denied. This position is represented by a number of authors and especially by those who see sociology as a protean science whose content changes every time one of its parts attains autonomy or whenever a neighbouring discipline modifies its sphere of activity.

Helmul Schelsky provides one example of this kind of response.[33] According to him, the polymorphism of sociology should be attributed to the fact that all the social sciences, with the exception of sociology, have considerably reduced their sphere of activity and have organised themselves, if we may be allowed to use our own terminology for the moment, around a small number of paradigms. This is the case for example with economics, whose current content, as we have seen, is much more restricted than that ascribed to it by seventeenth and eighteenth century authors. The same is true of course with linguistics which, being dominated by the structuralist paradigm, is far more concerned with the analysis of the structure of languages than, for example, with the relationships between language and society. So it is not by chance that the reduction of linguistics' sphere of activity has given birth to new disciplines such as psycholinguistics and sociologuistics. As far as philosophy is concerned, it has progressively specialised in three areas, ontology, logic and the theory of knowledge, and lastly the history of philosophy. So there is a need for the problems left unsolved both by the philosophical tradition and disciplines like linguistics or economics in their original form to be taken up by an alternative discipline.

Although we have arrived there by a different route, this conclusion is similar to Jean Baechler's in the epistemological reflections which open his book on *Les phénomènes révolutionnaires*.[34] For Baechler, the niche traditionally occupied by the social sciences is destined to disappear. It is the product of contingencies and lacks logical justification: "meaning any discipline in the whole range of the social sciences which is based on the question of how an object can be separated out in the infinite flux of human phenomena . . . . There already exist sciences of economics, population, war and international relations, politics, myth, language, etc. but the list is not complete and probably never will be."[35] This latter phrase shows quite clearly that, for Baechler, while linguistics, economics or demography are autonomous social sciences one can expect to see what is traditionally called sociology break down into a group of disciplines each based on a properly defined question. Sociology, then, for Baechler as for Schelsky, is a residual and hence composite science.

Many people will be deeply irritated by such analyses. It is true that they place the sociologist in a singularly uncomfortable position but should their validity be denied for all that? It is impossible in our view to remain unaffected by an argument like Schelsky's. Nevertheless it only provides an incomplete solution to the question we raised earlier. If we assume that sociology is indeed the receptacle for problems left unsolved by other disciplines, the question is why some of these problems, unlike those in linguistics and economics, fail to re-group around a small number of paradigms, thus forming disciplines with distinct contours and a linear tradition of research. Our response to this question, which is in no way incompatible – quite the contrary – with the preceding analyses, would be that some elements of sociology, like linguistics or economics, have or could have this potential for autonomisation within a group of guiding paradigms. However, in many cases this potential is reduced by the epistemological uncertainties which characterise sociology as a whole. A typical example of this is the so-called "sociology of organisations". This certainly appears to be a case in which research is dominated by a group of guiding paradigms which are widely accepted by students of organisation and rich enough to support a research tradition ensured of a certain longevity. At the present time it could be said that the work of authors such as Simon or Crozier is located within a coherent intellectual framework. Nevertheless, by the very fact that these sociologists of organisation are perceived and perceive themselves as sociologists in a more general sense, they are unable to resist the temptation to extrapolate and to search for a general image of society in their models of organisation.[36]

There is another "part" of sociology which could lay claim to the same autonomy, namely the part which deals with the distribution and the circulation of individuals between levels in the social hierarchy or, in traditional language the sociology of stratification and social mobility.[37] However, we saw in the first part of this chapter that a series of factors (both of a "diffuse" and institutional as well as an epistemological kind) help give studies in this field either a descriptive or a speculative cast. To which it must be added that the heritage of nineteenth century sociology which is still widely present in modern sociology leads many to identify mobility and stratification as the major sociological problem around which all the others revolve. So that the idea of isolating mobility phenomena in the way economics "isolates" economic cycles, ignoring their concrete historical and social context, meets with strong resistance.

Comparable symptoms of autonomisation are to be found in another area of sociology in what could be called the theory of social interaction, to use a general term. Clausewitz's studies of war, the sociology of international relations, game theory and the theory of interpersonal relations within small groups all point to the possibility of a general theory of relationships of competition, conflict and co-operation.

To avoid being carried away in a speculative direction we will end this list here, stressing our view that Schelsky's resigned position has significant critical merits: by underlining the artificial character of the unity which has traditionally been called sociology, it invites the sociologist to study the genuine logical unities which comprise his discipline and to disentangle them from the deceptive taxonomies which are used to define its scope.

We should further point out that the "active" and the "resigned" position are in no way contradictory, as can be seen from the foregoing observations. It is not difficult to think of authors who occupy the middle ground, as it were, between the two. Lazarsfeld, for example, is one who both recognises sociology's residual character and who in his theoretical and empirical studies emphasises his concern to develop a science of action transcending the traditional classifications of the social sciences.[38]

The third solution to the epistemological problems encountered in sociology could be called "dogmatic". It consists in an attempt to create an apparent unity in sociology by giving preference to one perspective or to one particular set of problems. In its crudest form it involves an appeal to sociology to study those problems which are made directly visible, *hic et nunc* by the influence of diffuse social factors. In a more elaborated version, it gives priority to certain phenomena or problems which, although they are not coterminous with sociology and are not especially likely to develop into guiding paradigms, do however have a unity of content (for example sociology as a science of cultural phenomena). Clearly this dogmatic solution is not of great interest. We refer to it here simply because it is quite common and therefore symptomatic and because the uncertainty about sociology which every sociologist experiences means that there is probably not one who escapes being more or less "dogmatic" in this sense.

The fourth solution to what we have termed sociology's latent crisis can be called the "critical" one. While it is largely our own, we must repeat that we do not underestimate the importance of the first two solutions with which it is quite compatible. It rests on the belief, shared by numerous authors, that a strategy for alleviating the crisis of sociology must involve a critical analysis of sociological language. One hardly needs to add that this critique must be positive and not normative. The main question therefore is not simply to denounce the flexibility of the concept of "theory" in sociology but rather to show first of all that the concept is applied differently in the majority of the other social sciences, and then to look into the reasons for this state of affairs. To take another example: one very often finds that sociologists put forward macrosociological propositions on the basis of microsociological observations which do not directly justify them. This is the case with those "theories" of social mobility which for example rely on surveys into the attitudes, choices, or behaviour of samples of students; it is also true of "theories" of stratification which rely on observations at the level of a particular collectivity or "community". Again, it is not so much a question of judging, but of realising this fact and analysing its meaning.

TOWARDS A CRITIQUE OF SOCIOLOGICAL INDUCTION

Parsons, as we recalled earlier, made the attempt at one point in his career to provide sociologists with an instrument analogous to the differential calculus which was used by the pioneers of modern economics and especially by those of the Lausanne School. In our opinion such a proposition contains both a profound intuitive insight and naivety. The naivety consists in the belief that the success of economics derives from the fact that this discipline had the good fortune to work with variables of the same kind as physics and that it was thus been able to use the instrumentation for its own ends. The profound intuition lies in the implicit affirmation that a nomothetic science cannot exist without a formal language. But what is a formal language if it is not a language whose assumptions have been made explicit, whose syntactic rules are perfectly understood and over which the speaker therefore by definition has complete control. Mathematics is obviously the typical example of such a language: it is impossible to move in this language from proposition p to proposition q, even if this is a long way from the first, without ensuring that the intermediate stages have been traversed correctly. By definition, if a mathematician has shown that q can be deduced from p, the whole mathematical community (without exception) and hence the wider public will be convinced without further discussion.

Although the language of mathematics has been applied with success to several sociological problems, it seems unreasonable at the present time to hope for a sociology as highly mathematised as physics or even economics. Even if this dream were one day to be realised as it was in economics, it would probably have to be by means of a restructuring and a considerable reduction in the area currently covered by sociology.

Thus we are confronted again with Parsons's problem. To emphasise its importance we will venture a rather free paraphrase: how can a sociologist ensure that when he puts forward a proposition or a theory, this is expressed in a language such that it has a chance of being accepted not only by those whose opinions it confirms, but by everybody?

Our reason for putting this serious question in a humorous way is in order to highlight the part which can be played by what can be called a "critique of sociological induction" in the development of sociology. In the absence of a formal language such a critique can give the sociologist better control of his language, make him aware of his assumptions, and consequently reduce sociology's susceptibility to external factors.

These reflections should be sufficient to illustrate what we have in mind when talking of a "critique of sociological induction". Roughly speaking, this critique incorporates a whole range of problems which are relevant to three disciplines: the sociology of sociology, epistemology and methodology.

(a) Sociology of Sociology

In the first part of this chapter we considered the evidence that the progress of sociology is subject to the influence of social factors which may be either diffuse or specific (institutional factors for instance). But we also drew attention to the important but probably less often acknowledged idea that these factors can affect the form or, as we would prefer to say, the language of sociology as well as its content. We must therefore try to establish the nature of these factors, firstly because to take cognizance of external influences on the language of sociology can only have positive results, and secondly because it is a prerequisite for any corrective action.

We have already mentioned some of these problems of the sociology of sociology and in any case the nature of these problems does not have to be described at length. Another brief example will suffice here. It is taken from an important institutional phase in this sociology of sociology and it has to do with the consequences of the establishment of sociology as an institution.

Other authors have shown that this factor played an important part in the development of European sociology in the nineteenth century.[39] Although at this time many sociologists perceived the possibility of making sociology a science based on the controlled observation of social reality, that is an experimental science in the broadest sense of the term, this type of research was not acknowledged or institutionalised until after the Second World War. Throughout the whole of the nineteenth century, investigations were carried out in one context or another. Some were undertaken by administrators, others were the outcome of sociologists' own initiatives. Certain authors, like Gabriel Tarde, even dreamt of a system of social accounting analogous to the observational systems already at the disposal of economists and demographers. He actually went so far as to anticipate, in a highly detailed manner, certain of the techniques which were to be developed later in survey research.[40] Even a sociologist like Max Weber was largely responsible for the preparation and analysis of several important surveys. However, the majority of sociologists were indifferent to survey technique. This approach had no place in traditional sociology which continued to preserve its absolute pre-eminence. It remained marginal and there were no visible attempts to inititutionalise its practice. After the First World War, when studies by certain sociologists – like Theodor Geiger for example – revealed an interest in what later came to be called "empirical research", they were the exception.

This phenomenon can be explained in different ways. But it is clear that part of the explanation lies in the essentially university-based development of sociology (in contrast with that of economics or demography) and the university role structure which was typical of all the European universities until the Second World War: the division of labour which is implied in the execution of a survey was particularly incompatible with the fragmentation implied by the notion of the professorial chair.

Today, university structures have undergone a fundamental re-shaping. However, it is still appropriate to ask, this time for the purposes of prediction rather than retrospective explanation, to what extent establishment of sociology as an institution affects its language. As we have said, one cannot help noticing that the questions which society asks of contemporary sociologists are often macrosociological. On the other hand, no one can deny the existence or the vitality of the macrosociological tradition especially in Europe. But at the same time a great proportion of the "empirical" work done today is still microsociological. The previously-mentioned case of the sociology of education is significant in this respect: for example, one can find macrosociological studies which have to do with the problem of the relation between economic development and schooling, or the problem of the relation between educational structures, levels of schooling and the degree of democratisation. But these studies are rarely the work of sociologists. Instead, they are the product of organisations like the OECD which are in a direct line of response to social demands. By the same token, these studies are generally descriptive in form.

Of course one should beware of hasty generalisations. Studies like those of Karl Deutsch for instance show that "empirical" macrosociology is better developed in the realm of political sociology.[41] But this in no way detracts from the fact that an "empirical" tradition encounters great difficulty in establishing itself in the realm of macrosociology, whereas it is well grounded in microsociology. It is important to try and discover the reasons for this.

It is worth repeating that the problem which we have just been addressing is only one example of numerous problems in the sociology of sociology which could have a direct bearing on the progress of sociology itself.

(b) Sociological epistemology

In this section we turn from the relationship between the language of sociology and the social factors that are capable of influencing it to the structures of this language itself. It is true that to define the notion of epistemology is a difficult problem, as Pierre Balibar and Pierre

Macherey have indicated. It is difficult to determine its place in the hierarchy of disciplines which runs from the theory of knowledge to the critical analysis of particular disciplines.[42]

Even sociological epistemology can be regarded in different ways. In a neo-Dilthean way, for example. In this case it would be an inquiry into questions of a general nature; for instance, knowing whether the object of sociology implies procedures that conform to those of the natural sciences, whether objective knowledge is possible in this realm, or whether the close connection between the observer and the observed gives sociology an irreducible specificity.

Another perspective, which is our own, conceives of sociological epistemology as a positive discipline, a discipline that is, which not only questions the relationship between an *idea* of sociology and an *idea* of its object, but which actually examines the language of sociology as spoken by sociologists. Once this is agreed the question becomes one of analysing the structures of this language.

Put in this way, the problem seems vague and poorly defined. Devices have to be invented which allow it to be tackled indirectly. One of these devices is to start out from the "errors", the curiosities and weaknesses of the language. This route is similar to the one taken by psychologists or doctors when they enlist the services of pathology in order to understand the normal. The advantage of this device is that it gives a clearer view of the logical weaknesses in the language of sociology and thereby helps to provide a remedy.

We could give a host of examples of these weaknesses. At the level of vocabulary, one finds that a number of concepts whose importance is attested by the frequency with which they are employed have confused or multiple meanings in sociology. The notion of structure is a particularly good case in point. But the same is true for the idea of function, system or action, for example.

At the syntactic level, one encounters the problem mentioned above the logical polymorphism of the entities which sociologists entitle "theories". In certain cases this notion really refers to what we have called "paradigms". These paradigms, can have different forms: they may be conceptual systems, systems of analogical propositions or formal paradigms. The analysis of uncertainties in the concept of theory in sociology does not only bring the benefits of logical classification. It also makes it possible to analyse the complex processes of what Karl Popper has called "the logic of scientific discovery".[43]

Other general logical notions – "model" or "type" for instance – are the object of similar confusion.

Resorting once more to the linguistic analogy, we would say that the weaknesses of the language of sociology can also be seen at the "semantic" level when it comes to comparing sociological "theories" or "models" with the reality to which they refer. At this level, the verification or validation of explanatory systems is the main problem encountered. In sociology this proves to be an exceedingly complex one and we have shown that the classic epistemological schemes derived – like those of Karl Popper – from the natural sciences and particularly the physical–chemical sciences can only be applied with difficulty to sociology.[44] Restating the problem in general terms, it could be said that the sociologist is involved with logical contexts which are extremely variable.

Of course there is nothing new in the problem of setting out proofs in sociology. But it seems to us that solutions have often been sought in *a priori* stances: either, at one extreme, in the reduction of the notion of verification to the statistical control of hypotheses, or, at the other extreme, in the enhancement of more or less clearly defined intuitive procedures. Obviously such solutions are inadequate and it is important for the development of sociology to look for ways of throwing light on this problem. Once again it seems to us that the correct method is to replace an *a priori* epistemology or an epistemology based on other disciplines with a critical approach based on the examination of sociology's actual products.

At the most superficial level one advantage of such an analysis would be the moderation of current polemics about the nature and meaning of the notion of sociology. At a deeper level, it would enable the problem of verification in sociology to be put in realistic terms, thus avoiding both the purely mechanical recourse to statistical proof (which in a great many cases is inadequate or even fallacious) and the excessive liberalism of methods of intuitive verification. From a general perspective, it seems that this problem, like all those we have mentioned, shows that the simple identification of a state of confusion, let alone its clarification, can have a considerable bearing in epistemological terms: there is no science without consciousness.

(c) Methodology

There is probably no need to stress the role of methodology in the development of sociology. We will simply point out here that methodology as we understand it, is not to be confused either with technology (the study of different techniques which sociology may employ), or with a normative methodology which mistakenly aspires to prescribe rules for research.[45] As with epistemology, it is a matter of a positive, not an *a priori*, discipline. The main difference is that the present study has to do with particular objects in the language of sociology, not with its general structure. To be quite explicit, we could say that the analysis of the distinction between theories and paradigms is a problem of epistemology in our terms whilst the logical analysis of any particular paradigm is a problem of methodology. We are not claiming that these definitions are better than any others. They have value simply because they allow certain distinctions to be introduced.

The problems of methodology are so numerous that we cannot even give a general idea of them here. A few specific examples will have to suffice.

In the first part of this chapter we alluded to the logical problem which arises when intergenerational mobility tables are interpreted. As is well known, these tables involve comparing the son's occupation with that of his father. A preliminary and very basic methodological question can be asked of this kind of structure, namely the extent to which class differences in fertility affect the result. In fact, as a rule these tables are derived from a sample of people who asked to give their father's occupation. The result is that class differences in fertility must introduce a bias into the pseudo-sample corresponding to the first generation.

A more interesting problem concerns the possibilities of measuring mobility using this kind of table. This problem is crucial in the comparative analysis of mobility tables. However, it is by no means certain that it has been satisfactorily solved to date. So we have here an example of a case in which the validity of an important set of results is governed by the solution to a precise methodological problem: as a Japanese sociologist has noted, the impression that mobility rates are similar in the majority of industrially advanced countries is possibly due to the fact that the indices which are generally used for measuring mobility are logically incorrect.[46]

But there is an even more fundamental problem which we have already emphasised: a mobility table is the outcome of a complex interplay between a number of variables (class differences in fertility, intergenerational evolution of the social structure, etc.). Therefore the problem is to know how much of the observed amount of mobility results "mechanically" from the interactions between these variables. In setting out to answer this question, one notices that, although an intuitive an analysis may do for the simplest cases, it is completely powerless when one comes to analyse the combined effects of the variables concerned. The methodological critique shows the need to construct a formal theory of the relations between these variables.

We have returned to this example because it clearly demonstrates the in-depth influence which the methodological critique can exert upon sociological analysis. Here, it shows that a direct reading of data as apparently straightforward as those contained in an intergenerational mobility table is practically impossible. The same example is an invitation to correct the "empiricist" leanings of this type of research with a greater concern for theorising.

In certain cases as in the previous example, methodological analysis may have to do with the relationship between a logical procedure and the object to which it is applied. In other cases it will apply to the formalisation or codification of a paradigm or research instrument, as in modern mathematical research into the problem of classification.[47] In further cases it may analyse the logical relationships governing a set of paradigms. Thus we ourselves have been able to show that a set of apparently very different methods, some of which were suggested by sociologists and others by psychologists or even biologists (Lazarsfeld's multivariate analysis, different types of so-called "causal" analysis, Guttman's radex, etc.) amount to a single general model.[48] This example illustrates another function of methodological criticism: it actually shows that in certain cases it can absorb the idiosyncrasies of particular disciplines and hence play an important interdisciplinary role.

We would not maintain that this *critical* perspective, with its three dimensions – sociology of sociology, epistemology and methodology – is the sufficient condition for progress in sociology. Progress in sociology, as in every science, comes about above all by imagination and invention. Now, whilst invention is largely inexplicable, the history of science teaches us to avoid an excessively romantic view of scientific creativity. It too is subject to a number of institutional and more broadly social parameters. Otherwise, it would be impossible to explain why the distribution of scientific discoveries follows precise statistical laws.

In our view one of the essential conditions for progress in sociology is the institutionalisation of the critique of sociological induction. This in turn depends on the development of sociology, epistemology and sociological methodology. Correctly conceived, these disciplines should contribute initially to the logical education of future sociologists. One only has to consult the curriculum of sociological studies in virtually any university to see how hesitant sociologists are about this problem. In the majority of cases it has been met conservatively by the introduction of elementary mathematical and statistical instruction. But this solution is clearly incomplete. Mathematical education is certainly indispensable for students of sociology. However, the selective character of mathematical applications to the social sciences at the present time means that mathematical education can only represent one aspect of this logical education. The methodology of physics has assumed an exclusively mathematical form. The same cannot be said of sociology. The result is that by reducing methodological training to an initiation into the language of mathematics the problem of the logical education of future researchers in sociology is only partly solved: this explains why students perceive instruction in mathematics and sociology to be devoid of interaction and complementarity and why the language of sociology generally seems to remain unaffected by this compulsory mathematical training. It is equally possible to envisage students of sociology acquiring this necessary logical education through contact with the history or philosophy of science. But there again the objective would only be achieved indirectly. For sociology cannot be other than what it is: in its present state profoundly distinct, logically and intellectually, not only from physics but from economics and linguistics. So much so that in our view the answer to Parsons's problem of finding an intellectual equivalent of differential calculus for sociology can only be found in the development and institutionalisation of an epistemological critique conceived as a rigorous discipline concerned with the language and products of sociology.

There is of course one further reason which militates in favour of the development of this epistemology, namely that sociology today is a science under threat. The propensity of certain sociologists to define it implicitly as an imaginative history of future society and the way in which others are tempted to reduce it to a technique of good social management seem to represent equal, complementary and even mutually reinforcing dangers. Will tomorrow's sociology be divided between prophecy and expertise? It is to be hoped not. The best way to reduce this risk must be to encourage sociologists to become masters of their own language, so that this language can be powerful enough to question social reality and clear enough for one sociologist's proof of a proposition to be a proof for all the others. Otherwise, how can we know, to repeat Durkheim's famous question, whether his thoughts convey social reality or merely reflect his own "preconceptions"?

Part One

The Sociology of Sociology

2. Sociology in the Year 2000

In 1969, as a result of space technology, three men landed on the moon and, if the fates do not decree otherwise, others are expected to step onto the surface of Mars by about 1985.

If the progress of sociology cannot be predicted quite so accurately, that is because it depends less on technical developments which lend themselves to extrapolation than it does on *structural* changes. This is why we are allowing an extra fifteen years for this scan of the future. The point of this look forwards – which is not to be confused with predictive techniques – is that it represents an original method for analysing the present rather than a way of reading the future.

The development of a science is always determined to a significant extent by the quality of the observations that are available to it. This quality in turn depends on two sets of factors: technical factors (equipment, instruments of observation) on the one hand and organisational factors on the other, their relative importance depending on the discipline. In the experimental sciences, technical factors predominate, at least in the earliest stages of scientific development. The role played by the microscope or the cathode tube need not be elaborated here.

In the observational sciences, on the other hand, organisational factors tend to predominate because the costs of observation can be very high. This is particularly true of demography and economics. Their development and their relative maturity derive essentially from the public authorities' preoccupation, dating from the eighteenth century, with the setting up of systems of demographic and economic accounting. This is why the State originated *statistics*: the word as well as the thing. In short, right from the beginning, the State shouldered most of the cost of the observations which demographers and economists require. Consequently, both of these disciplines first developed in the framework of specialist institutes which were more or less directly tied to the Administration before they were admitted to the University. In fact, although demography has long since been an accredited subject, the creation of university chairs in demography is a recent development.

33

Sociology has evolved quite differently. It came to be recognised as a specific discipline when the first university chairs in sociology were created. In France the occupant of the first chair in Sociology was Emile Durkheim, who is considered to be the leading figure in the French school of Sociology and one of the founding fathers of the discipline.

The installation of sociology in the universities at a time when institutions of higher education had practically no resources for the purposes of research, meant that it developed in a way completely different from demography or economics. It had to rely on data produced by 'observatories' over which it had no control – rather as if astronomy had had to develop without astronomers having any say in the collection of data from their observatories. This is why at the end of the nineteenth century there emerged a significant tradition in the sociology of crime: because societies had been preoccupied since the beginning of the nineteenth century with drawing up accounts of court cases, sociologists, again thanks to the State, had access to crime statistics which were relatively comprehensive in the majority of European countries. But where government interests did not lead to the creation of social observatories such as the criminal statistics service, there was no observational data.

The result was that the transformation of sociology into a positive discipline occurred less smoothy than in the case of demography and in multiple fashion: there were quantitative analyses in cases where statistics were available (as with Durkheim's *Suicide*), descriptive studies of social objects which could be observed without difficulty by a small university team, such as rural communities; monographic studies conducted on a limited scale. In addition, the difficulty of gathering pertinent information combined with the pressing nature of certain social problems to produce an essayist style of sociology.

Even today this situation has not changed radically. Certain books, including some of the most popular, show that in terms of a range of social problems, sociology has hardly matured beyond the level of Malthus's or even Montesquieu's demography because of the paucity of available information. Consider, for example, David Riesman's *The Lonely Crowd* which enjoyed considerable success for a number of years in Europe as well as in the United States. Riesman brilliantly describes how the development of industrial societies leads to the growing isolation of the individual, how the family itself is threatened by competition for social status and by the increasing dehumanisation of work. But we lack sufficiently workable bases of information to test these hypotheses. Everyday observation seems to confirm that family relationships, whether between spouses or between parents and children, are subject to a slow evolutionary process in the advanced industrial societies. But we know as little about the exact nature of this transformation as about its causes and consequences. It may even be that everyday observation is leading us at this point to an error of judgement like that of Montesquieu who, before the development of demographic observatories, was convinced that the earth was becoming depopulated.

Similarly, in 1969 one could give a thousand examples of cases where social problems and sociological analyses are treated in essay form, or by reflection and speculation, simply because observational data are lacking. Thus, at a time when education is becoming widely diffused, we have available only the scantiest information about the educational system in France and elsewhere. It is true that government interests in most countries has led to the creation of statistical observatories in this area. But these observatories are mostly of recent origin and nearly all are post-Second World War. They therefore tend to be rudimentary: it is very hard for instance to extract such apparently simple information as the measure of rates of failure in higher education.

In many respects, sociology has still to experience its Copernican or Galilean revolution. Some sociologists still have an image of their discipline which is more reminiscent of Aristotelian physics than Galilean physics: their unstated and sometimes unconscious belief is that sociological analysis has more to do with the methods to which Aristotle and the Middle Ages gave the name "rhetoric" and "dialectics" than with controlled observation. Or when they use observational data it is for the purposes of illustration rather than demonstration. But this image is itself a consequence of the underdevelopment of social observatories.

THE PROGRESS OF OBSERVATION

There are, however, several current tendencies which lead one to suspect that before the end of the century sociology will have a different appearance.

In the first place, this is because the good political management of industrial societies increasingly requires highly developed social accounting. Governments of the eighteenth century introduced economic and demographic accounting. Those of the nineteenth century introduced accounting for crime. Those of the twentieth century have initiated the statistical observation of educational phenomena and will perhaps introduce observational systems relevant to other aspects of the social order (health, leisure, etc.). It is not unlikely that sociologists will become more closely involved in the construction, management and utilisation of these observatories.

A second important factor is the development of sociological research and surveys in university or para-university organisations, especially in the postwar years. Historically, this process did not occur without difficulty and it is interesting to analyse the problems it encountered, even in the United States. The extension of university research has had important consequences: first, it has expanded our knowledge considerably; second, it has led to a significant improvement in the instruments of observation and analysis. Nevertheless, it is almost universally weak by being limited in scope – a fault which derives from the restrictions of the framework within which it operates. This means, paradoxically, that it is often difficult for this research to confront sociology's crucial problem, that of the influence of social structures on the behaviour of individuals. So we still do not know exactly how far the social composition of educational institutions (and hence their *positioning* which largely determines their social composition) affects educational achievement. To discover this, it would be necessary to carry out extensive surveys using two kinds of sample (institutions, pupils), a task which for financial and organisational reasons the university research centres are hardly equipped. In spite of these reservations, the development of sociological research in the university context, sometimes referred to as "empirical sociology", is a considerable step forward. Perhaps in future we will even see the universities developing permanent research centres which, like astronomical laboratories, will permit observations both synchronised in space and regularly repeated through time. This would provide both an empirical basis for the analysis of social change and improve our knowledge of the differential effects of social structures.

Thirdly, the development of centres of opinion research should be mentioned. By means of regular surveys of phenomena which are usually but not exclusively related to opinion, they are accumulating an irreplaceable fund of information for the understanding of social phenomena. Better coordination between these centres and the university centres of sociology is called for to fulfil an essential role in the development of sociology. Currently they seek above all to meet a short term demand. But even so they provide indispensable *documentation* for the analysis of social change. For example, many of the hypotheses formulated by authors such as Riesman or C. Wright Mills on the consequences of industrial development could be tested by analysing the findings of opinion research.

Fourthly and finally, since the early 1960s there has emerged a superstructure which embraces both the opinion research centres and the university centres of sociology. These are the *data banks* designed to record, catalogue and codify, and also to make easily recoverable and useable, the manifold investigations carried out in one or another framework.

This very recent innovation will undoubtedly have significance for sociology in the year 2000. For example, it will make it possible to construct a sociology of social change which will rely on observation, where often today we have only an impressionistic social philosophy more or less inspired by the great evolutionary social theories of the nineteenth century. It will also facilitate the logical coordination of separate observations and will play an important role in the building of a more satisfactory sociological *theory*. Finally, it will have a *feedback* effect on the quality of observation itself.

As far as we can see at the present time, these four tendencies which we have briefly described will generally contribute to a *formalisation* of sociological language at the theoretical no less than the analytical level. In the long term, the image of sociology, like the nature of sociological work and sociological education, should undergo a profound transformation.

THE OBSCURANTIST REACTION

It must be admitted that gloomy spirits are unsettled by these developments. While some decry the political misuse of opinion polls, others, fearing that research is being dehumanised by the standardisation of information, denounce the misuse of questionnaires and other quantitative techniques in sociology and propose a return to observational methods closer to "lived reality". In certain cases these denunciations may perhaps have some foundation but they are first and foremost a symptom of the obscurantist reaction which history shows is nearly always associated with scientific change.

In fact there is no prospect of appreciable improvement in sociological theory as long as it continues to rely on either limited and fragmentary observations or on the data of everyday experience. These methods can scarcely improve on the theories of social change produced in the nineteenth century in the absence of an observational system capable of recording the traces of this change. Although imperfect and still rudimentary, polls, surveys and data banks are attempts to create a permanent system of observation such as is available to demography but which the sociologist still lacks.

When it does exist – about the year 2000, all being well   the type of sociology, still flourishing in France, which depends like Aristotelian science on "rhetoric" and "dialectics" and the glossing of new sacred texts will probably belong to the past or – more likely – will carry another name.

3. The Three Basic Paradigms of Macrosociology: Functionalism, Neo-Marxism and Interaction Analysis[1]

Macrosociology is probably the least developed part of sociology. While macroeconomics is a well-organised body of knowledge which can be and is actually presented in textbooks which include a set of logically articulated topics, a treatise in macrosociology typically has the same appearance as philosophy texts; its chapters include presentations of A. Comte's, Durkheim's and Weber's sociology, just as a philosophy text includes chapters on Hobbes, Hume, Kant, Hegel, etc. Why is this so? My contention in this paper is that the primary explanation for the difficulty experienced by sociologists in their attempt to give macrosociology a firm foundation derives chiefly from the coexistence in sociology of three basic paradigms which can scarcely be reconciled with one another. A second and complementary reason is that, while among these three paradigms – functionalism, neo-Marxism and interaction analysis – the third one is probably the most fruitful, at least potentially, although it has attracted less attention among sociologists than the others. In the present paper I will primarily refer to contemporary Western sociology, that is, to sociological works written after the Second World War and produced in Western countries.

In a paper on macrosociology prepared for a volume published under the auspices of the International Council of Social Sciences, Paul Lazarsfeld, an eminent sociologist, who has been active essentially in the field of microsociology contends that macrosociology, is dominated by two paradigms (which he incidentally calls – improperly in my

opinion — *theories*): Marxism and functionalism.[2] Leaving aside for a
moment the fact that a third essential paradigm is omitted in this
account, the question is to give a workable definition of functionalism
and Marxism or, more precisely of the form of neo-Marxism which is
found in the work of Western sociologists. For, if most sociologists
would agree on the existence of the two distinct paradigms, there
probably would be little consensus as to their definitions. I do not want
to go into the details of this discussion in the present paper. Let me only
mention that those who consider themselves "Marxists" stress the
importance of conflicts in social life, while they construe "functionalists" as those who are interested in the analysis of consensus.
Functionalists would not likely agree with this description. They would
mention a work by an outstanding "functionalist", Lewis Coser's *The
Functions of Social Conflict*, the title of which indicates that one can be a
functionalist and still stress the importance of social conflicts.[3] So,
functionalists would not agree with Marxists that functionalism deals
mainly with consensus and equilibrium, while disequilibrium and
conflict is the Marxists' domain. Also, functionalists would find it
difficult to perceive a logical unity in the paradigm followed by those
who call themselves Marxist sociologists. The philosopher Hannah
Arendt has provided an excellent analysis of the crucial theoretical
differenes between such pioneers of Marxism as Marx and Lenin.[4]
While Marx, according to Arendt, closely following Hegel, thought that
the capitalistic state is involved in a process of self-destruction, Lenin
insisted, contrary to Marx, on the indispensability of exogenous
recourse to violence to shatter the capitalistic state. In this respect,
contemporary neo-Marxist sociologists are much closer to Lenin (and to
Mao who follows Lenin on this point) than to Marx. Thus, the French
sociologist Poulantzas contends that the capitalistic state plays an
essential role in the maintenance of capitalism.[5] According to the third
book of *Capital*, capitalism is threatened by the iron law of the
decreasing rate of profit. The function of the capitalistic state is
accordingly to remedy this self-destructive process. One need not be a
sophisticated expert in Marxism to see that such a theory is definitely at
variance with Marx's original views. The intervention of the English
government during the last half of the nineteenth century, as it is
described in *Capital*, consisted in instituting measures such as the
reduction of the length of the work day, a measure which had the direct
consequence, according to Marx's analysis, of diminishing the rate of
surplus value. Generally, the modern view of Marxist sociologists that
the capitalist state could effectively oppose the decomposition process of

capitalism is contradictory to the original Marxian dialectical analysis.

So functionalists are interested in consensus but also in conflicts and disequilibrium. Moreover, there are probably as many forms of functionalism as there are sociologists who classify themselves, or are classified by others, as functionalists. In another context, I have tried to show that for Merton, for instance, analysing the functions of an institution amounts to analysing the needs of those groups which it serves. While for Parsons an institution is functional with respect to a given social system if it is compatible with the other institutions of the system which in turn must be compatible with one another. Thus, the nuclear family is functional in modern industrial societies because it is the only form of family compatible with the requirement of a high degree of mobility, of a clear-cut separation between family and economic roles, etc. On the other hand, there are as many forms of Marxism as there are Marxist sociologists.

Nonetheless, it is not impossible to give both a fair and rather precise definition of neo-Marxism and functionalism; that is, a definition giving a clear account of the common logical and sociological denominator of each of the two paradigms which goes beyond the diversity of the works which employ these models. In order to present this definition, I will use a diagrammatic device which was inspired by Rawls's *A Theory of Justice*.[7]

Let us suppose we are able to list a number of fundamental goods, that is goods the availability of which justify for an individual his acceptation of the social contract. Such goods may be wealth, power, prestige, opportunities for self-realisation, etc. Let us then suppose that these goods are unevenly distributed. A convenient way of representing this distribution is to draw two perpendicular axes and to represent on one axis the share of an individual belonging to worse-off class or stratum, while the share of a representative of the better-off class is represented on the other axis. Suppose we observe for some *good* a distribution such as illustrated in Figure 3.1: the share of the better-off is a_1; the share of the worse-off a_2.

For the sake of simplicity, I will assume there is no problem of interpersonal comparisons of utility; that is, I_2 knows that he has less of the good than I_1; I_1 knows that he has more; both prefer to have more rather than less of the *good*.

Let us now consider the typical neo-Marxist and functionalist analyses of such a state of affair. On the functionalist side, two types of theories are generally developed: the theories of *individual* and of *collective* equilibrium. A functionalist, working along the line of

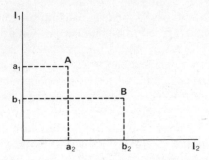

FIGURE 3.1 The distribution A and B of two *goods* G_A and G_B

individual equilibrium will, for instance, try to show that individual I_1 (the one belonging to the better-off category) has paid for his better share with respect to the considered *good*, G_A. This reward in terms of the *good* G_A is higher than that for the other individual, but this is compensated for by the fact that his share of some other *good* G_B is, or has been, smaller than that of individual I_2. For instance, I_1 (the one currently better-off) has spent more years in the educational system; in other words, he has refrained longer from consuming and this restraint is compensated for by a better income, assuming G_A is income. This kind of explanation can be found for instance in a classic of functionalism: Kingsley Davis's and Wilbert Moore's "Some Principles of Strati-fication?" The basic assumption of their analysis can be described as that of the proportionate investments and rewards. This proportioning is of course not necessarily satisfactory, so that social conflicts can appear and actually do appear. But in this perspective social conflicts are, so to say, adjustment conflicts; all members hold the common views that investments and rewards should be proportionate. Conflicts arise when the adjustment is not satisfactorily realised. Analyses and empirical investigations along this line are numerous. Homans has observed, for instance, that poorly paid workers displayed a limited dissatisfaction with their absolute level of wages, but were very sensitive to the fact that other workers had a slightly higher income, though their job included less responsibility.[9] From a number of observations of this kind, he concluded that people can very well tolerate being worse-off with regard to one *good* provided this is compensated for by a better situation with regard to some other *good*. I will accept for instance lower pay provided that I have less responsibility. I will accept less prestige if I have not invested in prestige-seeking endeavors. Basically, the functio-nalist analysis in terms of individual equilibrium consists in explaining the uneven distribution of one *good* by showing that some other *good(s)* is (are) also unevenly but symmetrically distributed, that is the unequal distribution of *good* G_A to be accepted a *good* G_B must exist with asymmetrical distribution *B*.

In what I called the functionalist theory of *collective* equilibrium, the line of reasoning is somewhat different, though related to the explanation in terms of individual equilibrium. The contention is that *A* is an equilibrium distribution of good G_A if any effort to depart from this equilibrium by one of the actors would have the effect of making the situation worse both for the worse-off and the better-off. In the language of game theory, explaining the income distribution *A* of a good G_A amounts to showing that *A* is a stable equilibrium. Here the "player" I_2 is a "frustrated" player but neither he nor the "satisfied player" would gain by departing from the equilibrium.[10] In a less restrictive version, explaining the uneven distribution *A* would consist in showing that *A* is a Pareto equilibrium, in the sense that departing from this equilibrium would make at least one of the players worse off. This less restrictive version is not often met in the sociological literature, however. This is so for an obvious reason: in the case where *no* player can gain from moving away from the distribution *A*, both players are likely to accept it, even though one of the players is a "frustrated" player; while in the case where one of the players can obtain a better share at the expense of the other, he may attempt to obtain it. This can be undesirable from the point of view of the public interest but not from the viewpoint of the worse-off player.

Examples of analyses along the line of what I called the collective equilibrium are numerous. They include functional analysis of authority and/or power which show that the uneven distribution of these goods increases the effectiveness of a social system and consequently the total amount of goods to be distributed to its members; functional analysis of stratification which show that the distribution of income, prestige, etc. according to contributions also maximises the total amount of goods and thus improves the situation of all including the worse-off.[11] Again, this collective equilibrium may not in practice be realised. In this case social conflicts are, according to standard functional analysis, likely to emerge. This type of analysis can be found not only among sociologists but also among historians. Thus, many interpreters of the French Revolution of 1789 insist that the compensations afforded the rising commercial bourgeoisie in terms of prestige and power did not match its contributions and thus hindered the economic and political development of the country.[12]

Let us now turn briefly to the neo-Marxist approach. Again, I am concerned here with that form of Marxism which is generally incorporated in the works of contemporary Western sociologists who consider themselves Marxists.. Essentially, within the neo-Marxist paradigm, the uneven distribution of a good is explained by the assumption that one group or several groups *dominate* another or several other groups. That is, one group or several groups are able to use *force* or, using the more current equivalent of this concept in contemporary literature, to exert violence on one or several groups. In this perspective, it is worth noting that the concept of violence has been recently substituted for the old concept of force which was common in classical political theory. Force implies the use of physical means of domination, while *violence*, in the current meaning of this term in neo-Marxist sociology can be exerted by one group upon another without physical force being used. Galtung's recent writings, for example, illustrate this new broader connotation in neo-Marxist sociology in contrast to the traditional use of the concept of violence.[13] Thus, inequality of educational opportunity is interpreted by neo-Marxists as the result of the domination of the dominant group(s) on the dominated group(s), alternatively, of the violence exerted by the dominant group(s) on the dominated group(s).

I am not sure all neo-Marxists would agree that *all goods* are unevenly distributed in industrial societies because one group is able to dominate the others. Many of them would agree that no social life is conceivable without authority and power. But the contributions of neo-Marxist sociologists amount typically to showing that the unequal distribution of some goods is to be interpreted as the product of the domination of one group or of one class, as they would rather say, by the other(s). Inequality of educational opportunity, as already mentioned, inequality of income, inequality in the power of influencing the course of policy-making etc., are interpreted as the consequence of this domination.

So far, I have presented, in a very broad and rough fashion, the basic assumptions used by functionalists and neo-Marxist sociologists for explaining the uneven distribution of fundamental *goods* in modern industrial societies. Later on, I will briefly consider their theories of social change. For the time being, I would like to suggest that, as opposed as they are, the systems of explanation used by neo-Marxists and functionalists may appear, at the static level, as legitimate in the sense that it is not difficult to find social phenomena which can definitely be more easily and convincingly explained within one paradigm than within the other. Incidentally, I should also mention that, by concentrating the discussion on the social production and distribution of *goods*, provided the concept of *good* is taken broadly enough so as to include the material as well as the non-material, public as well as private, *goods* (or evils) as well as services (or disservices), no limitation of the traditional scope of sociology is introduced. After all, the implicit purpose of all sociologists is to evaluate social structures in terms of the quality and quantity of *goods* (in the broad sense) which they are able to distribute to individuals and of the manner in which they distribute these *goods*.

As one example of a social phenomenon not easily explainable within the functionalist framework, one can once more mention the tremendous amount of inequality of educational opportunity which can be observed in all industrial societies. By inequality of educational opportunity, I mean, the probability of a worker's son reaching the college level compared with the prospects of a lawyer's son doing so. Even in a country like the US where inequality of educational opportunity is relatively low the probability of a worker's son getting a college degree is about one-tenth the probability of a professional's son getting a degree. This fact is scarcely explainable by a functionalist analysis, for at the individual level there is no compensation for the lesser access of the lower classes to education, and at the collective level, inequality of educational opportunity entails a waste of talents and consequently a collective deficit. The inability of functional analysis to explain inequality of educational opportunity is obviously correlated with the success of neo-Marxist explanations. Because the lesser access of the lower classes to education is not compensated by a greater share of some other *good*, Marxists cannot perceive this inequality as legitimate. This inequality is not justified from a collective viewpoint either, because of the overall collective deficit entailed by inequality of educational opportunity. This shows, according to neo-Marxist analysis, that one group, the dominant group, has the power of imposing a state of affairs redounding exclusively to his own advantage. However, at this point, the neo-Marxist explanation is confronted with a difficulty. All empirical studies show that the members of lower classes tend to value education as a way of success less than members of higher classes do. Typically, this difficulty is eliminated by introducing the assumption that the cultural system, being under the control of the dominant groups makes the school culture appear to the members of lower classes as at variance with their own subculture, whence they conclude that school is not for them. A major logical problem is raised by this kind of explanation, however, for in Popperian language, such assumptions are not falsifiable.

Equally it is not difficult to discover social facts which can be more easily explained within the framework of functional rather than the neo-Marxist analysis. Surveys and empirical observations of wage claims, satisfaction and dissatisfaction with social rewards, and so on are much more easily accounted for using the functional theory of individual equilibrium between contributions and compensations, investment and reward, than by the neo-Marxist approach. The neo-Marxists would, of course, object that lower class people are "alienated", that is, that they do not perceive that they serve the interests of the dominant class, rather through a 'rationalisation' process they unconsciously limit their legitimate claims to goods available. Such an interpretation fails again to meet the Popperian requirement of falsifiability. In short, this neo-Marxist account is believed but not verified.

I have shown so far, considering the current explanations of static inequalities in the distribution of fundamental goods, that the functional approach typically includes two types of theories: individual and collective equilibrium analyses. Neo-Marxist interpretations are charac-terised by the key concept of domination. It should be noted, however, that the domination of one class by another is generally not a matter of direct observational evidence. Rather, it is indirectly deduced by the neo-Marxist from the observation of certain types of inequalities such as educational inequalities, which cannot be easily explained by the traditional functional theories of individual and/or collective equilib-rium. Generally speaking, it should be noted that the neo-Marxist approach has been especially applied to what economists, using the concept coined I believe by Jean-Jacques Rousseau, call *public evils*. Public evils are states of affairs which are disadvantageous for all members of a society.[14] Inequality of educational opportunity is an example of public evil for it generates a waste of talents harmful to the member of society, individually and collectively. Pollution, the waste of natural resources, the deterioration of the quality of life are other examples of public evils. Functional analysis cannot be easily applied to such phenomena, because the very concept of public evil implies a suboptimal state in the Pareto sense; that is, a collective disequilibrium: everybody is made worse off by the presence of the public evil. Clearly, public evils constitute fruitful fields of investigation for neo-Marxist sociologists whose typical line of reasoning may be formalised as follows:

(a) A public evil, by definition, is harmful to all members of society.
(b) If all members had equal power, they would collectively eliminate the public evil; if they were called to vote upon the issue, a majority would vote for its eradication.
(c) Hence, the existence of a public evil has to be accounted for by the fact that it is beneficial to some members in the sense that the profit they acquire from the public evil is, by reason of their socio-economic role in society, larger than the deficit they suffer from its existence as members of the society at large.
(d) The previous statement implies that these members, which, by definition, constitute the dominant class, have the power of imposing their will upon the rest of the collective.

As already stated, this line of argument is typical of neo-Marxist explanations of educational inequalities. It would be easy to show that it is typical as well of neo-Marxist urban sociology, of the neo-Marxist analysis of economic inequalities, etc.[15]

Let us now turn to the dynamic aspects both of functional and of neo-Marxist sociology; that is, to the theories of social change which each of these two approaches is likely to generate and actually do generate. Of course, as in the above comments on the static explanatory schemes offered by the two pradigms, I will be interested less in providing an exhaustive, detailed and accurate survey of the theories of social change proposed by neo-Marxists and functionalists, than in identifying the main ideal-typical theories of social change produced within the framework of the two basic paradigms.

Once more, the diagrammatic device of Rawls, will be useful. Let us suppose A represents the distribution of some fundamental *good* in a given society at some time. As above, the two axes are used to measure the shares of a representative respectively of the worse-off and of the better-off classes. As easily verified, OM includes all the distributions for which the shares of the two individuals would be equal. OP includes the set of distributions whose degree of inequality is identical to the degree of inequality of A. That is, suppose B represents the distribution of some good G_R. Since both A and B are located on OP thh degree of inequality in the distribution of the two goods is identical; in other words, the ratio of the share of I_1 (the better-off individual) to the share of I_2 (the worse-off) is the same in the two ases. QR includes the set of distributions for which the total quantity of good distributed to I_1 and I_2 is constant. Let us, for instance, compare distributions A and C. In the two cases the sum of the shares distributed to I_1 and to I_2 is the same. Finally ST and UV

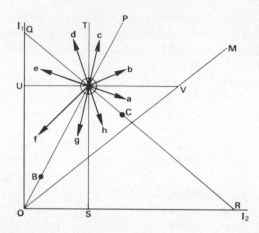

FIGURE 3.2 Typical paths of change in the distribution *A* of a good G_A

include the distributions for which the shares respectively of I_1 and I_2 are constant. That is, all distributions located on the line ST are characterised by the common property that the share of I_2 is constant and equal to OS. Similarly the share of I_1 is constant and equal to OU on the line UV. Again, such a representation implicitly introduces a number of simplifying assumptions: that goods are measurable, that utility is proportional to the quantity of good, that interpersonal comparison of utilities raises no problem, etc. Such assumptions would be highly undesirable in another context. But here they are harmless and help in visualising the various types of theories of social change produced by the two paradigms under consideration.

The lines OM, OP, . . . , UV cut the open space included between the axis OI_1 and OM into a number of areas. Let us suppose the distribution of the *good G_A* follows the direction *Aa* (area RAV) from one period to the next. In that case, the total quantity of the good *A* increases and the distribution becomes more equalitarian; the share of the worse-off becomes greater, the share of the better-off becomes smaller. The trend is the same in area VAP, except that the share of the better-off becomes greater. In area PAT, the trend is the same as in VAP except that the distribution becomes more inequalitarian. In TAQ, the distribution becomes more unequal and the share of the worse-off also declines. In QAU, the same properties hold as in the previous area, but the total quantity of good dwindles. In UAO, the same holds, except that the share of the better-off person declines. In this area inequality increases, the total quantity of good G_A declines, and both the better-off and the worse-off individuals become worse-off. The situation is almost as bad in area OAS except that inequality decreases. In SAR, the last area to be considered, the total production of the good declines, the share of the better-off declines, but equality increases and the share of the worse-off increases.

We shall now examine the typical predictions about the change in the production and distribution of primary goods made by the functional and the neo-Marxist sociologists. Let us consider functionalism. first.

As stated above, a stable distribution is typically characterised in functional analysis by the fact that moving away from this equilibrium would have the effect of making everyone's situation, that is I_1's and I_2's, worse-off. Reciprocally, an unstable distribution is characterised by the fact that it is possible to move away from this situation and, by so doing, to improve the situation of at least one of the two representatives, I_1 or I_2. Consequently, a typical change resulting from the move from a disequilibrium to an equilibrium situation will follow paths such as Ab or Ac in Figure 3.2. That is, typical paths of change will be located in one of the two areas VAP or PAT so that inequality can increase or decrease, but the situation of no one will become worse. Although sociological functional investigations seldom make this kind of analysis explicit, it is often implicitly present. Thus, Nieburg's analysis of violence in modern societies attempts to show that violence has often the effect of making the relative situation of two opposing groups better off.[16] He shows that the present calm of American ghettos, which contrasts with the turmoil of the early 1960s, is probably the consequence, less of the general political action in favor of minorities taken by the Democratic administration, than that the wave of violence in the 1960s has allowed the blacks to accumulate stocks of weapons. As a consequence, the police have to be more careful and respectful when dealing with the ghetto population and this is advantageous to both parties. Generally, violence is frequently used by one group, according to Nieburg's analysis, with the purpose not of destroying the opposing group, but rather of gaining recognition from that group. Once this aim is achieved, the resulting situation is better both for the group which has used violence and for the group against which the acts of violence were directed.

The same kind of analysis can be found, at a more general level in the aforementioned work of Lewis Coser which is a classical functional analysis of social conflicts.[17] Coser's main contention is that conflicts are most likely to appear in the context of disequilibrium situations.

That is, whenever two opposing groups are in a situation such that moving away from the situation can be expected to result in an advantage for at least one of the parties without harming either one of the parties, conflict occurs. This explains why union leaders often require exactly what they can get. In this context, many pieces of research about social conflicts can be mentioned in which conflicts are analysed as cooperative games but have the appearance of games of conflict. As an example, I would like to quote an analysis based upon a report by a British trade union team on American unionism in which the greater productivity of American industry is analysed as resulting from well-calculated social conflicts:

> The statement is made by the British team that the American unions do not, as a rule, seek wage increases by means of nationally negotiated agreements. On the contrary, negotiations take place firm by firm. The most prosperous firm in the industry is usually tackled first. They usually secure from them a higher rate of wages than the poorer firm in an industry would find it possible to pay. The leading firm in an industry running at a high output rate and making very large profits, is in a particularly vulnerable position to trade union attacks. They are always worried at the possibility of a strike with all their competitors remaining in full production.
>
> Less efficient firms are tackled later. In the end they usually pay the same or slightly lower rates than the more efficient firms. This British trade union team grasped the all important fact that the difference in efficiency between the best and the least efficient firm in the same industry is much smaller in the United States than in Great Britain. They add, and rightly, that as a direct result the average efficiency of American production is high.[18]

So, conflicts, by raising productivity, contribute to raising both wages and profits. As shown by Figure 3.2, this move from one equilibrium to the next is represented by vectors such as *Ab* and *Ac*.

Actually, this beautiful piece of sociological analysis due to non-professional sociologists is closer to the paradigm of the analysis of interaction which I will sketchily develop in the second part of this paper than it is to traditional functional analysis. I will come back to this point later.

I will mention, as a last example of a macrosociological functional analysis of change, one essential part of Rawls's *A Theory of Justice*, a part which is obviously very much influenced by the functionalist paradigm. In this recent and renowned book, Rawls presents a typical functional static analysis of inequalities: an unequal distribution of good is legitimate if and only if a decrease in the inequality would make the share of the worse-off still smaller. This analysis is encapsulated in the concept of contribution curve. Typically, according to Rawls, the distribution and production of a good are linked to one another by a curve such as OMP in Figure 3.3. That is, there is one point (M) such that the share of the worse-off is greatest; this point coincides neither with the point Q, corresponding to the greatest total sum of the good, nor with the point N, corresponding to a greater degree of equality, but to a lesser share for the two participants. Let us now suppose that the set of possible (realisable) states are effectively located on the contribution curve. Obviously, neither I_1 nor I_2 would select distributions such as N as optimal since other points represent a larger share of the good for both participants. Q would not be an equilibrium point either since, although total production is maximum at this point, the share of the worse-off is smaller than it could be. In a situation where none of the participants has the power of imposing on the other a distribution he would not be ready to accept, the point which would be selected is M.

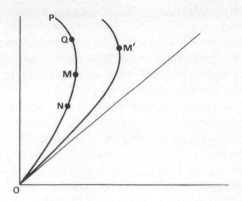

FIGURE 3.3 Contribution curves (Rawls)

As regards change, Rawls assumes that the contribution curves will tend to shift to the right over time (curve OM'). If the assumption is correct, the new equilibrium point will be M', with the consequence that, from M to M', the distribution becomes more equalitarian and the share of both participants increases. As shown by Figure 3.2, according to

Rawls, change in industrial democratic societies typically follows a path such as *Ab*. I will not discuss here the assumptions of Rawls's analysis. Let me only mention that the shape of the contribution curve can be considered as a broad generalisation of findings mainly from the sociology of organisation and economics. Economists have attempted to show that total production and distribution of economic goods are functionally related; organisation sociologists have attempted to show that efficiency and distribution of power are functionally related. But my main point is that Rawls's theory, as most theories inspired by the functional paradigm, concludes that social change in industrial societies should typically follow paths such as *Ab* or eventually *Ac* in Figure 3.2. That is, the share both of the worse-off and of the better-off should increase. Also, the assumption that none of the participants in the social game has the power of imposing his will on any other leads, in the most optimistic versions of functionalism, to the conclusion that the share of the better-off should increase more slowly than the share of the worse-off.

Obviously, such analysis can hardly account for public evils. Hence the success of neo-Marxist theories of social change in the recent years, since they show beyond any doubt, that public evils such as crime, pollution, etc. are produced by industrial societies, usually in increasing quantities. Referring to Figure 3.2, the typical predictions of neo-Marxist theorists concerning social change in industrial societies leads to the conclusion that change should follow paths such as *Ad*, *Ae*, *Af* or *Ag*. Again, I do not want to go into a detailed analysis, but simply to identify the main theoretical ideal types.

As mentioned earlier, at the static level, neo-Marxist theorists generally introduce the basic assumption that one class (the dominant class) has the power of imposing its will on the other classes (the dominated class(es)). This assumption is deduced from the very existence of public evils. A logical consequence is that the share of those in the worse-off class becomes relatively smaller over time. Typical of this analysis is Mills's theory of power.[19] The development of big corporations, more generally the development of the industrial civilisation, has the consequence that power is increasingly unevenly distributed over time; thus, the distribution of power follows a path such as *Ad* in Figure 3.2. Another interesting example is the neo-Marxist analysis of income distribution. It is a fact that income distribution does not show any "natural" tendency to become less inequalitarian in Western societies during the last decades.[20] While economic growth has contributed to increasing the income of all, inequalities still remain. If one assumes that inequalities of income distribution are not legitimate in the functional sense but derive rather from domination, one deduces that the members of the lower class should consider differences of income as illegitimate. In other words, lower class individuals should pay attention not only to their absolute income and to its variation over time but to the difference between their income and the income of the better-off. These inequalities being illegitimate give rise to envy, so that, even if the income of the worse-off increases, envy and dissatisfaction remain at best constant.

Neo-Marxist urban sociology also provides interesting examples. Roughly, the main line of argument is that the deterioration of the quality of life in modern cities would be impossible if the members of the dominant group did not find it more advantageous than disadvantageous in contributing to this deterioration, consequently this public evil is essentially suffered by the dominated group(s). The typical interpretation is that the distribution of the good 'quality of urban life', moves along paths such as Ae: the total quantity of the good decreases and this decrease is essentially supported by the worse-off.[21]

Perhaps the most interesting theories are those which contend that the basic structure of industrial capitalistic societies should give rise to change in the production of fundamental goods following paths such as Af and Ag. Typical, in this respect, are analyses such as Marcuse's and Goodman's, according to which the logic of capitalism has the consequence that all members of capitalistic societies are progressively deprived of fundamental goods such as the opportunity of self-realisation (the "one-dimensional" man).[22] Of course the system continues to operate because it allows the members of the dominant group to draw more than proportional benefits in terms of other goods.

I will conclude this sketchy inventory here. It shows that, in spite of the heterogeneity of neo-Marxist as well a functionalist contemporary sociological works, it is not impossible to give a precise description of the two paradigms. Basically, the functional paradigm assumes that no one is able to impose his will upon others by force or violence. Hence a state of inequality is an equilibrium if and only if moving away from this equilibrium would make the share of at least one participant worse (in an alternative version: worsen the share of the worse-off). From a dynamic point of view, change is characterised by a move from a disequilibrium state to an equilibrium state. Consequently typical changes will follow paths such as Ab and Ac in Figure 3.2. Inequality may eventually increase, but the share both of the worse-off and of the better-off increase.

In the neo-Marxist paradigm, domination of one class by another is the crucial assumption. The popularity of this paradigm in contemporary Western sociology certainly is related to the inability of functional theories to cope with such problems as public evils. From a dynamic point of view, the prediction of neo-Marxist theories are pessimistic as far as Western industrial societies are concerned. Here change typically follows paths such as *Ad* or *Ae* or eventually *Af* or *Ag*.

I will now very sketchily develop a third paradigm which is less frequently used by sociologists. I will call it *interaction analysis* or, perhaps better, analysis of the *aggregation of actions*. The main defect of the functional paradigm is that it is generally unable to account for undesirable social outcomes. The main defect of the neo-Marxist paradigm is that it uses the strong assumption that the dominant group(s) is (are) able to impose (its) (their) will upon the dominated group(s). A strong argument in favor of the interaction paradigm is that it is able to explain undesirable social outcomes without introducing the expensive assumption of domination.

The general methodology principle underlying this third paradigm is that macrosociological phenomena, even though they appear by definition at the societal level, should be analysed as resulting from the aggregation of elementary actions. Each of these actions is guided by its own rationality, with rationality being dependent on the existing institutions. Rather than an abstract definition, examples of applications of the paradigm would be more useful.

The first example will deal with social mobility. Empirical observations of mobility in all Western societies show that these societies are all characterised by a non-negligible amount of social heritage; this heritage has remained rather constant over the last decades. More precisely, let us suppose we can define three social classes – C_1, C_2, C_3, from the highest to the lowest. By a large amount of social heritage, I mean that siblings from families belonging to class C_1 have a greater chance of belonging themselves to C_1, than siblings from C_2 families and still more so than siblings from C_3. Similarly siblings from C_3 family are much more likely to belong to C_3 than siblings from C_2 and still more so than siblings from C_1 families.

Typically, this state of affair is explained by theories formulated within the functional paradigm by the assumption that both more or less mobility than observed would be costly both individually and collectively. Parsons contends, for example, that long range individual upward as well as downward mobility entail high costs for the individual due to the weakening of family ties, to the necessity of adopting a new style of social relations, etc. On the other hand, the industrial structure of Western societies requires a greater amount of mobility than traditional societies.[23] Beyond any doubt, Parsons's analysis of mobility as well as the analysis of another functionalist, Svalastoga, is centred on the assumption of equilibrium.[24]

On the neo-Marxist side, the diagnosis is that social heritage is a public evil. The social positions achieved by individuals are largely determined by the status of their orientation family, so that the freedom of choice is restricted for all. But, of course, while this restriction of freedom corresponds to a net deficit for the individuals born in the lower classes, it is beneficial to the siblings from the higher classes, because they have a greater chance of keeping the high status of their family. So, social heritage is to be explained by the domination of the lower classes by the upper classes. Of course, my presentation of the functionalist, as well as the neo-Marxist, views of mobility are sketchy. But the statement that they correspond exactly to the description of the two paradigms given in the first part of this paper is certainly fair.

The two interpretations raise, however, a serious problem. The structure of social mobility as observed at the macrosociological level is the complex result of a multitude of elementary decisions and actions: decisions such as to continue or leave school at a particular point in the curriculum, decisions to take certain courses, decisions to look for special kinds of jobs, etc. Accordingly, a question which can be addressed to both the functionalist and to the neo-Marxist theorist is whether it is possible to ignore these elementary components. In other words should the analysis of macrosociological phenomenon ignore its microsociological components? (interactionism

I have attempted to show elsewhere that a much better understanding of the existence and persistence over time of social heritage is gained by using the aggregation of actions-paradigm.[25] I do not intend to go into the details of this model here but I will simply give a rough idea of it. A first crucial assumption is that individuals measure the interest of an investment in education in terms of their resources; that is, going to school one more year represents a cost to the student (costs proper plus foregone earnings). But the disutility of this cost is obviously a function of current family earnings; it is greater, the smaller the family income. A similar assumption holds as to expected gains.[26] An important result of a model developed along this line is that it explains one major public evil, i.e. the inequality of educational opportunity, simply as the result of the aggregation of individual actions in which everybody attempts to serve his own interest in the best way. Another important result is that this model obviously gives a simple answer to the question why a non-negligible amount of social heritage is observed in Western societies. Indeed, assuming that the level of education is rewarded in terms of social status, the aggregation of decisions about schooling generate, at the macrosociological level, a correlation not only between family status and level of education, but also between family status and achieved status.

But perhaps the most important result is that the model developed along this line explains empirical observations which can hardly be accounted for by the other models. Neo-Marxist sociologists contend, for example, that social heritage results from the dominant class's control of the educational system. A difficult question is raised against this interpretation, however, by the fact that, according to observation, educational inequality has decreased steadily non-negligibly in all Western societies over the last decades. How is this fact to be reconciled with the other observation that the structure of social mobility, that is of social heritage, appears constant over the same period of time? This question has no simple answer in the functional or neo-Marxist paradigm. It can be answered by the aggregation approach, though the exact proof requires the building of a model. I cannot, of course, present this model nor even give a summary of it here. I will only say that the solution of this apparent paradox results from the fact that when somebody wants more education than a comparable individual would have demanded previously this has the effect of modifying, though infinitesimally, the social expectations of all other members of the same and of neighbouring age group. When *each* individual demands more education than comparable individuals would have demanded previously the aggregation of these changes, each of which has an infinitesimal affect, results in a macrosociological change in the structure of social expectations associated with each educational level. Obviously this global change is complicated. One reason for the complexity is that change in the demand for education is not distributed in a uniform fashion. Once a model is built, it turns out that the resulting aggregated change in the structure of expectations has the consequence of neutralising the potential effects on mobility of the increase in educational equality.

Again, my purpose here is not to develop the details of the model but rather to show that it is based upon a paradigm entirely different than the functional and neo-Marxist paradigms. Roughly speaking, the model generates several socially undesirable outcomes which are shown to result from the aggregation of elementary decisions, each of which is assumed reasonable or rational in the economic sense. The fact that everybody demands, over time, more education is desirable, both individually and socially. The fact that lower class people increase their demand for education faster than higher class people do is also socially desirable, because this results in a more balanced distribution of education. But the aggregation model shows that these desirable events necessarily generate undesirable ones. Among these are: no increase in the chance of upward mobility for lower class youngsters, more years of education are required to maintain the same chance of moving upward; also – this is one of the strangest outcome of the model – more income inequality.

The clock-like diagram of Figure 3.2 can be used to visualise one of the outcomes of the model, viz., inequality of education decreases over time. In other words, education is distributed more evenly and also in greater quantity over time; this trend follows a path such as Ab. A second outcome is that although overall increase in the demand for education is probably to some extent responsible for economic growth the model shows that this result also has inequalitarian effects; that is, when education follows a path such as Ab, economic rewards follow a path such as Ac. A third outcome is that a decrease in inequality of educational opportunity does not necessarily generate a decrease in social heritage. If A is assumed to represent the probability of reaching the higher class for the individuals belonging respectively to the higher and to the lower class according to their orientation family, this outcome of the model would be represented by a loop going from A to A for the probabilities characterising social heritage do not change over time. A fourth outcome is that all individuals require more education over time to maintain the same chance of moving upward, alternatively of not moving downward; hence all individuals are exposed over time to an increasingly stronger pressure to acquire more education. This outcome is represented by a path such as Af where everybody becomes worse-off over time.

This shows that the over time change in the demand for education in industrial societies have generated over the last decades a bundle of *goods* and *evils* which go together: *goods* cannot be acquired without the simultaneous acquisition of evils.

Such an analysis brings us far from the key concepts of both functionalism and of neo-Marxism. This analysis shows that the general increase in the demand for education has made everybody worse-off in some respect, including siblings from the higher classes; but in some respect siblings from the lower classes have gained a relative advantage. Those outcomes are scarcely reconcilable with the assumption of total control of the educational system by the dominant group. In regard to functionalism, our analysis shows that the key concept of equilibrium can be unworkable. For here over time people have simultaneously gotten both a greater share of some *goods* and a smaller share of some others. As these *goods* can hardly be measured in terms of a common unit, it is difficult to state whether the initial bundle of goods provided by the "system" is closer to equilibrium than the final one. By system, I mean the outcome of the aggregation of a set of individual actions taken within a given institutional framework. As in this case people are exposed to an increasingly strong pressure to get more education over time, not because the economic system requires more educated people nor because the dominant class draws more than its proportional benefits from economic growth, but rather because everybody finds it reasonable to try to get more education than socially similar persons would have demanded some time previously.

Let us now very briefly develop another example. Neo-Marxist sociologists have widely propagated the idea that institutions such as advertising give rise exclusively to public evils and to private benefits advantageous to the dominant group(s). Why this kind of analysis has gained wide acceptance can easily be understood. The public evil effect is more than visible, TV and the countryside would be more pleasant without advertising. The private benefit effect is also well-known. Hence the traditional neo-Marxist way of reasoning: the occurrence of a public evil and of a private benefit shows that those who get the benefit are able to impose their will upon others.

My opinion is that an analysis following the aggregation of action paradigm would be more illuminating. This would consist in developing a series of models in which the effects of advertising would be analysed as the result of the aggregation of actions in given empirical conditions; then, in attempting to see which of these models better fit reality. Here is, sketchily developed, one of these models. Let us suppose two firms produce a given consumption good and one of them decides to advertise its product. Suppose further advertising is effective and that the market is saturated; that is, total consumption of the good is not likely to increase. Still, because advertising is supposed to be effective, it is rational for each firm to advertise its product. If the first firm does so it will attract some of the customers of the second firm and the second firm will likely react by advertising its product. In this case, the net outcome will be a net increase in the costs of production. Accordingly the aggregation of two rational actions will result in a net public evil. If the firms are able to increase the price of their product without decreasing consumption of this product this public evil will be supported by the public. In that case, the effect of the actions taken by the firms would be to create a kind of meaningless indirect tax benefiting the advertising industry. This is a pure public evil effect still more absurd than the neo-Marxist critics of advertising have ever imagined. It is probable that, in some cases, such a model fits reality.

Let us now devise another model. Two firms produce some consumption good. The productivity of the first firm is higher than the second. The product is sold at a price equal to the marginal cost of production of the firm with lower productivity, which thus contributes to creating additional profits for the other firm. Let us now suppose that the firm with the higher productivity invests a part of its additional profits in advertising and that this advertising is effective. As a result, the firm with lower productivity will lose some of its customers and will be stimulated to increase its productivity. The final outcome in such a case could be to transfer to the public a portion of the additional profits collected by the firm with higher productivity. In this situation a public good is generated by advertising.

These sketchy examples are sufficient to show that the effects of advertising with regard to the public interest are rather complex. The first model generates a pure public evil; the second one a pure public good. Obviously the effects on prices are not the only ones. More complicated models could be devised which, just as the educational model described above, would generate a mixture of effects, some of them desirable, some undesirable.

It seems to me a fascinating research project for a sociologist, or rather a team including a sociologist and an economist, to develop systematically models of the potential effects of institutions such as advertising on the public interest and further attempt to fit these models to reality. This would be more beneficial than simply stating that TV would be better without advertising.

The above two examples are probably sufficient to give the reader an idea of the "aggregation of action" paradigm. Obviously, this paradigm is of crucial importance in economics. Actually, a large part of the economic theory follows this paradigm. There is no reason whatsoever why it should not play an important role in sociology as well. After all it is crucial in the work of one of the greatest pioneers of sociology, Jean-Jacques Rousseau. The basic idea of the *Social Contract* derives from the fact that when everybody acts freely without consulting each other the result can be disastrous for all, even if one introduces the assumption that men are basically friendly to one another. In other words, as shown by W. G. Runciman and A. K. Sen the crucial intuition upon which the *Social Contract* rests is nothing other than what was later called the "Prisoner's Dilemma".[27] Now, the "Prisoner's Dilemma" effect appears not only, as sociologists often believe, in international relations, an area in which the participants can follow their own will without being constrained by a higher authority. It also appears in everyday social life as well, because many types of behavior are not constrained by a contract. For example, anybody can choose to spend one more year in the educational system without consulting his neighbor. However, by so doing, he contributes to decreasing the social expectations associated with the degree his neighbor has reached. As we saw earlier, when such individual decisions are aggregated, they result in a "Prisoner's Dilemma" effect. That is, everybody has to get more education to keep the same expectations. The second example of advertising also generates a "Prisoner's Dilemma" effect. By deciding rationally and unilaterally to advertise their product the firms can generate a disastrous effect either for themselves or for the public. Now the problem, as well known since Rousseau, is that eradicating such effects is always costly. The prisoners caught in the "Prisoner's Dilemma" can be saved from themselves if and only if they are *forced* to play the strategy they would otherwise not choose. In other words eradicating a "Prisoner's Dilemma" effect always means introducing a constraint on the players. As shown by Rousseau the players may freely accept to constrain themselves, that is, they may discover it is beneficial to trade their liberty of action so that they may escape the disastrous consequences of the dilemma. But Rousseau's meaningful ambiguity in his evaluation of the "social contract" is worth recalling. Sometimes he writes that the "social contract" has made men free; sometimes he suggests it has made them slaves. This means that it is not easy to compare the cost of the eradication of a "Prisoner's Dilemma" effect with the benefits that might accrue from this eradication.

Another difficulty derives from the fact that "Prisoner's Dilemma" effects can appear in social reality in combination with positive effects. The first example concerning education is typical in this respect; the freedom given anyone in liberal educational systems to "choose" his level of education simultaneously generates public (and private) *goods* and *evils*. Consequently eradicating the public evils by controlling the demand for education in an authoritarian fashion would have the effect not only of introducing constraints but also of eradicating the positive effects of the system.

I spent some time commenting on Rousseau to prevent a possible objection from sociologists to the aggregation of actions paradigm; that is, the claim that the paradigm is good for economists, but not good for sociologists. Rousseau's work is sufficient for showing the weakness of such an objection. Also, the example concerning education shows that this paradigm can be fruitfully applied to problems such as the inequality of educational opportunity and social mobility which traditionally are of interest to sociologists. Other examples could be mentioned as well. Schelling's and Hirschman's work contain many suggestive analyses in terms of the action paradigm of social phenomena of direct concern to sociologists. They explain phenomena such as norms, loyalty, and so on as pseudo-contracts agreed to by participants in order to diminish the public evils which would otherwise result from certain systems of interaction.[28] Schelling has shown that social segregation can be more convincingly analysed in terms of the aggregation than by the domination paradigm. So, there is no doubt that, from Rousseau on, the action paradigm has been fruitfully used to analyse social phenomena traditionally of interest to sociologists.

Why many contemporary sociologists simply ignore this paradigm and prefer other paradigms often less powerful is a difficult question which would require a separate analysis.

4. Tarde's 'Psychological Statistics'[1]

We have lost the habit of reading Tarde, and certainly not just recently. Even very old sociology textbooks include scarcely more on Tarde than a more or less paraphrased version of Durkheim's critique. The same applies to a recently published work.[2] The treatment Tarde gets from these authors is little worse than that accorded to Durkheim himself. They make repeated comments about the "psychologism" of the one and the "sociologism" of the other and endlessly discuss the ontological level at which the "conscience collective" is to be understood; they do get round to a discussion of "imitation", recognising that the notion is less naive and therefore more inaccessible than is generally believed.

In recent years, however, there has been something of a revival in the reading of Durkheim in other countries. Alessandro Pizzorno recently contributed a brilliant essay to the *European Journal of Sociology* which showed that certain problems of what for convenience can be called contemporary sociological theory – problems to which systems like that of Parsons provide specific solutions – are present in Durkheim, provided that one is careful to grasp the movement of his thought and not simply the dogmatic forms in which he expressed it.[3] Pizzorno teaches us to think of *Suicide*, the preface to the second edition of *The Division of Labour* and other texts in a new light. In the United States, the Columbia School, whose influence on the methodology of the social sciences goes far beyond the American context, together with Hyman and then Selvin, became aware that the most modern methods have their roots in Durkheim.[4] Why has it taken such a long time to discover Durkheimian methodology? Why should it have become apparent to those who had rediscovered it by other means? The explanation, which has more to do with research practice than theoretical exposition, is that it is not found in the place one would expect. Methodologically speaking, the *Rules* are very far removed from *Suicide*. Whilst contemporary sociologists hardly learn to read the former, the latter is increasingly becoming a fundamental book not only for the theory but above all for the method.

The explanation of this paradox? Basically it is very simple: to express a methodological practice in doctrinal terms presupposes that an appropriate logical language be formulated and recognised. The only language of this kind which was available to Durkheim was that of Stuart Mill. In such a language it is extremely difficult to explain ideas which we would now express quite naturally in statistical terms – the ideas of correlation, partial and total correlation, the non-additivity of factors, etc. All these ideas are found to underlie the methodological practice of *Suicide*; Durkheim makes use of them in practice without acknowledging or describing them as such. He falls to name them simply because they cannot be explained in the language of classical logic.

If this is the case, learning again to read an author such as Durkheim will involve transcending the apparent dogmatism in order to grasp the movement of empirical research – such an unusual procedure that it seems almost too obvious. A by-product of this approach which helps to reveal methodological procedures is the clarification of certain controversial concepts like "conscience collective", for example. There is little doubt that Durkheim, from *The Division of Labour* onwards, was quite convinced of the "validity" of the concept. But is it not in *Suicide* that one finds an operational justification? In order to explain the behaviour of an individual, one is actually forced to introduce a number of factors which – because of their logical definition and not because of their obviously debatable ontological status – are supra-individual. Perhaps the expression "conscience collective" is badly chosen. In any event, one must unavoidably recognise the existence of statistics in determining individual behaviour using general factors.[5]

We could elaborate on the way in which this methodological approach can shed light on concepts such as "conscience collective" which are generally discussed in purely ontological terms, but that is not our present aim. What we hope to show is that it would also be useful to re-read Tarde, taking the empirical research as it appears in his criminological writings as a starting point instead of the concept of "imitation", the "psychologism" of the *Lois*, etc. For it is in this area in particular that he is forced to bring a more or less controlled interpretation to a collection of raw data. One finds that some of the dogmatic statements which are so vulnerable in criticism begin to disintegrate and become as it were the projection of a particular practice, after the fashion of the "conscience collective". Another consequence of the stress on methodology is to highlight certain pages which are generally overlooked by historians of sociology; pages in which Tarde sometimes appears as a no less original forerunner than Durkheim. The change of perspective also seems to make it easier to integrate a number of aspects of Tardian thought whose unity is obscured when one sees nothing but psychological dogmatism.

Unlike Durkheim, Tarde did not provide a systematic statement of his methodology. However, here and there, one can find a number of statements of principle and several fundamental choices which clarify his whole empirical approach, especially in the study of crime. Like Durkheim, Tarde worked with empirical data which were the products of social accounting, or the *Compte général de la justice* to be precise. Essentially, there are two possible ways of exploiting this raw material: the customary correlation analysis which seeks to demonstrate the unvarying factors of a phenomenon – a type of analysis illustrated by *Suicide* – or the analysis of tendencies to vary: in other words, synchronic analysis or diachronic analysis. The two procedures obviously presuppose specific instruments: the former implies what we would call multivariate analysis while the latter relates to correlation analysis – with the special difficulties involved with temporal data – and the theory of processes. Tarde had no hesitation in rejecting the first type of analysis. This is not because he was unaware of the instruments needed to carry it out. There are clear examples in fact where he uses the technique of correlation to determine the influence of a given factor, as when he demonstrates the causality of imitation in the recidivist by relating the growth of recidivism in a given period to rates of urbanisation.[6] However, he rejects synchronic causal analysis except in cases like this where it helps to show the action of a temporal process:

Consider, as a matter for philosophical reflection, the map of crime in France, department by department, and the rising curve of recidivism over the last fifty years. Now contrast the proportion of the urban population compared with the rural population, department by department, with the proportion of this urban population year by year: to see, for instance, that between 1851 and 1882 the latter proportion rose from 25 per cent to 33 per cent, that is from a quarter to a third, following a regular and uninterrupted progression, is to understand the effect of a determined social cause, whilst there is very little to be learned from a comparison of the proportion of 26 per cent and the proportion of 28 per cent between two neighbouring departments. Similarly, a table showing the increase in civil burials in the last ten years in Paris would be meaningful, but a comparison of the number of civil burials in France, in England and in Germany at a given time would have scarcely any value.[7]

It would clearly be hard to dismiss the charge of dogmatism here. Despite the availability of suitable instruments, Tarde renounces synchronic analysis. However, it would be a mistake to attribute this choice to a principled psychologism, which would be an explanation of a purely verbal kind. It is better to see this affirmation of both a methodology of process and psychologism as the simultaneous expression or product of Tarde's scientific interests.[8] We propose to examine his criminology, which is that part of his work where he appears as the rigorous analyst of a certain kind of social information and not as a speculative philosopher. In particular, one finds that he pays less attention to the unchanging causes of crime than towards the mechanisms of repression and, conversely, impunity. This is understandable: unchanging causes imply necessary evil, which is why Durkheim was led to consider that pathological social phenomena may not be inconsistent with society in its normal state provided they are contained within certain limits. Clearly such a proposition was guaranteed to arouse Tarde's horror because he was well aware that a highly embarrassing problem of principle is linked with any causal explanation of crime. Is not a causal explanation in terms of fixed factors rather than processes a kind of *justification* or, at least, essentially an abdication from the means of action? This is why Tarde was less preoccupied with explaining crime than with analysing repression, because at the level of justice there are possibilities for action. Moreover, even if one does not contemplate this direct action on the processes disclosed by means of statistical time series, the very analysis of these series provides a social forecast which can at least orientate action. Such is Tarde's insistence on this idea that it is hard to avoid the conclusion that Tardian psychologism is linked with the desire to inaugurate a social *future*. In Tardian criminology one therefore sees two fundamental themes emerging: the theme of impunity attributable to the apparatus of repression and, conversely, the diffuse theme of what can be called the "productivity" of justice. We will return to these themes later.

Subsequent opposition to Durkheim's synchronic analysis and Tarde's diachronic analysis partly reflects the contrast between the two personalities. There is no doubt that Durkheim dreamed of action — re-read, for example, the preface to the second edition of *The Division of Labour* and recall the celebrated formula which states that a purely speculative science is not worth an hour's trouble. However, his own participation in the society he was analysing was in a university context: after the Ecole normale, Durkheim followed the classic professorial career. Tarde on the other hand came from the magistracy and only entered higher education very much later, by way of the Collège de France. One can see therefore that they both adapt their sphere of action to their experience, their prospective career or their "situation"; which is nothing unusual, especially as a social science divorced from action was less conceivable in the last quarter of the nineteenth century than perhaps at any other time. This is why ultimately the treatment of pathological social states for Durkheim has to proceed by way of society itself and for Tarde – at least as far as crime is concerned – it has to proceed by way of the administration of justice.

Thus far there is no hint of dogmatism except in the justification of the choice of the field of research. In fact, once this has been defined, one merely has to look at a few of the series examined in the *Compte général de la justice* to discover that crime can be treated not simply as such but as a raw material which the repressive apparatus converts into a "finished" product, namely: the classifications unsolved, punished, acquitted, etc. For example, the regularities in the statistical tables taken from the *Compte* and reproduced in *Les délits impoursuivis*[9] do not derive from crime *per se* – or not from it alone – but from the treatment which is administered by the courts, at least according to Tarde. Indeed, what is the judicial system if not a collection of people occupying certain roles, who exercise reciprocal control over one another and who possess a capacity for anticipating each other's decisions. etc.? We will see later that although this modern language is different from Tarde's it does not deny what he is saying: the only difference is in the words. The same is true of Durkheim's dogmatic assertions about the "conscience collective", which sometimes appear to be a crude reification of the subtle analyses Pizzorno has taught us to look for, and the idea of "imitation". They both conceal the various forms of "interaction" – the term we would normally use today – between persons occupying determinate roles. In practice, once the object of research has been defined as the treatment of infringements by the judicial apparatus, the notion of interaction becomes indispensable. As for the crude expression "imitation", it is probably a sacrifice to the system: it should be remembered that the philosophical origins of sociology provided strong incentives to systematisation at the time when Tarde was writing. However, in line with the approach we adopted at the outset, we will regard the dogmatism of imitation as a residue. Instead, we will concentrate on those texts where imitation appears – under various names – to possess the power to explain empirical facts. Put another way, this is to say that a "contemporary reading" of Tarde ought to begin with the *Criminalité comparée*, *Les délits impoursuivis*, Chapter XII of the *Lois de l'imitation* on "L'archéologie et la statistique" and, for reasons which will be seen

later, several fragments from "La croyance et le désir" from the
Philosophie pénale etc. After which one could look at the *Lois* as a whole.

Our present purpose is not to analyse systematically Tarde's criminological writing but simply to show from a few examples how a
"psychologistic" type of explanation and reliance on mechanisms which
Tarde simply chose to label "imitation", at least in the dogmatic texts,
appear quite naturally in the analysis of criminal statistics. This point
forms the object of the present section. However, even when the
explanatory concepts and mechanisms are set out in this way, one finds
that Tarde is still not fully satisfied methodologically and tries to
improve the validity of his interpretations or, more precisely, tries to
define a research strategy capable of observing the phenomena which are
simply postulated by the analysis of series. In fact, the approach of *La
criminalité comparée*, especially in Chapter II (la statistique criminelle
du dernier demi-siècle) which is of special interest to us, involves the
induction of an explanatory model from criminal statistics without
conclusive proof of the link between the two. Tarde had a presentiment
of this problem and thought he had discovered the solution – at least in
part – in the idea of a "psychological statistics", which we will examine
in the following section.

In studying the functioning of the judiciary, a distinction immediately
asserts itself: that between actors who interact reciprocally and actors
who, whilst having some influence on the course of justice, are not
strictly speaking found in situations of interaction. The first category
includes magistrates, the second the accused, prisoners, etc. and also
non-professional judges. Presence and absence of the phenomena of
interaction in the first and second cases respectively should not be
understood in an absolute sense; it would be more accurate to
differentiate between the types of interaction which give rise to temporal
processes and those whose action does not contribute to any cumulative
effects. This distinction makes it possible to explain, for example, the
graphs which show appeals over time.[10] Tarde establishes that the
proportion of convicted prisoners who appeal against the decision of the
petty sessional courts remains stable over time whilst the proportion
of appeals lodged by the prosecution is decreasing throughout the period
in question: 'the prosecuting magistrates are using one another as
examples". Tarde does not speak of "imitation" here but he does use a
synonymous term. However, in a strict logical sense it is by no means
obvious why this imitation should cause a decrease in appeals lodged by
the public prosecutor. For, in order for this effect to occur, it is clearly
necessary for imitation to take as its model those prosecutors who –
sponte sua – tend to avoid appeals. However naturally it may seem to

relate to the phenomenon under investigation, the notion imprisons
Tarde's thought: the proposed explanatory model is quite obviously
incomplete. In parenthesis, note that this inadequacy leads directly to a
problem of empirical research which as far as we know has scarcely
received any attention: is it possible to discern from the statistics of the
Compte the prosecutors who, by virtue of their importance or whatever
reason, might have influenced the decline in appeals? The existence of
"sources of radiance" – to use one of Tarde's favourite phrases – has a
clear connection with other phenomena. For example, the report
presented by the Garde des Sceaux to the President of the Republic in
1909 shows that the diffusion of the innovation of the reprieve made very
uneven progress according to the sphere of authority of the appeal
court.[11] It is all the more strange that Tarde made no attempt to examine
this problem which he constantly analysed in his theoretical writing,
namely the development of a process like that of diffusion from one or
from several centres.[12]

The explanation of this difficulty possibly lies in the fact that imitation
appeared in *La criminalité comparée* as an instrument of analysis and
not as an explicit outworking of the abstract and over-general schema
presented in the *Lois*. Tarde is forced to give it a more subtly
differentiated form nearer that of contemporary analyses of the process
of interaction between persons who occupy certain roles because of their
position within a system. In this context, the explanation of the decline
in assize acquittal rates appears to make good sense:

. . . the magistracy is constantly forced to adjust itself in anticipation
or to adapt, as a Spencerian would say, to the weaknesses of the jury
which are becoming increasingly well understood . . . . "For fear of
an acquittal", as the expression goes in the public prosecutor's office,
the magistrate's office and the arraignment chambers, one finds the
public prosecutor, the examining magistrates and counsels becoming
progressively more exacting in their demands for proof, which is of
course often highly commendable. This is responsible for the ever-
decreasing proportion of criminal cases ending in a negative verdict.
The proportion of charges completely rejected by the jury has
gradually fallen from 82 per cent to 17 per cent. Since it is well known
that juries are no more rigorous than in the past, this outcome can
only be attributed to the "increasingly scrupulous attention which the
magistrates are paying to the examination of charges before referring
them to competent jurisdiction".

This gradual adaptation of the magistracy to the jury, I would argue, explains the genuine decrease of certain types of charge which I would call secondary; the charge of false testimony, for example, which dropped from 49 or 101 to 4 or 1. I doubt whether one could persuade any examining magistrate that this decrease is due to a significant improvement in the truthfulness of witnesses. The reason must be that less and less useless effort is spent in pursuing false witnesses. Similarly, less and less time is spent pursuing arsonists, who are so difficult to apprehend. If, in spite of this, the number of charges against the malicious starting of fires has risen appreciably, it must be because crimes of this type have grown enormously.[13]

Here imitation gives way to a more subtly differentiated process: "adapt", "adjust in anticipation" are substituted for "using as examples" and the substitution undoubtedly introduces a very important element. The magistrate does not simply "imitate", he also tries to assess the chances of a case which comes to court ending in an acquittal which would be unprofitable for the judicial system. In the process he occasionally adjusts his "anticipation" — as we would say — in the light of the actual verdict reached at the trial by the jury. In this context, the expressions "increasingly well understood", "gradual adaptation" leave no room for doubt. Imitation has the form of an iterative process where the anticipation of results in period t is determined, at least in part, by the results actually observed at $t - 1$. Tarde's schema is clear enough to be formalised without difficulty: if P_t and P_{t-1} represent the proportion of cases taken to court out of the total of those known to the public prosecutor during period t and period $t - 1$ and if A_t and A_{t-1} represent the proportion of acquittals, one way to translate the passage from Tarde would be as follows:

$$P_t = a(1 - A_{t-1}) + bP_{t-1}$$
$$A_t = cP_t$$

A model of this kind describes the graph of acquittals as a decelerated decreasing functions — in the present case — with a tendency towards equilibrium.[14] Today we are in a better position than Tarde to construct and verify models of this type because we have formal instruments which were unknown to him. But that is another problem. There are other respects in which the mechanism described in the quoted passage is more complex than the one described by the above equations. In fact, where arson was concerned, Tarde introduced another variable into the system which referred to the aggregate of declared infringements. Once again it is as though the concept of role were implicit, because although the prosecuting or examining magistrate *has to* amend the functioning of the judicial system (the *obligation* being a simple expression of repeated anticipation), he also has an essentially repressive function and has to base his decisions on the body of recognised crimes. The introduction of this new variable immediately makes the model complicated enough for its formulation and solution to be a difficult problem, even for contemporary statistics. Without laying stress on the technical problems, it is enough to state that, when one follows Tarde in his analysis of criminological data, the governing idea of "imitation" has a subtly differentiated operational form which evokes the concepts of modern sociological "theory".

The decrease in assize acquittals is not the only phenomenon which can be explained by this set of concepts. The shrinking proportion of indictments and charges dismissed without sufficient grounds can be explained in a similar way.[15] Again, although Tarde is less explicit on this point, it is likely that he had in mind an anticipatory mechanism similar to the previous one and involving public prosecutors and examining magistrates. Once again, phrases such as "to be better and better adjusted", "gradually increasing harmony" and "more and more closely fitting" which reflect a psychologically and sociologically more complex theory are substituted for the global term "imitation". The "stochastic process" – as we would call it – which explains the fall in the number of acquittals in criminal cases can also be used without modification to explain many other time series drawn from the *Compte*. In every case, one can see lengthy and unproductive judicial proceedings (examination terminated by a dismissal of charges, acquittal, appeal, etc.) declining in proportion.[16]

Fewer and fewer cases brought by the public prosecutor before the magistrates and even before the jury are ending in acquittals. The proportion of acquittals by the magistrates was 139 in a thousand; it has fallen to 58. Before the jury it was 37 per cent in 1831; now it is no greater than 17 per cent. One could of course equally contend that cases in petty sessions with private individuals prosecuting (in the role of public prosecutor, as it were) are more successful than previously in that they more often lead to sentences, which is a similar trend to the first. Absurd though it may seem, it would appear to follow that as well as congratulating the magistracy one should also commend the growing wisdom of the public. In reality, should we not really applaud the magistrates for using the foresight gained in their experience and application of case law to take preventative action against impassioned lawsuits undertaken lightly on private initiative which are happily becoming less and less numerous? This is the reason for the gradually increasing harmony between the bench and the public, for there is no denying that this process is occurring: "the decisions of the high court judges have been accepted to a greater and greater extent by the public prosecutors and private parties; the number of appeals lodged has constantly decreased". Not only then are the numerous cogs of the judicial machine becoming better and better adjusted to one another – jury and assize court, public prosecutor's office and examining magistrate's office, this office and the defending lawyer's, etc. – but they are also fitting more and more closely to the needs of those subject to the judicial process and consequently to their most cherished traditions.[17]

In contrast, the decisions of those actors whose role does not imply interaction, in the sense that its effects are immediately spent without contributing to any cumulative process, can be described by a static causal analysis. Again we find Tarde having recourse to the technique of correlation as used by Durkheim. The absence of a dynamic process or the absence of interaction with repeated effects between roles, which amounts to the same thing in Tardian theory, can be translated graphically into the uniformity of temporal curves.[18] Here one can see clearly why Tarde showed little interest in non-temporal causality: it is something other than a *datum* or the basis for the "imitative" processes which represent genuine progress:

The jury is always influenced to the same extent (the agreement between the percentage figures is striking) by the sex, age and educational level of the accused. They are more severe towards the accused when they are older and less well educated, more severe towards men than women, and towards crimes against property than crimes against the person. Juries are evidently gallant and property-owning. Joking apart, this does not mean that there is an unconscious process of law but that on average, for persons of similar status from the same country and the same time, it is as though fate had decreed fixed quantities of aggravating and extenuating circumstances, which hardly vary. In fact, when people act in isolation without copying each other and one adds up these actions which are of the same type, one invariably ends up with figures which scarcely change between one period and another. Why? Because the forces, the motive powers which they respond to are fuelled by an unchanging racial constitution, or a national character which changes extremely slowly, or the ideas and morality of the century which, although less slow to change, can be regarded as if immutable in the short span encompassed by our statistics.[19]

From another passage one can infer indirectly the reasons that led Tarde to opt for dynamic processes as opposed to synchronic causal analysis. There is no doubt that "causes" of this type are an object of science; but reduced to themselves, they can scarcely predict more than the present, whereas the object of both sociological and natural science – for Tarde did not believe that one could make fundamental distinctions between the categories of knowledge – is prediction. But changes which are rapid enough to be observable in the statistical series which are available and which can be predicted from these series – in short, changes which have implications for practical action – proceed from "radiation from imitative sources". Not in passing that the middle range temporal horizon which Tarde grants to science and to social action seems to conform much more closely to our own views than to the sociological systems more or less pervaded by historicism:

> Some say: there is no science without the capacity for prediction. We say: yes, without the capacity for *conditional* prediction . . . the physicist can tell us that a gun fired now will be heard in a certain number of seconds at such a distance, provided that nothing interrupts the sound in its passage or that, after a certain length of time a louder noise like a cannon shot for example will cease to be heard. Well, it is by precisely the same token that the sociologist merits the title of scientist, in the strict sense; given the existence of a number of sources of imitative radiance and the approximate strength of their separate or concurrent influence, it is possible to predict what the state of society will be in ten years or twenty years, on condition that no political reform or revolution comes to interrupt this expansion and that no rival sources emerge.[20]

If we now consider Tarde's doctrinal expositions of his methodology, we find that they are infrequent and sketchy: the lack of available formal instruments at the time when he was writing was the main reason for this. A half-century later, the methodology proposed by Simiand for the identical analysis of time series was hardly more substantial, despite its greater volume.[21] An appropriate formal language had still been neither specified nor constructed. We will therefore limit ourselves to a brief examination of one of Tarde's "methodological" passages which appears to be the most explicit, although still desperately vague.[22] This does not mean that one should neglect Tarde's methodological efforts. Although he did not direct his efforts towards statistical induction for the very good reason that this type of research hardly existed, he did try another strategy which was naturally suggested by the ideas of *decision-making*, *mechanism* and *interaction* which appear in his analyses of crime without being labelled as such. In fact, given that the phenomena which ultimately explain the time series of the *Compte* are individual phenomena, would not a method of analysing them constitute a "psychological statistics"[23] or a way of measuring subjective quantities? As it happens, the period furnished Tarde with a series of studies from which he was able to forge his own instruments: namely the research of the psychophysical school. The key text here is the second part of "la croyance et le désir", an article which appeared in 1888 in Ribot's *Revue Philosophique*.[24]

Here again, the preoccupations of the sociologist and the experience of the magistrate go hand in hand: on several occasions Tarde describes the mechanism of decision-making — with special reference to the experience of the magistrate having to understand a file — as a process of oscillation between two opposing poles which eventually arrives at a balance. A decision is made when a certain threshold is reached in the perceived difference between the reasons for preferring one or other term of the alternative.[25] As we have seen, one important consequence of the processes of interaction, the effects of which are revealed in the statistics of the functioning of the repressive apparatus, is a gradual displacement of the thresholds. This is why the need to find a "measure" of individual states analogous to the measure of average states of opinion in "ordinary statistics" appears very early in Tarde and almost as an obsession. For these reasons, even when the analysis concerns statistical indices of opinion rather than criminal trends and the functioning of the judiciary which they describe, Tarde, who is generally prepared to see their practical utility and accept them, judges them to be inadequate.[26] Again, he proceeds to radicalise a point of view which follows naturally from his distinctive criminological perspective:

A psychological statistics which registered the individual increases and decreases in particular beliefs and particular needs initiated by an innovator would *alone* be capable, if it were practically possible, of providing the underlying reason for the figures given by ordinary statistics. These carry little weight, for they are nothing more than a count of transactions, purchases, sales, products made, products consumed, crimes, trials, etc.[27]

Thus, one needs not simply to know that the judge's decision emerges from a series of oscillations; one also needs to be able to measure his internal states in order to localise the threshold from which the decision was taken. The idea flowed too naturally from Tarde's empirical preoccupations and his personal experience for him not to have tried to put it into practice – well aware though he was that he would only find a faint echo.

Initially he considered Bentham's moral arithmetic[28] and the calculation of probabilities.[29] He objected to these instruments on the grounds – which seem obvious today but which were less so at the time – that they only gave "the mathematical reasons for belief" or desire and that their attempt to provide the basis for a system of measuring internal quantities was unsuccessful. "Credibility" or "desirability" are neither belief nor desire. At best it is possible to regard the former quantities as being related to the latter by a certain function:

> . . . *in fact*, these mathematical reasons for belief to which I made reference have the same relationship to belief as, according to the psychophysicists, the amount of external stimulation like luminous intensity, for example, has to the degree of sensitivity to the quantity of light.[30]

The idea of a "psychological statistics" in Tarde therefore seems to be tied to a consideration of the work of the psychophysicists who quite clearly impressed him, although in the end psychophysics failed to solve the problem he was posing: Fechner's law explaining sensation – a non-measurable quantity – as proportional to the logarithm of stimulation – a measurable quantity – supplied in effect, a means of indirectly measuring the first.[31] However, Tarde did not believe that it was possible "to extend the celebrated logarithm of sensations to this new case", a conclusion which is supported by contemporary research. But he does retain and give greater depth to the idea of a function relating an observable quantity to a non-observable quantity. Without proposing an explicit functional form, he is able to state, with reference to specific examples, the properties of the function which binds the manifest to the unobservable.[32] Several passages even suggest precise laboratory experiments of the kind which are performed in contemporary social psychology:

The inhabitants of a town of 10,000 people, where ten cases of cholera
have occurred, begin to get alarmed; if, on the next day there are
twenty more cases, their alarm will have more than doubled, whereas,
if from the beginning the number of sick had been twenty, the initial
alarm would not have been noticeably different. Suppose I have ten
lottery tickets and I buy another ten, will my hopes of a win have
simply doubled?[33]

This, incidentally, is a reminder of how close Tarde comes to contemporary studies, not only in these examples, but in all of his reflections
on "psychological statistics". The idea is present in the "characteristic
scale"[34] which binds the probability of the occurrence of a behaviour to
an unobservable variable: it directly envisages the notions behind
Guttman scales, linear scales, scales to show saturation effects, etc. In
short, Tarde had the idea of generalising the psychophysical schema in
two senses, in the first place when he sought to apply it to new situations
and secondly when he caught a glimpse of types of functional
relationship between observable and non-observable quantities different from the logarithmic relationship of the psychophysicists.
However, the functional indeterminacy which he introduced for the best
of reasons was to remain for him an insurmountable obstacle. The first
steps towards a solution to this problem were not made until 1927 with
the work of Thurstone, and research is still going on today.

Convinced of the importance of this problem, but brought to a
standstill by its difficulties, Tarde pressed forward in another direction:
towards the *direct* measurement of internal quantities – especially belief
and desire – which seemed to him to supply the conceptual pair capable
of explaining the decision-making process.[35]

We will quote from a particularly noteworthy passage in which Tarde
sets out to define an isomorphism between the system of numbers and
certain systems of belief by means of a procedure which makes it
possible to experimentally combine a measurement with a non-
observable quantity on the grounds of an affirmation, by the subject, of
a relationship of equality or inequality between his beliefs. The
psychophysical inspiration is present in the idea of using subjectively
perceived *differences*, but this time the suggested experimental procedure is totally original and owes nothing to the psychophysical
tradition:

For example, my belief in theory A, theories B, C, D, etc. which are
quite distinct from one another, is not equal. What is the mathemati-

cal relationship between my belief and each of the theories? I observe that, if one of the inferences from B seems to contradict C, I am inclined to doubt, and all the more so if C happens to contradict D or E, etc. I conclude from this the degree of confidence which can be placed in B, C, D, E. If a contradiction now becomes apparent between A and B, and my confidence in A holds, albeit impaired; and if, having been contradicted by B, theory A is also contradicted by C and then by D, and that only with this third contradiction do I begin to have fundamental doubts about theory A, do I not have grounds for thinking that my belief in theory A is three times greater than my belief in B or in C or in D?[36]

Why did Tarde fail to pursue these intuitions which apparently provided a way to experimentally study the mechanics of decision-making which are so important for deciphering the primary phenomena which in aggregate form the statistical series of the *Compte*? "Impracticable" procedures are part of the answer. An understanding of this obviously depends to a large extent on Tarde's contemporary context and scientific milieu. If one excludes the biologists and physicists, the psychophysicists were alone among scholars in placing man in a laboratory situation. The main elements of an explanation would doubtless include: the inadequacy of the solutions provided for the problem as set; the specific and restricting character of these solutions; the idiosyncracy of the Tardian intuitions.[37]

There may appear to be a disappointing quality about this short excursion into Tarde's empirical work. The problems which he actually solved were very few. His intuitions have a premature quality. However, the questions which he posed – by which we mean the most general questions dealing with methods and the doctrine of science itself rather than questions of detail – are by and large still relevant: the explanatory models put forward in *La criminalité comparée* have never, to our knowledge, been fully elaborated. Similarly, Tarde's reflections on the mechanisms of decision-making in *La criminalité*, in "*la croyance et le désir*" and elsewhere, have had descendants in contemporary social psychology: research into attitude measurement, laboratory experiments on the utility function, etc. The sociology of crime can obviously still derive some benefit from the Tardian suggestions by trying to follow them through with the help of an improved methodology. At the very least, reading Tarde is helpful and stimulating. It is cause for regret that this pioneer of French sociology is only accessible through the old editions. A collection of selected passages, for which the texts used and quoted here could perhaps serve as a point of departure, would be desirable.[38] It would help to rectify the over-simplified image of Tarde and his role in the scientific evolution of sociology which historians of sociology are inclined to present. For if, beginning with Tarde's experiences and preoccupations, one sees the field of research which he identified and one follows him in his empirical analyses and methodological reflections, one cannot but see the psychological dogmatism, the somewhat crude character of "imitation" as it appears in the dogmatic expositions of the *system*, as residues of minor importance.

5. Lazarsfeld's Metasociology[1]

The reader of this *Philosophie des sciences sociales* should not expect to find a comprehensive selection of Lazarsfeld's works. A collection of readings presupposes that every aspect of an author's output is taken into account. In the present volume, an entire portion of the output has been deliberately excluded, naturally with the author's permission. Even so, the reader may well be surprised that there are no extracts from *The People's Choice*, *Voting*, *Personal Influence* or the *Academic Mind*. We have chosen not to include any extracts from these major sociological studies of consumption, electoral behaviour and the sociology of education although they have achieved wide recognition among social science specialists, not to mention a general audience, for they have been widely translated, but not unfortunately into French.

This exclusion is the result of a deliberate policy. The *Philosophie des sciences sociales* which follows is not an anthology but a book. Paradoxically, it is a book which Lazarsfeld has authored in a genuine and original sense although he did not actually write it. In a sense it is an imaginary book. Placed side by side, the extracts presented here have the appearance of a constantly interrupted reflection on a small number of fundamental themes and perhaps on the single theme of the unity of the social sciences. For Lazarsfeld's obsession is not so much with the quantitative, with electoral behaviour or a methodology based on the *ars probandi*, as is sometimes believed, as with something more profound: finding the key to a longed-for but elusive formal kinship behind the fragmentation and dispersal of the social sciences.

In order to translate this obsession as accurately as possible we have decided to eliminate from the final section any passages which refer to one or other aspect of the social, whether it be consumption, mass communication or dectoral behaviour. This is because in a certain sense, these concrete or "empirical" studies are rooted in this fundamental obsession. Lazarsfeld actually declares this himself, both paradoxically and aggressively, in "An episode in the history of social research: a memoir".[2] Explaining why, after his Viennese period, he devoted part of his activities to the study of the market he states that it was "a result of the methodological equivalence between the socialist vote and the consumption of soap". By this he meant that both cases require analysis of a decision-making process; it may be that the sociologist finds it more interesting or more reputable to study political rather than consumer behaviour; but from a formal point of view it is still true that there is a definite analogy between the two types of study.

Therefore, the common denominator between all the extracts assembled here is that they all refer to the social sciences as a whole and not just to particular aspects of social reality. These are not simply sociological texts but articles about sociology and the social sciences more generally. More pedantically, one could say that this is a work of *metasociology*, or one could simply paraphrase the title which Lazarsfeld gave to a selection of readings which he edited and call it a book about the *language of the social sciences*.

THE LANGUAGE OF THE SOCIAL SCIENCES

The obsession which time and again made Lazarsfeld reflect on the problem of the language of the social sciences and their dispersal is one which the majority of sociologists share. The same questioning can be found in Durkheim, in *The Rules of Sociological Method* naturally, but in other places too: in Weber, in the *Aufsätze zur Wissenschaftslehre* and elsewhere, and in Parsons, especially in *Towards a General Theory of Action*.

Does this recurrent questioning derive from the uniqueness of the social scientific mode of knowledge, as Dilthey or Auguste Comte believed? Does it come from the fact that the sciences of nature have, by the thought which they have provoked among philosophers, led to the formation of an epistemology which the social sciences would have some difficulty subscribing to? Is it because the social sciences have yet to find their philosopher or historian – a theme which appears more than once in the articles published here? It is difficult to say what part these different factors play.

At least there is one point on which it would be hard to disagree with Lazarsfeld. It is that before giving a verdict on the social sciences, before declaring them to be the same as or different from the natural sciences and before conceiving a theory of sociological knowledge or any other grand design *ejusdem farinae*, it is necessary to carry out a precise analysis of the sociologist's work and a proper history of the social sciences. If we now have a number of precise ideas about the logic of the natural sciences or about the "structure of scientific discoveries", to use Thomas Kuhn's expression, this is not because of abstract speculations about the nature of experimentation or the subject—object relationship which characterises research in the natural sciences, but because historians have devoted attention to the history of a number of scientific discoveries, and because philosophers of science cannot avoid spending several years familiarising themselves with the language of science before they can begin to extract propositions of a general kind.

The social sciences perhaps do suffer from one disadvantage compared with the natural sciences: namely their exoteric quality. The fact that a good deal of sociological writing can be read without any special preparation may discourage the philosopher from doing the kind of preliminary informative work which he could scarcely neglect if he were interested in the natural sciences. On the other hand, the historian of science may be put off by the impression of discontinuity which the social sciences give. The cumulative and linear nature of mathematics or physics seems to contrast strongly with the discontinuity of the social sciences. Kuhn observed that to gauge the difference between the two kinds of discipline it was enough to look at what Lazarsfeld would call a preferential index: whilst the reputation of a socioligist or an anthropologist increases with the number of books he publishes, it is rare for a physicist to write a book. Or if he does write one, it is likely to be a textbook which will hardly add to his reputation in the scientific community.

We will leave aside the question of whether the natural sciences have experienced a development as linear as is sometimes supposed. For the record we will simply mention the findings of the sociology of science which seem to show that even development in this domain is not just the outcome of internal forces generated by the accumulation of knowledge, but also the product of social relationships within the scientific community and many other social factors.

If the development of the natural sciences is perhaps less linear than is acknowledged by popular histories, then conversely the development of the social sciences is perhaps less discontinuous and anarchic than a certain tradition in the history of the social sciences is prepared to admit — a tradition which often reduces this history to a succession of *doctrines*, systems or at least highly individualised products, and represents them in a form analogous to the history of philosophy.

An important task for anyone who is interested in the language of the social sciences is therefore to abandon the cultivation of generalities which may have made some sense in Dilthey's time but which hardly remain serviceable to either the social sciences themselves or to the philosophy of science.

Lazarsfeld's intuition is that the function of reflection on, or more precisely research into, the language of the social sciences is not simply speculative. On the contrary, this function is secondary. The main function of this research is to provide an essential catalyst to scientific progress. This intuition, which amounts to an obsession, is based on a consideration of the natural sciences. On several occasions, in the autobiographical fragment cited above which, unfortunately for reasons of space we have been unable to include here, and also in his presidential address on "The Sociology of Empirical Sociology", Lazarsfeld recalls how the discovery of the theory of relativity (which he was to use in his doctoral thesis in applied mathematics) represented for him a key experience. In particular he describes the intellectual joy which he felt on discovering that the notion of simultaneity had to be called into question when it was applied to two events, one occurring on the moon and another on the earth. The expressions "the notion of . . ." and "called into question" show clearly that Lazarsfeld saw the theory of relativity less as a discovery about the real world than as a discovery about the language of science – a physicist's discovery about his own language.

In short, Lazarsfeld took from the theory of relativity the idea that scientific progress often follows from criticism of the language used by the experts. Naturally, this is criticism in the positive sense of the term, or a classification of language, to use one of Lazarsfeld's favourite expressions. *Methodology* is the name he gives to this positive critique of scientific language.

This attraction for clarification and clarity of language is undoubtedly one of the dominant traits in Lazarsfeld's intellectual personality. Even C. Wright Mills, who in *The Sociological Imagination* is highly critical of Lazarsfeld's work, concedes this point. He says, with a touch of admiration, that one has to acknowledge this as one of Lazarsfeld's qualities: every proposition has a perfect clarity and he has probably never written a phrase which is not perfectly intelligible.

This taste for the clarity of language, this conviction that scientific progress is made when the language is made plain, is shared by a good many sociologists. In Durkheim, for example, one can sense feeling of scandal when he comments on those authors who claim to have discovered a relationship between suicide rates and cosmic phenomena and make the latter a cause of the former. This feeling of scandal is resolved by a critique of the scientific *language* used by the Italian positivists. With unprecedented clarity, Durkheim shows that a statistical relationship can never ever be interpreted directly as a causal relationship, but only in some cases as an outcome of more complex relationships.

In Vienna, when he encountered the theory of relativity, Lazarsfeld had no knowledge of Durkheim. When he later made this discovery, he paid homage to the progress which Durkheim had brought about in the language of the social sciences, especially in *Suicide*.

Because clarity of language may seem to be a banal objective, it is worth noting that the idea that the classification of language can contribute to progress is perhaps less generally admitted by sociologists than might be expected. According to his biographers, Durkheim felt ill at ease among his contemporaries at the Ecole Normale who were much more dazzling than he and more adept at using the dissertation style. Even today, the idea of the importance of methodology is often given a poor welcome. It is blamed, just as Lazarsfeld was blamed by Mills, for substituting rigour for imagination, the art of description for the art of explanation and, finally for sterilising research. When carried to their extreme, these objections justify the replacement of research with verbosity and the language of the dissertation, which have only a slender chance of contributing to scientific progress.

Lazarsfeld himself on more than one occasion shows his irritation with the fine phrases and rhetoric which often serve only to retard the progress of the social sciences. In several places (in the chapter on "Max Weber and empirical research in sociology" reproduced below and in "The philosophy of science and empirical research in sociology"), he takes issue with the notion of *ideal type*, which he says is as obscure and as elusive as it is famous; so obscure that Weber himself never attempted to define it. To Lazarsfeld, the myth of the ideal type seems all the more irritating when set against important passages, usually neglected by traditional histories of sociology, in which Max Weber enunciates the problem of typology construction in terms which are logically far more satisfying. In other articles, including one not reproduced here but available in French,[3] he is annoyed to see certain sociologists refusing to acknowledge the value of any research which does not incorporate an account of social *structures* or which fails to grasp the *totality* of a particular social situation, without being able to explain what they mean by *structure* or by *totality*. According to Lazarsfeld, such remarks cannot generate even modest progress until they attempt to define more clearly the meaning of the words they use.

What we have said so far should be enough to convince the reader that the present volume is not going to provide solutions to the so-called epistemological issues which are hotly debated in the social sciences. Are qualitative methods to be preferred to quantitative methods, or "ethnological" methods to statistical methods? Does structuralism represent a scientific revolution in the social sciences? Lazarsfeld's response would involve replacing these questions – which are dialectical in the Aristotelian sense of the term – by others that rely on an analytical treatment. Instead of extolling the virtues of qualitative methods, it is preferable to examine the underlying logic of these methods and to examine the kinds of situation to which they are applicable, to analyse the problem of how to apply proofs in cases where statistical induction is impossible and to distinguish between the varieties of qualitative method. Likewise, before declaring oneself to be a structuralist one needs to know what structuralism means. We will return to this point in the context of the specific comments which we will be making in this introduction. But it is worth mentioning now simply to illustrate the type of analysis which Lazarsfeld is recommending to his readers, for this is where his methodology has led to a spectacular proposition: in fact he has demonstrated that Jakobson's phonological structuralism is formally – we would not dare to say structurally – indistinguishable from a logical operation frequently used in sociology, an operation which Lazarsfeld has called the "substruction of an attribute space" and which Max Weber himself applied in a rudimentary form.

Lazarsfeld's methodology itself rests upon a methodology. It is a method which he sometimes describes in terms of the French expression "explication de texte" (on this, see for example the presidential address on "The Sociology of empirical sociology"). Instead of asking what might make qualitative methods *a priori* generally preferable to quantitative methods (or the opposite) he takes a sample of investigations using qualitative methods and submits them to an *explication de texte*. In place of a general inquiry into the limits of the application of statistics to the social sciences like Sutherland's in *The Principles of Criminology* and Sorokin's in *Fads and Foibles of Contemporary American Sociology*, or numerous contemporary critiques like Martindale's in "Limits to the uses of methematics in the study of sociology",[4] he proceeds by way of an exposition of research which uses statistics, so as to give a detailed diagnosis of the problems encountered.

The reader who is especially interested in this problem of statistical applications will find an example of a diagnosis based on an *explication de texte* in the article on "The Interpretation of statistical relationships as a research procedure" reproduced below. It will be seen that the apparent dilemmas which Sutherland and others describe as being involved in the use of statistics in the social sciences actually arise because the statistical method is incorrectly used. Thus Sutherland declared that it was pointless to prove with any amount of figures that a relationship existed between juvenile crime and parental alcoholism because it is impossible to be sure whether the apparent effects of alcoholism on criminality are actually a result of the emotional deficiencies which it brings about, the weakening of the parents' sense of morality, or the material conditions which cause the acoholism of the child's parents; assuming that the relation between alcoholism and criminality is not simply due to the fact that both phenomena occur more frequently in the milieux of deprivation.

In fact Lazarsfeld's diagnosis does not refer directly to this argument of Sutherland's which is convenient because it poses the problem with exceptional clarity, but to other arguments which pose similar problems. His response is that difficulties of this kind should not be seen as a limitation to statistical method, but rather as an invitation to improvement. Indeed the ambiguity of results like those in Sutherland's example can be resolved if, instead of restricting oneself to the analysis of the relationship between the two discrete variables, one examines the conditional relationships between these variables and each of the "intervening variables" whose concurrence makes the original relation ambiguous (in Sutherland's example, the intervening variables would be the social milieu, the degradation of material conditions, etc.).

Another interesting diagnosis, which relates equally to the problems of statistical applications, is highlighted in a passage which we have been able to include here. It is Lazarsfeld's preface to the posthumous volume by Samuel Stouffer, *Social Research to Test Ideas*.[5] In particular Lazarsfeld analyses the difficulties which sociologists encounter when they try to make textbook applications of statistical methods, without realising that cross fertilisation between the two disciplines presupposes both clarification of sociological language and an awareness of the logical properties of statistical instrumentation. This is why sociologists have reached deadlock when they have unquestioningly applied the notion of partial correlation, without realising that it presupposes a linear theory of correlation.

Although the expression *explication de texte* is borrowed from teaching in the humanities, the method may have suggested itself to Lazarsfeld as part of his scientific education. It invites the methodologist to proceed from the particular to the general. It is precisely this analysis of limited and particular problems or difficulties which is the source of progress in the natural sciences. The corpuscular theory of light was not replaced by an improved theory following a general discussion of its merits, but by the discovery of the phenomenon of interferences. By the same token, it was the failure of the Michelson – Morley experiment which led to the theory of relativity. In short, progress in the language of science most often results from the analysis of limited and particular phenomena, strategically important though they may be.

These banal propositions are rarely applied in the social sciences, where one frequently encounters a quite different "preconception" which involves the belief that only general debates can generate progress and that methodological criticism is scarcely capable of more than a secondary contribution. Perhaps this tendency to deal directly with the general is that trait which sets the "social scientist" furthest apart from his colleagues in the natural sciences. The result is a proliferation of nouns ending in "ism", a proliferation which clearly has no parallel in the natural sciences: marxism, positivism, behaviourism, structuralism, functionalism, structural–functionalism.

Lazarsfeld's work suggests that the correct strategy is to take the road in the opposite direction, and to move, as in the natural sciences, from the particular to the general. This proposition is confirmed by the discoveries of the social sciences: the Hawthorne effect, the curiosities of marriage rules in primitive societies and the strangeness of magical practices have certainly contributed more to the advance of these disciplines than all the general debates. It is similarly confirmed by metasociological and methodological discoveries: the detailed interpretation of passages from Fromm or from Redfield, which led Lazarsfeld to his theory of typology construction, throws far more light on the problem of concept construction in the social sciences than most attempts at speculative theory.

Several of the passages reproduced below will show the reader how Lazarsfeld's attempts at clarification based on circumscribed problems has another consequence: it makes it possible to identify unsuspected relationships between research areas which are usually regarded as belonging to separate compartments. The example of Lazarsfeld's methodological reflection on the problem of typology construction is again significant in this respect. As we shall see in more detail below, not only does it make it possible to decipher the common underlying logic of various conceptual systems belonging to classical sociological theory (such as the types of authority in Fromm, the opposition between "organic solidarity" and "mechanical solidarity" in Durkheim, the types of deviance elaborated by Merton, Tönnies[1] *Gesellschaft–Gemeinschaft* opposition, etc.) but it also reveals – as we recalled earlier – an unexpected link between structural linguistics and the practices of sociology.

Similarly, the methodology of measurement in the social sciences elaborated by Lazarsfeld revealed unexpected ties between sociology and psychology, behaviourist though it was. In fact, in a very brilliant passage, Lazarsfeld shows how behaviourist objectivism rapidly became untenable. Even in the interpretation of animal behaviour, the behaviourist is quickly forced to introduce, in order to interpret the observed relationships between the stimulus and the response, intervening variables that possess the threefold property of being hypothetical inobservable and, to a certain extent, anthropomorphic. The idea is quite easy to grasp: I watch a small spider run across my page. I lift my finger in an attempt to crush it. It changes its direction of movement and increases its speed. The phenomenon is repeated with every attempt I make. Naturally, I would interpret this behaviour with the help of a hypothetical, unobservable and to some extent anthropomorphic variable by speaking of escape or evasive behaviour. A banal enough observation, but one which despatches with a single blow both strict behaviourism and naive scientism. As Lazarsfeld demonstrates with great precision in his "Theoretical observations on the construction and measurement of concepts in the behavioural sciences", behaviourists such as Tolman were forced to explain the response not as a function of the stimulus alone but as a function of the stimulus and a more or less extensive set of interviewing variables.

This historical analysis not only has the effect of diluting the pure doctrine of behaviourism to the weakest of solutions and thereby reducing its isolation, but it also reveals the structural affinity between the logical procedure of the experimental psychologist and that of the sociologist. In fact it is a procedure similar to the one used by Adorno and his collaborators for example in their study of *The Authoritarian Personality*: the concept of authoritarianism is likewise unobservable, hypothetical and, if not anthropomorphic, at least grounded in everyday experience. Like the psychologists' intervening variables, Adorno's "authoritarianism" is located between a group of stimuli (the projective questions used by the authors of *The Authoritarian Personality*) and the subjects' responses. Naturally, this variable had to be tested for validity, as in the case of experimental psychology. But that is another question. For the moment it must simply be said that the intervening variables which the behaviourists had to introduce in spite of themselves – in spite of their general *doctrine* – are no less indispensable to the sociologist than to the psychologist. Neither intelligence nor authoritarianism nor bureaucracy are notions that can be observed directly. However, that does not mean that they have to be excluded from research which is prepared to accept the judgement of the facts. It simply means that they have to be incorporated within a logical chain, the ends of which are made up of observable elements. Weber, for example, who sought to establish the ten indices of bureaucracy (to use Lazarsfeld's language) was well aware of this and was on the verge of realising the need to postulate a probabilistic relationship between a concept and its indices.

Thus the analysis reveals the logical connections between apparently unrelated disciplines and between authors as apparently far apart as Max Weber and Tolman.

THE REVERSE SIDE OF THE HISTORY OF THE SOCIAL SCIENCES

This example clearly helps to explain why *history* as well as methodology should have such an important place in Lazarsfeld's reflections and research on the language of the social sciences. Quantitatively speaking, the most important part of this book consists of a series of passages relating to the history of the social sciences. Contrary to the impression which might be gained from a superficial look, this is not the product of a sort of hobby or pastime. On the contrary, according to Lazarsfeld, the two activities, the methodological and the historical, are intimately linked. Methodology directed him towards his theory of measurement, formalised in the analysis of latent structures, which involves the idea of a mathematical connection between the unobserved hypothetical variables and the observable variables or indices. Historical analysis enabled him to see that the problem which he was trying to solve in the analysis of latent structures was just as prominent in psychology. Similarly, the methodology of typology construction leads to the conception of all typologies as constructed from a Cartesian space of classificatory dimensions (whether this space is explicit or only implicit). The historical analysis is able to show the connection between this formalisation and the general problem of the construction of conceptual systems in the social sciences.

In short, Lazarsfeld's basic obsession led him simultaneously to methodology and to history. Alternatively, one might say that he developed an interest in both the *genesis* and *structure* of the language of the social sciences. The two approaches in fact represent two convergent ways of grasping the problem of the unity of the social sciences which was always present on the horizon of Lazarsfeld's thought. This is why, in the pages which follow, one finds parallel developments regardless of the problem being considered; some of them belong to the category of methodology, others to the category of history. The codification of correlation analysis, which Lazarsfeld calls multivariate analysis, is echoed in an interpretation of Durkheim; the analysis of latent structures is echoed in the history of the introduction of the notion of probability into the social sciences; attitude measurement finds an echo in early efforts to construct a theory of measurement in the social sciences like that of Quételet's, for example; the methodology of the construction of types is prefigured in the outline proposals on the subject by a Max Weber who is unfamiliar to historians of sociology; qualitative methodology is echoed in a close reading of LePlay and his school.

The historical sections which are presented in the first part therefore share a similar objective to the methodological passages in the second. Sometimes it is a question of unveiling the practically hidden relationships which exist between patterns of thinking in this or that discipline; sometimes of tracing connections where the academic history of the social sciences tends only to see doctrinal divisions and oppositions. The historical task that Lazarsfeld assumes is so important to him that he makes no attempt to avoid that thankless yet unavoidable phase of the historian's work, which is the discovery, collection and the critical reading of little known or inaccessible writings. Surely few sociologists or even historians of sociology can boast of having studied Hermann Conring, Süssmilch or Petty. Few books about Max Weber make mention of the fact that he was directly involved in extensive empirical surveys. Few sociologists are committed to analysing in detail the meaning of Halbwachs's objections to Quételet's "average man".

Moreover, Lazarsfeld is not simply content to analyse in minute detail an important mass of writings be they from little known pioneers or from authors neglected by the academic tradition. In several cases he has also done his utmost to outline the history and sociology of intellectual milieux, analysing for example the exchanges and relationships between Conring and Leibniz or the avatars of the LePlay school.

Therefore, the reader who is pressed for time will at least derive some benefit from reading the historical passages in the first part: he will find there an unrecognised Max Weber. He will learn of the difficult gestation of the notion of quantitative statistics in Germany. He will make acquaintance with a Tolman who has little concern for rigid behaviourism. He will see how sociological surveys, which are now common currency throughout the world, first received an institutional framework in Vienna. He will also find out that the institutionalisation of this survey research occurred in the United States much less easily than is generally believed. He will discover too how the majority of the elements of what is sometimes called "American sociology" originated in Europe, and that what many Europeans currently consider to be a foreign import is generally a re-import. Why did "empirical sociology", the elements of which are all European, fail to take root in Europe? Why have Europeans acquired the habit of seeing nothing in Durkheim but the theoretician of collective consciousness and in Max Weber nothing but the author of *The Protestant Ethic*? The answers to these problems remain uncertain and probably cannot be given exactly without the help of very detailed historical research.

In this connection it is interesting to observe a footnote in the fragment of autobiography that we have already alluded to: in this, Lazarsfeld points out that he did not become a sociologist until relatively late, when he was appointed to the chair of sociology which he still occupies at Columbia University. Previously, neither in Vienna, nor in Newark, nor in Princeton did he officially carry the title of sociologist. The note of course contain a hint of irony, to the extent that it points to Lazarsfeld's refusal to become enclosed within a discipline, sociology, even though its limits and specificity are more difficult to define than those of any other discipline in the realm of the social sciences. For one of Lazarsfeld's major intuitions is that the methodological equivalence which unites analysis of both the socialist vote and the consumption of soap, also exists between theory or conceptualisation and research and between psychology and sociology, economics and sociology, history and sociology.

Lazarsfeld's willingness to cross disciplinary boundaries comes perhaps from the intellectual climate which he experienced in Vienna, at the time when he became preoccupied with the social sciences. On this point, it is best to allow a passage from the autobiographical fragment to speak for itself:

I have mentioned some of the turns of fortune which drove me into empirical research. Given this inclination, it is now useful to describe the form which it took in the intellectual climate which surrounded me when I took my first steps in the social sciences. This will help to explain the role which I was destined to play subsequently in the United States.

The Bühlers, within the framework of the institute for psychology which had just been created at the University of Vienna, had begun to concern themselves with the integration of the theoretical perspectives which governed psychology. This attempt is well illustrated by Karl Bühler's important study, *Die Krise der Psychologie*. Karl Bühler achieved fame as an introspectionist psychologist, but he had an equally wide knowledge of the philosophy of culture. His philosophical education gave him close familiarity with the thought of Wilhelm Dilthey. Moreover, a visit to the United States brought him into contact with behaviourism. His book is an attempt to analyse three sources of psychological knowledge: introspection; the interpretation of cultural products like art, folklore, biographies or private diaries; and the observation of behaviour. But there is no doubt that the key to Bühler's thought lies in a need to go beyond particular perspectives or particular groups of facts and to arrive at a comprehensive conceptual integration.

It is difficult for me to say how much I was influenced by this ecumenical intellect. At least I never missed an opportunity of showing that studies, even "trivial" ones, could lead to important results, as long as they were suitably interpreted and integrated. By "important", I mean "implying a high degree of generalisation".[6]

Lazarsfeld's passion for observation, combined with the intellectual ecumenicity conveyed to him by the Bühlers, meant that he too was always seeking to relocate particular studies within a general conceptual framework. The affirmation that apparently humble and unoriginal studies can lead to important generalisations is illustrated by the analysis he conducted of number of market research studies, at the time when he was involved in this type of survey. This analysis allowed him to formulate the concept of the "proletarian consumer" who embodies an important combination of characteristics. It is worth quoting a passage from this analysis:

The proletarian consumer is psychologically less mobile, less active and more inhibited in his behaviour. He conducts his purchases within a smaller radius. He supplies himself with greater frequency from the same place. His dietary habits are more rigid and less subject to seasonal variations. As a result of the lowering of his psychological horizon, his sole interest is in basics; the lower the social class of consumers the more vague and the less frequent are demands for quality, presentation and variety of goods.

The passage is interesting for more than one reason, because it is typical of Lazarsfeld's approach. On the one hand there is proof of the affirmation that very ordinary studies can be lead to general concepts and to important results. On the other hand, one sees evidence of one of Lazarsfeld's fundamental methodological preoccupations: the embodiment of a set of particular traits within a general category. This preoccupation led him to the idea of *matrix formulation* (see for example on this concept "Several functions of qualitative research"), to the mathematical analysis of the relationship between indices and *latent* variables in the analysis of latent structures and to the problem of typology construction. It is also typical in that it expresses Lazarsfeld's long-held interest in the historical analysis of concept formation.

However the conceptual integration of descriptive materials and the concern to find the structures the language of social research by way of methodology, simply represent two levels of the "need for generalisation" which is Lazarsfeld's as much as it was Karl Bühler's. Earlier, we noted the irony with which he stated that he officially became a sociologist because Columbia, who had a vacant chair in sociology, wished to employ him. The same irony reappears more than once in references to the problem of defining sociology. This is why he describes the general framework of his own research activity as "the empirical analysis of action" instead of relying on the scarcely definable framework of sociology.

It is well to stress this point. For, if one wished to summarise Lazarsfeld's thinking in the broadest possible terms, one could say that his attempt to endow the social sciences with a universal language is sustained by three key ideas:

(a) The quest for the *structures* of the language of the social sciences, which he calls methodology;
(b) Research into the *genesis* of this language, and
(c) The idea that a wide range of studies in various disciplines have a common denominator in the notion of *action*.

It is true that a basic theme of the economic theory of decision-making, like the psychological theory of socialisation, studies of the market and political sociology is the analysis of action. Lazarsfeld's "need for generalisation", which is expressed in his twofold interest in methodology and the history of the social sciences, is expressed at another level by his impulse to use the denominator of action to coordinate research carried out in the framework of the different social sciences. Incidentally, this is why the majority of "empirical research" that he carried out has to do with that pivotal moment of action called *decision-making*: purchasing or consumer decisions in *Personal Influence*, voting decisions in *The People's Choice* and in *Voting*. This is also why he did not find it beneath him to take an interest in studies of the market, because they involve the empirical study of decisions which are more easily observable than others because they are made in the short term. Other decisions, like occupational choice, which Lazarsfeld studied in one of his earliest publications, *Jugend und Beruf*, pose more serious methodological problems.

> In the final analysis, the study of purchasing decisions is one particular way of posing a problem which attracted a great deal of respect in the European humanist tradition: *die Handlung*, action. Bühler himself wrote a fundamental article on language as a particular form of action. When I came to the United States, it was also within the framework of action analysis that I presented the results of the market studies carried out in Austria. In my communication on "The psychological aspects of market research" (1934) I included a half-dozen pages dealing with the "structure of the act of purchasing". . . . The general idea was that "the act of buying is strongly articulated" and that it involves a distinguishable sequence of phases or elements.[7]

Finally, market studies confirmed for Lazarsfeld two propositions which he was never to renounce. The first states that action is an object of research which should not just be observed but also analysed structurally with the help of theoretical schemas: "it would have been unacceptable to state that x per cent of the observed subjects did or thought this or that. The task was to combine scattered findings with the help of a small number of integrating constructs." The second proposition is that the notion of action itself plays an essential integrating role to the extent that it transcends particular disciplines and methodologies.

The centrality of the notion of action accounts for Lazarsfeld's constant return to it, not only in his empirical research but also in numerous historical passages and in passages of a general kind. Note that the reader will find a general passage of the theory of action ("Some historical observations on the analysis of action") in the first section. From the original, unpublished English text, we have excluded the passages whose substance is covered in other extracts. In the historical section the reader will also notice that a large part of the piece on Max Weber ("Max Weber and empirical research in sociology") has to do with the theory of action and analyses Weber's position in relation to the German philosophy of action. The theme of the theory of action is taken up again specifically in a passage in the third section ("Reflections on business life") and, more diffusely, in a passage in the first section ("Theoretical observations on the formation and the measurement of concepts in the behavioural sciences") which is concerned especially with the history of experimental psychology and the avatars of behaviourism, but which is located within the perspective of the empirical analysis of action, as Lazarsfeld conceived it from contact with the Bühlers.

THE SOCIOLOGY OF YESTERDAY AND TOMORROW

Lazarsfeld's historical studies — the principles of which are presented in the first section of this volume — naturally led him to confront certain problems in the sociology of knowledge. Firstly, why this discordance between the academic and quasi-official history of the social sciences — especially sociology — and this *rediscovered history* set out in the passage on Weber or the notes on quantification? Why this discontinuity in the history of the European social sciences?

After achieving fame and founding a school which was to survive for several generations, LePlay fell from grace, a state from which he has never escaped. Quételet founded no school, but he was so prolific that, even during his lifetime, a catalogue of his work was published with cross-references to allow the reader to find his way through the labyrinth. In this abundant output there are such remarkable innovations and actual foreshadowings of modern sociology that Lazarsfeld, on receiving the supreme distinction which American universities grant to their most celebrated professors, chose the title "Quételet Professor of Sociology". Now Quételet is scarcely referred to in the histories of sociology. Why did Max Weber apparently fail to understand the importance of systematic observation for knowledge of the social? Why did Durkheim persist, as do many contemporary sociologists, in artificially individualising sociology, in order to make it epistemologically specific at all costs? Finally, why was it that the innovations which multiplied from the seventeenth, and especially from the nineteenth century, failed to bring about the institutionalisation of empirical research in the social sciences in Europe until very much later?

Lazarsfeld provides elements of an answer to these questions. The LePlay school was in fact a sect, depending largely on the charismatic authority of its leader, then its founder. The result was that when a critical mind penetrated the sect, LePlay's authority began to pass into the hands of the abbé deTourville and eventually disintegrated completely. As far as Max Weber is concerned, the explanation perhaps lies in the fact that the German tradition was hardly prepared for what Lazarsfeld calls the empirical analysis of action. Action (*die Handlung*) was a concept whose intellectual provenance was essentially jurdical, so that the analysis of action basically originated in the philosophy of law. The obscurity which Gabriel Tarde, another innovator of genius, fell into is perhaps due to the monopoly which Durkheimian sociology exercised in France for a period.

In a more general way, it could be said that at the end of the nineteenth century, the social science in European universities was dominated by a sociology with philosophical origins and a macrosociological orientation. This sociology preferred to work with global units (societies, states, nations) rather than individual units. This is doubtless why Tarde was so misunderstood. Meanwhile, the individual was reinstated by another discipline, psychology, whether it was introspective or experimental. Thus the paradigms of scientific research in social science were on the one hand experimentation as practised by psychologists, on the other, analysis of cultural products, and finally, analysis of statistics of administrative origin. Durkheim's *Elementary Forms* illustrates the second paradigm, while *Suicide* and numerous products of the Durkheimian school illustrate the third. It remained to invent another paradigm, that of sociological or social psychological surveys, involving standardised observations of social reality carried out by the sociologist himself. More precisely, it remained to be *institutionalised*, because it had been forseen by Tarde, used by LePlay, and had begun to be institutionalised in Vienna, at the psychological institute directed by the Bühlers.

Perhaps the main reason why the institutionalisation of "empirical sociology" ran aground in Europe is possibly because it presupposed an organisational innovation which the universities were reluctant to adopt, especially in Europe – at least this is what Lazarsfeld suggests in "The sociology of empirical sociology" and "An episode in the history of social research". In fact, "empirical sociology" assumes, on the part of the university dedicated to it, at least as much an aptitude for management as an aptitude for research. Neither experimental psychology nor traditional sociology encounter this problem of management to the same extent. In these disciplines the organisational model is congruent with that of the university organisation. A director can conduct a programme of experimental research with the help of his assistants. In contrast, the organisation of a sociological survey presupposes a more complex division of labour because the abilities involved are more diverse, ranging from awareness of human relations to theoretical or statistical competences. Further, a survey of this kind is more burdensome, both financially and by virtue of the stages and time involved, than work of an experimental nature (at least in the case of psychology). Finally, the financing, collection of data and the application of findings generally involve the sociologist in relationships and transactions with the world outside the university – another factor which hardly ever intervenes in the case of experimental psychology.

All of these reasons help to explain why the institutionalisation of empirical sociology – of survey sociology – encountered such difficulties. In effect, it presupposed a new university type, to which Lazarsfeld gave the name "managerial scholar". The link between this new social "role" and the development of empirical sociology possibly explains to a large extent why the majority of European innovations leading in the direction of systematic observation of social conduct were quickly stifled. For the European universities and societies were perhaps less prepared to adopt and to allow this new role, which appeared to contradict the traditional structure of university roles. The recent history of French sociology is significant in this regard: after the withering away of the Durkheimian school whose work was very well adapted to university structures, the renaissance of the social sciences after the Second World War was impelled above all by non-university institutions such as the Centre Nationale de la Recherche Scientifique or the Ecole Pratique des Hautes Etudes. The effectiveness of these institutes is explained by the fact that they adopted "laboratory" structures much more favourable to the development of "empirical sociology" than departmental chairs. This is doubtless why "empirical sociology" became established as a kind of norm among the new generation of French sociologists in the space of a few years.

This conflict between the structure of university roles and the new roles associated with empirical research, particularly strongly pronounced as it was in Europe, was not absent from the United States. On

several occasions, in his presidential address to the American
Sociological Association and elsewhere, Lazarsfeld recalls that when he
arrived in the United States, there was not a single institute of empirical
research in existence apart from the one in Odum at the University of
North Carolina. It was only by slow degrees that the idea became
accepted. The reader who is interested in this historical problem can
refer to "An episode in the history of social research".[8] But what
interests us here is that the difficulties involved in establishing empirical
sociology in the United States, like the discontinuities in the history of
empirical sociology in Europe, and the rapid development of this kind of
research in France after the Second World War, tend to confirm the
importance, from the sociology of knowledge point of view, of the
organisational model associated with empirical sociology.

It is no accident that Lazarsfeld returned to this theme on a number of
occasions. Sometimes it was to underline its importance for the
"sociology of sociology" and for the interpretation of the history of the
social sciences and sometimes to stress the relationship between the
quality of the organisational model adopted by a research institute and
the quality of methodological work: because the effectiveness of the
methodology depends directly on the quality of the division of labour.

In short, Lazarsfeld's thinking on the organisation of the social
sciences, which is summarised in his presidential address on the
"Sociology of empirical sociology", stands in a direct relationship both
to his methodological work and to his research into the history of the
social sciences.

The third section of the present volume, apart from this general
passage on the organisation of sociology and its relationship to
methodology, consists of a collection of writings which are a modulation
of the fundamental theme of the unity of the social sciences. We will
come back to these contributions below, because there is one point
which we would like to underline in relation to this series of articles on
"empirical sociology", namely the *open* character of the kinds of
research which Lazarsfeld indicates by this expression.

We gave a reminder earlier of the ease with which "empirical
sociology" became established in France once the institutional obstacles
had been removed. Nevertheless, this development still had to overcome
a certain amount of resistance and reticence. And not only in France.
For example, Lazarsfeld recalls the attacks by Arthur Vidich and his
collaboraters in *Reflections on Community Studies* which accused
empirical sociology of being unilateral and restricting. One may also cite
those of C. Wright Mills.

But Lazarsfeld would certainly be the last to admit that all research should make use of questionnaires and take the path of "survey research". In 1933 he published a methodological article in which he insisted on the need to vary the sources of data:

(a) For every phenomenon observed, objective observations should be available as well as introspective accounts.
(b) Case studies should be combined pertinently with statistical information.
(c) Information gathered *hic et nunc* should be complemented by information about the subsequent phases of the phenomenon under investigation.
(d) Experimental data should be combined with natural data.[9]

On this last point, he adds that, by *experimental* data, he means chiefly answers to questionnaires or other types of data *solicited* by the investigator and, by *natural* data, those data simply gathered by the observer without any intervention on his part.

The passage on qualitative methods ("Several functions of qualitative analysis in sociology") recalls after a lapse of several years that there is no reason in principle why statistical methodology should predominate over qualitative methods.

The accusation of partiality and dogmatism is no less justified than the accusation that Lazarsfeld's research would tend to produce a restrictive view of the social sciences. We have stressed this point enough for further repetition to be unnecessary: quite the opposite, Lazarsfeld's obsession has been to replace the enclosed fields which make up the social science landscape with a discipline without frontiers.

Hence the importance which he attached to perfecting the surveys used in empirical sociology so as to eliminate the atomistic and individualistic character which they had often been accused of possessing. Thus, Blumer, in a famous attack on surveys declared that they could never be of much use in sociology because they only studied an abstraction: the individual detached from his social context.[10] In summarising Blumer's thinking one may say that atomistic surveys have as an object a sort of *homo sociopsychologicus* representing an abstraction analogous to the *homo œconomicus* of economic theory. In reality, in the survey research practised at the time when Blumer was writing, the sampling was done exclusively from a collection of individuals, which meant that the researcher gained very little information about the social milieu of the individual. One may well ask, for instance, whether there is much use in knowing a worker's opinions about trade unions if one does not know the majority opinion in the occupational milieu to which he belongs.

Responding to these objections, Lazarsfeld develops the notion of contextual analysis which shows that the *homo sociopsychologicus* was not a product of survey research itself, but of the atomistic character of the sampling designs in general use. In this form of analysis, the individual is not only defined by a collection of individual variables (age, sex, opinions about this or that, level of education, occupation, etc.) but by a collection of variables typical of the milieu to which he belongs. In this case, the survey loses its "atomistic" character and can, by means of a proper elaboration of the observational design, connect up with the macrosociological tradition of the Durkheimian type.

It is therefore quite definitely false to assume that Lazarsfeld's methodology gives rise to a restrictive conception of research, which has no capacity to respond to the preoccupations of macrosociology. At the level of his *intentions* at any rate, Lazarsfeld's aim has always been the opposite one of refining this methodology in such a way that "empirical" sociology is in a position to respond to those exigencies which sociologists are so fond of proclaiming, the need to take account of "social structures" or the "totality" of situations. He has always endeavoured to analyse these imperatives in a precise fashion, in order to translate them into an operational language. Invariably, the outcome has been that the objection of sociologists hostile to his style of research could be dispelled by progress of a methodological kind. Appropriately translated and clarified, the imperatives relating to the "totality of social situations" or to "social structures" can in fact be transposed into the language of variables and relationships between variables. The objection can be met by showing sufficient methodological imagination in the elaboration of the observational design. So that methodology rather than being a source of division should be a source of harmonisation and progress.

Lack of space prevents us from reproducing a series of articles illustrating the care with which Lazarsfeld has expanded the methodology of sociological surveys so as to respond to this kind of imperative. Only one of the passages in the second section ("Problems of methodology") provides some material on this subject. If we have preferred this to other passages, it is because a large number of these methodological passages have already been published in French.

It should, however, be recognised that one of the things Lazarsfeld does omit to mention is that numerous questions which quite clearly belong to the realm of sociology cannot be analysed by way of surveys alone, whichever the degree of refinement of the observational design or the diversity of the data gathered. How can macrosociology or historical sociology be made sciences of observation? These are crucial questions to which he has scarcely tried to respond. Perhaps this arises from the fact that sociology has always appeared to him as it were through psychological spectacles. So that reconciliation with an author like Max Weber, whose own perception was distorted by law, was scarcely possible.

The articles in the third section, especially "The historian and the surveyor of populations", and the "Reflections on business life", provide a further testimony to Lazarsfeld's ecumencial intention: they show that empirical sociology may not only attempt to respond to the intellectual imperatives of classical sociology but can also collaborate usefully with the historian and the economist and thereby thrust aside the frontiers between disciplines.

The time has come, following this general survey of Lazarsfeld's *metasociology*, to introduce the passages published in the present volume by underlining their main points and re-integrating them with the general project which we have been attempting to outline in the first part of this introduction, without always being exactly sure of reproducing the author's own thought on this or that point.

On reading the preceding pages, the reader will perhaps have gained an impression of repetition and the interlacing of themes, the reason being that it is difficult to explain Lazarsfeld's thinking in a linear form. The same themes and the same obsessions are repeated in different settings: the setting of the empirical analysis of action, the setting of methodology, the setting of the history of the social sciences and of the sociology of knowledge. One has to deal with a sort of musical structure, involving a simultaneous development of parts which are both independent and connected. This structure is evident in the composition of the texts themselves, which involve numerous shifts from one key to another, sometimes explicitly entitled "digressions", as in a passage from the "Reflections on business life". The result, which hardly makes the commentator's task any easier, is that the same themes or the *Leitmotive* reappear sometimes in different guises, sometimes in the same guise in a number of passages. The theme of typology construction receives a systematic methodological treatment in "The construction of typologies", but is similarly developed in a historical form in the "Notes on the history of quantification", in the article on Max Weber, in the

"Reflections on business life" and in several others. The theme of measurement and conceptualisation is likewise omnipresent. Occasionally, a single theme even appears under different names. Thus, in many ways, the concepts of "intervening" variable ("The formation of concepts"), of "latent" variable, of "expressive" index ("Problems of methodology") at least refer to a common problematic even if they are not synonymous.

These observations perhaps justify the rhetorical imperfections of the first part of this introduction. They also explain why we must now look at each contribution individually. An additional reason which justifies this mode of procedure is that Lazarsfeld is, paradoxically, both an author of perfect clarity and, at the same time, a difficult one. His phobia of hastily advanced generalities and imperfectly clarified concepts or propositions means that he is content to allow his examples to speak for themselves and avoids drawing as many conclusions as he might. The result is that an article by Lazarsfeld is always an excellent opportunity to practise the exercise of explication de texte which he himself ardently recommends.

The *Notes on the History of Quantification in Sociology: sources, tendencies, major problems* begin with a significant prefatory statement. "The title of this present essay, it is stated, relies on three terms which have been unable to escape from a certain imprecision." In fact, the word *quantification* is equivocal, because it describes procedures which run from simple enumeration to those mathematical models, some of them highly sophisticated, which have been in use for several years in the social sciences. The word *history* is equally ambiguous. In fact, the history which Lazarsfeld sets out to describe is a history full of discontinuities, a series of episodes which were for the most part quickly interrupted and which never experienced a revival. Now history almost inevitably presupposes, if not continuity, at least an explanation of the passage from one state to the next. But the history of the social sciences – that which cannot be reduced to the major doctrines – has been so little studied that the researcher who undertakes to study it has to begin by writing descriptive monographs which will constitute the raw materials of a future history rather than a history in the full sense. In fact, the reader can choose between two interpretations of these *Notes*: he can either see in them a succession of descriptive monographs or an attempt to write the prehistory of the types of research which Lazarsfeld labels "empirical sociology".

The third ambiguity contained in the title again brings us face to face with one of Lazarsfeld's favourite and repeatedly discussed ideas: the undeniable truth that, despite touching but vain attempts by certain sociologists to define the specificity of their discipline at all costs, the limits of *sociology* are less definite than those of any other discipline. The analysis of attitudes is a problem common to both psychology and sociology. The analysis of family budgets, which LePlay systematically conducted, is of as much interest to the economist as to the sociologist. The third ambiguity – which has to do with the applicability of the name sociology – thus echoes one of Lazarsfeld's permanent preoccupations: that of transcending disciplinary frontiers.

This prefatory statement is enough to show that the problem addressed by this article is more a question of the history of observation and the analysis of social problems in general than the history of quantification. It has more to do with the problem of the language of the social sciences than the development of quantitative techniques. Lazarsfeld himself is obviously aware of this: if it were essentially a text on the history of quantification, the long final passage devoted to LePlay and his school would not be justified.

Therefore, the reader will be encountering what is above all a programmatic article illustrating the discontinuity of the development of the social sciences, providing several searchlight beams on important innovations and thereby implying that a systematic history remains to be written. Lazarsfeld returns to this theme on various occasions in his work: the history of the social sciences has so far – without exception – failed to interest any historian or, for that matter, any philosopher. Not that the materials are lacking. There are enough "classical" authors. There are probably also enough unknown or insufficiently known authors, like those discussed by Lazarsfeld. The reasons for this lack of interest by historians in the social sciences are therefore of another order and have to do with certain hypotheses we referred to earlier. What one cannot fail to observe is that the history of the social sciences is generally the work of sociologists, psychologists or of other categories of social scientists who, because they themselves are implicated in the judgement that they seek to bring, tend to reproduce conventional images rather than undertaken the meticulous work which historical research de- mands. On this point, one can only agree with Lazarsfeld. This circumstance explains for example the exaggerated part played by the theory of collective consciousness in the presentation of Durkheimian sociology. For clearly this phenomenon is accounted for less by the importance of the notion in Durkheim's work than by the fact that it affords a particularly convenient purchase for a philosophically-trained sociologist.

Lazarsfeld himself is evidently both judge and defendent when he investigates the origins of empirical sociology. For example, there is no doubt that the image which he presents of authors like Durkheim or Weber is strongly marked – not to say distorted – by his own point of view. But, on the one hand, his historical writings bear witness to a meticulous concern for detail and on the other hand, they have the considerable advantage of seeing the history of the social sciences from another point of view from that of the history of ideas, concepts, doctrines or systems.

The first searchlight beam is turned on the early attempts to articulate the idea of *statistics* from the seventeenth to the nineteenth century. Here Lazarsfeld examines the opposition between German university statistics, initiated by Heimann Conring in the seventeenth century, and English political arithmetic associated with the name of William Petty. The history of this opposition is interesting because in it one can see the coming together and clash between two originally highly contrasting conceptions of the idea of statistics, in terms of their content if not their outcome.

At the outset, at the time of its foundation by Conring, statistics was regarded in Germany as the science of the State. The universities in Germany were still impregnated with Aristotelianism. Latin was still the language of instruction. These circumstances explain why Conring chose to articulate the elements of statistics in terms of the Aristotelian theory of causality. The study of the purposes of the State therefore involved the analysis of the goals of the State as a body (*final* cause); analysis of population and goods (*material* cause); study of the constitution and law (*formal* cause); and study of the administrative process and the activities of the elite (*efficient* cause).

The combination of the modern idea of "statistics" and this scholastic scheme may seem surprising to contemporary intellects. However, Conring's categories were later to be refined, in particular by the Göttingen school (the University of Göttingen was opened in 1737) and by one of its most eminent representatives: Achenwall. Ultimately, this meant that Conring's schema had two consequences: on the one hand, it provided an impetus to the gathering of more and more numerous data on the functioning of States. On the other hand, it had the effect of maintaining the tradition and intellectual continuity of "German university statistics", by providing it with a conceptual framework which could be simultaneously perfected, completed and filled out. Incidently the connection between the refinements made to the classifications originally proposed by Conring and the accumulation of data led some of Achenwall's successors to astonishingly modern ideas. Thus it was the Göttingen "statisticians" who were the first to use a tool which eventually came to occupy an important role in the social sciences: matrices. The purpose of these matrices was to classify the international data which had begun to accumulate. The rows related to the countries under comparison; the columns set out the categories of information collected. To begin with, these matrices contained information of a qualitative kind. But they developed into "statistical tables" as their detractors liked to call them.

It was at this time that the struggle between the German tradition and English tradition of arithmetical politics reached its culmination – precisely at the moment when the two traditions, after being so part apart at the beginning, had eventually come together.

The second searchlight beam is focused on Quételet. It is actually with Adolphe Quételet, the Belgian mathematician, astronomer and so-ciologist, that one encounters what was probably the first attempt to found a quantitative social science. In *La Physique sociale* especially, one already finds a relatively elaborated theory of measurement in the social sciences. Apart from direct measurements (of size, for example) Quételet identifies two categories of indirect measurement. The first applies "when qualities are such that their effects are approximately the same and when they are proportional to the frequency of these effects". This is so in the case of "women's fertility" or "drunkenness". The second applies "when causes are such that it is necessary to take as much account of the frequency as the strenght of the effects". This is the case with "moral and intellectual qualities" or what we would today call *attitudes*, like "prudence, courage, imagination". The solutions which Quételet proposes to this latter problem – the one which modern theories of attitude measurement deal with – are relatively simple. Nevertheless, certain of the basic ideas in this theory are present in *La Physique sociale*: in fact Quételet clearly perceives that the problem posed by the measurement of "moral qualities" can only be resolved by postulating a mathematical relationship between "the cause and the effect" or, as we would tend to say in our language, between the variable to be measured and its indices.

Thus, the frequency of crimes can serve to measure the "propensity to crime", if one postulates a determinate relationship between the two variables. The fact that Quételet always postulates a linear re-lationship – which is obviously questionable – is less important than the general idea that the unobservable can become measurable provided one admits to the existence of mathematical relationships between observable properties and non-observable variables.

Another important intuition of Quételet's which modern sociology has made ample use of, is the idea that it is possible to "substitute an isolated observation of a large quantity of persons for repeated observations of the same person". This postulate is fundamental to the interpretation of a considerable proportion of sociological surveys.

The third searchlight beam is directed towards LePlay, whose monographs on the family are of crucial importance for the history of observational techniques in the social sciences and who, in spite of his opposition to statistics, originated an important quantitative method: the analysis of family budgets. But these are just the most well known aspects of LePlay's work. A complete history of the Playist movement, which would have to include an inspection of the 40,000 pages of *La réforme sociale*, has still to be written. This history would be a fascinating one because the Playist movement is dominated by a strange contradiction: though strongly marked with ideology, dogmatism and even sectarianism, it nevertheless played an important role in the development of a positive social science and proved to be amazingly innovative from the point of view of observational methods.

In the autobiographical fragment which we referred to on several occasions in the first part of this introduction, Lazarsfeld is at pains to stress the influences of the Bühlers on his intellectual development. In the extracts reproduced here from *Some historical observations on the analysis of action*, one finds a description of the intellectual climate which led him to concentrate his efforts on the problems of decision-making (in voting, consumption, etc.) and on what he called the "empirical analysis of action". The sections of the original article which are omitted here have principally to do with the relationship between Max Weber and the theory of action. As this problem is dealt with in an article on Max Weber at the end of the first section, we have decided to include mainly those parts concerned with the Würzburg School, on the one hand, and the works of the Bühlers and Lewin, on the other.

Lazarsfeld's general purpose in this article is to show how a new research tradition, the empirical analysis of action, became established via criticism of the prevailing schools of thought. The first of these schools is behaviourism, which rejected the notion of action for implying a subjective moment. The Bühlers, in elaborating this notion, avoided introducing positivism at the very high price which behaviourism agreed to pay from the conceptual point of view. At the same time, they were keenly concerned to avoid the dangers of subjectivism and of introspection. This reluctance may make the project seem banal to us. But it is important to see that historically it involved an important innovation. Between two psychological traditions, Wundt's psychophysics and behaviourism on the one side, which sought to give psychology a scientific status at the price of a reductionist epistemology, and the tradition of individual clinical psychology, hardly free from its humanist origins on the other side, the Bühlers inserted an entirely new tradition of research. The *action* paradigm allowed them to retain the subjective moment in behaviour and led them to introduce a category of concepts which later became widely diffused, namely dispositional concepts (attitudes etc.). At the same time they retained the idea, taken from experimental psychology, of underwriting the logical bases of induction by standardising observation and employing statistical techniques.

It was by this third route, characterised by a *method*, standardised quasi-experimental observation and the action *paradigm*, that both Kurt Lewin and Lazarsfeld became involved.

In short, what Lazarsfeld owes to the Bühlers is firstly the action paradigm. Secondly, it is the idea that a positive attitude in the analysis of social phenomena does not imply the elimination of subjectivity or, more generally, the exclusion of unobservable variables. Similarly, he retained the idea, which was to occupy an important place in his work, that one of the fundamental problems of the social sciences was the problem of *conceptualisation* – the idea of the association between scientifically strategic concepts and sets of observable elements. In this sense, both the analysis of latent structures, which formalises the relationship between "indices" and latent (unobservable) variables, and the elaboration of the notion of type derive from the epistemology of the social sciences which Karl Bühler arrived at in his *Krise der Psychologie*. Finally, Lazarsfeld took from the Bühlers the idea that the experimental procedures used by psychologists could be extended by standardised observation which, because it allows the use of statistical techniques, can greatly benefit from the logical advantages of experimentation whilst avoiding most of its difficulties.

If one does not take account of the intellectual terrain on which Lazarsfeld made, as he put it, "his first steps in the social sciences" it is difficult to understand several important aspects of his work: his lasting enthusiasm for the analysis of the decision-making process, for instance, no less than certain of his most notable methodological contributions. Thus, the so-called panel technique, which involves observing the same sample of individuals on several occasions, clearly derives directly from the Viennese intellectual environment. For it represents the best logical approximation to experimental techniques which it is possible to envisage. But by remaining a technique of *observation*, it avoids the artificial character of experimentation. The latter, despite its advantages from the point of view of inductive logic, in fact presents serious drawbacks when it is used to analyse concrete social processes.

What interested Lazarsfeld – in Vienna and subsequently – was precisely the analysis of concrete social phenomena. In Vienna he belonged to the socialist movement and his interest in the social sciences was at least partly awakened, if we are to believe the autobiographical fragment, by social preoccupations. The methodological orientation which he acquired from the Bühlers enabled him to respond to this preoccupation and define his fundamental scientific project: to study the individual in his natural social milieu. The third route opened up by the Bühlers actually led to sociology, although it derived from a critique of psychology. But, it must be noted that this was a sociology centred on the individual and organised around the idea of action, for this is the feature which exhibits both its strength and weakness. Would Lazarsfeld have stayed with this vision of sociology if, after leaving Vienna, he had not become immersed in the typically pragmatist climate of the American intellectual universe? This is a natural question to ask but one which is difficult to answer.

At the same time, the action paradigm offered the advantage, as we have seen, of transcending disciplinary boundaries. For all the social sciences are concerned with the analysis of action, whether it be with the theory of economic decision-making, or the psychological analysis of behaviour. But what still had to be invented was the positive and empirical analysis of action. The economic theory of decision-making is by nature speculative and *a priorist*. It consists in spelling out the consequences which follow from the axioms which define *homo oeconomicus*. As for experimental psychology, it has the disadvantage of relying on the abstraction which is the individual as observed under laboratory conditions. Lazarsfeld's intuition was that there was room for an empirical analysis of action in a variety of social science sectors isolated from one another by the compartmentalisation of disciplines.

It is the same theme of the methodological unity of the social sciences which is Lazarsfeld's preoccupation in the article "Theoretical observations on the formation and measurement of concepts in the behavioural sciences".

It sets out to show how the development of experimental psychology led to the utilisation of "intervening variables" situated between the stimulus and the response, as identified by the researcher. Although they were not open to direct observation, they were still indispensable for the interpretation of relationships. These unobservable "intervening variables" clearly belong to the same logical category as "latent" variables, a notion which Lazarsfeld developed in the analysis of latent structures. Generally speaking, all the social sciences were obliged to introduce concepts which, unlike typical concepts in the natural sciences, corresponded neither to observable variables nor to relationships between observable variables. The notion of "intelligence" and the notions of "anomie", "bureaucracy" or "authoritarianism" are obviously useful, even indispensable, to the description of reality. But unlike the notions of length or acceleration, they do not correspond to observable variables.[11] They imply the idea of degree or intensity, but they are not directly measurable.

Variables of this kind, which are to some extent, but not entirely, typical of the social sciences, appeared very early in experimental psychology. Thus whilst Weber's law describes a pure relationship between the stimulus and the response, Fechner in his reformulation introduces an "intervening variable", namely the notion of the "intensity of feeling". This notion clearly corresponds to an unobservable and non-measurable variable which offers certain logical advantages.

At the time when the social sciences began to make some claims to scientificity and appropriated the epistemological model of the natural sciences or at least what they thought this model to be, the tendency was towards an objectivism which aspired to eliminate variables of this type. Behaviourism is the most well known and systematic example of this tendency.

Lazarsfeld had more than one reason for dwelling on the history of behaviourism. The first is that behaviourism attempted to eliminate the concept of action. The second, corresponding reason is that, following Bühler, it was precisely the critique of behaviourism which allowed him to introduce the idea of the empirical analysis of action. The third and most important reason which expresses one of the central theses of the present article, is that behaviourism actually failed to maintain its radical objectivism for very long and was forced to reintroduce the action schema. (Note that one can give a formal definition of *objectivism*: in the present case, it involves excluding from scientific language all propositions except those which contain exclusively descriptive concepts, whether of stimulation or response. In this sense Weber's law is objectivist; Fechner's or Weber–Fechner's, as it is still referred to, is not).

The example of Tolman is typical of the evolution of behaviourism. The fact is that after an initial absorbing interest in animal psychology he went on to make an important contribution to Parsons's and Shils's interdisciplinary enterprise, *Towards a General Theory of Action*. Although he had been regarded as an important authority in the behaviourist movement, he originally considered that animal psychology – which appeared to be a suitable candidate for the application of strict behaviourism – could not help but introduce concepts which did not correspond to directly observable phenomena, namely anthropomorphically-based concepts such as need, caution, etc. In short, he quickly became aware that, to interpret relationships between stimulus and response, an objectivist language according to the above definition was inappropriate. It was necessary to open up this language and make room for unobservable variables situated in an *intermediate* position between the stimulus and the response in the syntax of propositions. This is why he refers to them as *intervening variables*.

The direction of Tolman's involvement has the same pattern in the case of Hull, who mathematically formalises the notion of intervening variable. Let us suppose that response is measured by p (probability of a correct response on the part of the subject) and that one wishes to study the relationship between p and n (number of trials rewarded). One can then try to observe the empirical relationship between p and n and attempt to find an analytical expression for it. However, in the majority of cases, several analytical expressions may correspond with the empirical distribution and it will be impossible to choose between them. In short, the objectivist language leads to an impasse. The other strategy consists of *elaborating* the relationship between p and n with the help of new propositions. But these propositions entail the introduction of new notions which do not belong to the vocabulary which describes stimulus and response. Starting out with the relationship $p = \emptyset\ (n)$, Hull first introduces the notion of speed in accomplishing the task (E), then the notion of desire (D), for example with regard to the food which serves as a reward, then the notion of habituation (H) to behaving in a manner likely to be rewarded. These notions are introduced in sequence of propositions:

$$p = h(\mathrm{E})$$
$$\mathrm{E} = g(\mathrm{D, H})$$
$$\mathrm{H} = f(n)$$
$$p = h[g(\mathrm{D, H})]$$
$$p = h\{g[D, f(n)]\}$$

Let us now suppose that reasonable hypotheses in the form of *f*, *g* and *h* can be put forward: it then becomes possible to *deduce* the analytical form of the relationship between *p* and *n* and to verify that it actually occurs. Therefore, the openness of the language does not rule out the possibilities of verification. On the contrary, it leads to an elaboration of the stimulus–response relationship.

Hull's work represents a relatively simple version of the developments which subsequently took place in learning theory. However, it is a good indicator of the direction these developments were to take.

As Lazarsfeld says, Tolman and Hull were the beginning of the end for behaviourism. Because the observable could only be explained by the unobservable, and because a certain degree of anthropomorphism was unavoidable even in animal psychology, the theory of animal behaviour ceased to appear as a privileged example of objective psychology. This is why Tolman's interests tended progressively towards the general problematic of the analysis of behaviour and action. Not only did psychology thereby cease to be divided into distinct areas but it even came to share the same language as the other social sciences.

We could take other subject areas and trace the development of the idea that scientific language (not only in the social sciences but in the natural sciences as well) inevitably consists of propositions expressing relationships between observable and unobservable variables. According to Lazarsfeld, this idea can be found in William James and Herbert Spencer; whilst R. Carnap and A. Kaplan give examples of its application in the natural sciences. It was the development of this fundamental epistemological proposition which eventually gave birth to the series of mathematical instruments which, like factor analysis or the models associated with the theory of learning, make it possible to analyse the structure of a set of observable variables as a function of a set of unobservable variables.

Naturally, this problem is a general one, common to all the social sciences: we would say that all of them without exception – despite the resistance of some like behavioural psychology – make use of strategic scientific concepts which do not correspond with directly observable variables. This is the case with the concept of *habituation* in psychology, the concept of *utility* in economics, or the concept of *anomie* in sociology.

To summarise, the history of behaviourism is like a kind of developer, in the photographic sense, of an underlying structure in the language of the social sciences.

In the article on Max Weber, "Max Weber and empirical research in sociology", Lazarsfeld once again takes up his reflections on the theme of the empirical analysis of action.

As we indicated in the first part of this introduction, this article holds an immediate interest: it presents the reader with a little known, if not unknown, image of Max Weber. Lazarsfeld describes how, on six separate occasions, Weber became involved in sociological surveys in industry and how this experience gave him an opportunity to reflect on what we today, following Lazarsfeld, would call the methodology of empirical sociology. It is remarkable to find Weber declaring that "only an in-depth analysis of the figures can guide the investigator towards the hypotheses which he needs to interpret his findings and to pose new problems" or to see him questioning the relevance of laboratory experiments applied to the analysis of the work conditions of industrial workers, and coming to a negative conclusion about the suggestion that the survey method be replaced by the experimental method; or again, to see him defending the application of a quantitative and statistical methodology in the construction of typologies.

In this article, one therefore finds a Weber committed to quantitative typologies, rather than the theoretician of the ideal type. Instead of the historicising sociologist, a sociologist who seems to be very close to the Durkheim of *Suicide*, for example, when he attempts a statistical analysis of the stabilising influence of marriage; over against the theoretician imbued with juridical thinking, a sociologist at pains to link conceptualisation with observation thought of in quasi-experimental terms.

This "rediscovered Weber" which Lazarsfeld presents raises a question. Why was this aspect of Weber's activity only a passing phase? Lazarsfeld's reply is twofold. Firstly, it is possible that, for various reasons, Weber harboured ambiguous feelings towards psychology (it is known that his scientific activity was interrupted for several years by mental illness), and that he sought to overcome the attraction which he felt for psychological problems by ignoring them. Secondly, and this is the interpretation favoured by Lazarsfeld, the problem of action within Weber's cultural milieu belonged primarily to the juridical realm and thence became part of the philosophy of law. When it entered the social sciences it was essentially by way of the history of civilisations. The connection between action and history is expressed with particular clarity in Wilhelm Dilthey, with whom Weber was closely familiar. His theory of action thus came under the constant influence of the Diltheyan idea that action is of no interest except in relation to history; hence his conviction that one of the key objectives of the social sciences is to carry out a "critique of historical reason".

The methodological essays in the second part echo the historical essays in the first. Through the medium of Weber's hesitations, the story of behaviourism, Quételet's intuitions or the lengthy gestation of the modern idea of statistics, one can see the slow formation of a language which, although it may not cover the whole of the social sciences at least broadly transcends their boundaries. In the second part, one can find descriptions of what may be called the basic structures or at least certain of the basic structures of this language.

This collection of articles consists of two contributions of a non-specific kind, firstly about methodology in general ("Problems of methodology"), secondly about qualitative methods ("Several functions of qualitative analysis in sociology"), and two contributions of a more specific nature, the first of which deals with the analysis of statistical relationships ("The interpretation of statistical relationships as a research procedure"), the second with the problem of typology construction ("Techniques of typology construction").

"Problems of Methodology" is one of the two opening chapters of the progress report which Merton and his collaborators published in 1959 under the title *Sociology Today*. The other chapter was by Parsons and dealt with sociological theory. Lazarsfeld's contribution is a general presentation of the problems of sociological methodology as they appeared at that time. Since then some of these problems have assumed a different form. However, to this day this contribution remains one of the best introductions to methodology and to the concept of methodology in particular. True to his usual practice, Lazarsfeld seeks to clarify this rather delicate notion by using a range of examples grouped into broad categories.

One of Lazarsfeld's chosen objectives in this article is to eliminate the numerous misunderstandings which have arisen concerning the concept of methodology. Methodology is not as is sometimes thought, a *normative* discipline. In no way does it seek to establish the ideal rules by which proper research should be carried out. Given the continual development of scientific language, such a "methodology" would tend towards sterility. Methodology in Lazarsfeld's sense is more a *positive* discipline. It does not aim to pass judgement on the work of the sociologist but to understand it in order to draw from it, and in some cases to codify or generalise its procedures.

As Lazarsfeld says, "sociology studies man in society, methodology studies the sociologist at work". The benefits of this positive discipline of methodology are twofold. On the one hand, it contains a speculative advantage which we stressed sufficiently in the first part of this introduction. It helps to throw light on the structures of the language of the social sciences, in something like the way in which logic was originally able to give form to patterns of everyday thinking. On the other hand, it presents a practical advantage to the extent that, in contributing to the formalisation and generalisation of research procedures, it facilitates their transmission and development.

One common source of confusion arises from the assimilation of methodology to what could be called *technology*. It is therefore important to distinguish clearly between these two notions. The second has to do with the acquisition and use of particular tools, whether the questionnaire, factor analysis, or scaling techniques. The manipulation of such techniques can be done without any references to a specific problem, hypotheses or object of research. Thus, one can learn to carry out a factor analysis using a imaginary correlation matrix. Methodology, on the other hand, involves the analysis of already completed research – or in some cases the programming of new research – in order to isolate the logical structures connected with the different phases of research.

It is interesting to note that the real meaning of the concept is being distorted even now and that methodology is often equated with technology. This is possibly a consequence of the phenomena of bureaucratisation which have accompanied the institutionalisation of research. It may indeed be true that the critical spirit has difficulty in maintaining itself in a bureaucratical context. But a critique, in the positive sense of the term, is precisely what methodology is.

Leaving the detailed study of the article up to the reader, we will illustrate the notion of methodology from one particular case, elaborating an example which Lazarsfeld himself uses, which he borrows from Clausen.

Very frequently, sociologists make use of correlations between variables defined, not in individual terms, but in terms of geographical or administrative areas. Thus one can make a connection between the percentage of workers and the percentage of Communist votes in an election within a group of communes. Or one can relate the proportion of mentally ill to a measurement of living standards on the basis of a particular territorial unit – urban districts, for instance – in order to see if the poorest among them are also those which have the highest rates of hospitalisation for mental illness. Once the data have been set out, one can calculate the corresponding coefficients. This operation is based on technology. It is possible to learn to calculate a correlation coefficient using imaginary data. Let us suppose, then, that the correlation coefficient obtained is very high or, in other words, that the poorest districts generally have the highest rates of hospitalisation. Should one conclude from this that bad living conditions have something to do with the probability of the development of psychopathological problems in the individual?

The answer is no. In fact, the interpretative hypothesis proposed in the question is only one of the possible hypotheses. One could also surmise, for example, that, when problems appear – which clearly happens in most cases well before hospitalisation – they lead to a disruption of occupational life which in turn leads to a degradation of the individual's standard of living, thereby increasing the probability of encountering the mentally ill in the deprived districts. An alternative supposition could be that material conditions do not strictly speaking exert any influence over the development of problems but that these occur because of the climate or because of the kinds of social relationship which prevail in the poor districts. In this case, the probability of an individual falling victim to mental problems will be independent of his personal living conditions and will depend solely on the social characteristics of the district. In short, it is possible to explain the observed correlation with the help of extremely diverse hypotheses.

But one can take a further step and inquire as to the source of this *ambiguity*; a significant ambiguity in that the same conclusions can be deduced from different hypotheses and the available data preclude any choice between them.

Formally, the data allow one to declare that a correlation exists at the level of an aggregate (the district); the poorer the *district* is, the higher the rates of hospitalisation. The question itself has to do with *individuals*: are material living conditions the source of mental problems in the *individual*? In short the question is to know whether one can interpret a relationship observed at the level of aggregates at the level of the *individual*. We can answer this question by constructing an arithmetical model. Let us assume that there are four districts characterised respectively by 3, 6, 9 and 12 per cent of hospitalised cases and having 20, 40, 60 and 80 per cent of their population belonging to deprived strata (naturally, these are imaginary figures constructed for the present purpose). We can then ask how the individuals are distributed in terms of the two variables to see if the observed relationship at the level of "aggregate" rates is necessarily maintained at the level of individuals.

The model can be translated into the following schema:

	Lower classes	Others	
Sick	0	3	3
Healthy	20	77	97
	20	80	100

	Lower classes	Others	
Sick	2	4	6
Healthy	38	56	94
	40	60	100

	Lower classes	Others	
Sick	6	3	9
Healthy	54	37	91
	60	40	100

	Lower classes	Others	
Sick	7	5	12
Healthy	73	15	88
	80	20	100

The figures which appear *inside* the table are purely imaginary. The only ones which are derived from the hypothesis are those at the *margins*. They reveal a possible, though fictitious, situation in which the fact of belonging to a lower class does not increase the probability of mental problems, despite the fact that mental problems occur more frequently when the proportion of individuals of lower class increases. In fact, the probability of the appearance of these problems in the lower classes is equal to $(0 + 2 + 6 + 7)/(20 + 40 + 60 + 80) = 7.5$ per cent. In the other classes it is equal to $(3 + 4 + 3 + 5)/(80 + 60 + 40 + 20) = 7.5$ per cent. In short, the arithmetical example shows that it is impossible, without taking precautions, to infer from a relationship at the level of aggregates to a relationship at the level of individuals: the existence of the former does not entail the latter.

This discussion may be regarded as a typical example of methodological analysis: taking a particular problem it raises a general logical problem and enables the investigator to become *aware* of the hypotheses brought into play in the analysis of relationships defined on an aggregate basis.

We have been at some pains to stress this familiar example because it provides a good illustration of the nature of methodology. The reader will find in Lazarsfeld's article numerous examples of methodological analysis applied to other aspects of research, whether it be problems of conceptualisation, comparison between techniques or the systematization of empirical research. The methodological procedure which Lazarsfeld advocates is shown to be very fruitful especially as far as the problems of conceptualisation are concerned. But we will have occasion to return to this problem when we come to the article on typologies.

In other respects, the article is a strong plea in defence of empirical sociology, demonstrating that its refinements, instead of betraying the ambitions of macrosociology and sociological theory, have contributed to their rediscovery and clarification through formalisation.

In our opinion, this defence is not entirely convincing. It has the weakness of relying on the postulate, which we find hard to accept, that macrosociological problems can always, in principle at least, be tackled by statistical or quasi-statistical methods. There is, however, one implication which could be termed *ethical*, to the extent that it invites the sociologist who is concerned with macrosociological problems to take up a reflexive attitude with regard to the mental processes he employs.

The following article, the *Interpretation of statistical relationships as a research procedure*, is another classic example of methodological analysis. In it, Lazarsfeld formalises the problem of the interpretation of statistical relationships. More precisely, he poses the question of the conditions for interpreting a statistical relationship within a set of propositions using causal language. The reader will see how a strong statistical relationship can, under certain circumstances, be associated with a complete absence of causal connection between the two variables in correlation. Conversely, a zero statistical connection does not necessarily imply the absence of any causal connection: one variable can have an effect on another without the state of the second appearing to be determined by the state of the first. The first of these two methodological propositions was clearly perceived by Durkheim. Indeed it was thanks to this methodological discovery that he succeeded in rescuing the quantitative study of suicide from the conflicting debates in which it had become embroiled. It is curious that Durkheim, who had a real genius for understanding the logical difficulties of interpreting statistical relationships, still failed to perceive the second of the stated propositions: he always interprets a zero correlation as indicating an absence of causal relationship which, as Lazarsfeld demonstrates, is not necessarily true.

This text has considerable importance. It has been translated and reproduced many times in a variety of publications. Its present widespread popularity among sociologists is such that, in order to get some idea of its methodological importance, it needs to be compared with a number of other texts that attempted to tackle the question in the nineteenth and twentieth centuries. Lazarsfeld never wrote the history of this problem. It would be a simple matter to do this, beginning with Stuart Mill's *Principles*, Durkheim's *Suicide* and *Rules*, Simiand's "Statistics and Experiment" or Sutherland's *Principles of Criminology*. One would find that the ideas that appear to us today to be relatively simple have taken the best part of a century to evolve. Moreover, Lazarsfeld's article came right at the beginning – it must be noted in the perspective of these historical remarks – of an important movement of methodological research which is still alive at the present time, which shows by its very existence that the apparently innocuous questions which he raises here lead to real logical and epistemological difficulties which have yet to be fully resolved.

The methodological examples alluded to in the preceding pages have to do with quantitative research. But there are two other articles which show that methodology is never, either in the spirit or the deed of Lazarsfeld's work, restricted to quantitative aspects alone.

Several functions of qualitative analysis in Sociology is an analysis of the structures of qualitative language. In particular, it contains a very illuminating description of types of classification and, if we may be allowed to use the expression, of the types of typology which are encountered in the sociological literature. These classifications run from syncretic distinctions to formal typologies constructed from a set of classificatory dimensions. Between these two extremes, it is possible to define a whole range of intermediate cases. Thus, the classification of forms of knowledge proposed by Max Scheler rests partly on an ordinal classificatory dimension which marks the growing levels of abstraction in the modes of knowledge and partly on a set of idiosyncratic attributes characteristic of each particular type and non-reducible to more general classificatory dimensions.

This analysis is a good illustration of Lazarsfeld's methodological project. In the first place, one can see the positive rather than normative character of the analysis. Secondly, one can see Lazarsfeld applying the fundamental procedure which his methodology implies: that of *explication de texte*. In fact, the present article is the product of a systematic analysis of an extensive sample of qualitative research. As such, it illustrates the functions of methodological analysis. It leads firstly to a realisation of the mechanisms behind the formation of certain types of concept and consequently to the systematisation and eventual formalisation of these mechanisms. Further it makes it possible to objectify and render communicable certain procedures which would otherwise have to be rediscovered by each researcher largely according to their intuition and flair. Lastly, it brings to light the general structures of the language of research in the social sciences. In this connection, it is significant that, in his classification of types of classification, Lazarsfeld takes his illustrations from authors as different as Louis Wirth, Max Scheler, Robert Merton, Talcott Parsons or C. Wright Mills. Simply listing these names illustrates the character of the methodological analysis. *A priori*, Mills's essayist and critical sociology, Scheler's moral philosophy or Parsons's taxonomic theories seem to be very distant from one another intellectually. However, it is possible to detect formally analogous processes of conceptualisation.

But conceptualisation derived from a classification or a typology – whether implicit or explicit – only corresponds to one particular class of the processes of conceptualisation identified by Lazarsfeld. Another of these processes – which can be found in very different kinds of research, in cultural anthropology no less than in macrosociological theory or social psychology – is the one to which Lazarsfeld gave the name of *matrix formulation*.

In this instance, conceptualisation seeks to subsume under a common title (the matrix) disparate but related elements. Thus, Ruth Benedict was impressed by a collection of traits in Zuni culture: the Zuni indians make limited use of drugs and alcohol; they relate to their gods in simultaneously casual and ceremonious ways, reveal great imaginative apathy, demonstrate great liberalism with regard to divorce, etc. Although these traits pertained to different spheres, they all appeared to Ruth Benedict as mutually reinforcing, in much the same way as symptoms reinforce one another and combine in a syndrome. Summarising her observations, she declared that the central theme of Zuni culture consisted in the "avoidance of all emotional excess" and turned this into the concept of "appollonian culture". An expression of this kind, "capable of summarising a set of particular observations in a single description concept" is precisely what Lazarsfeld calls a matrix formulation.

This is another form of conceptualisation which can develop into a typification at a later stage in research. In analysing the qualitative sociological literature which he brought together, Lazarsfeld was able to show that this procedure of *matrix formulation* actually appears in very diverse contexts. For instance, numerous concepts in classical socio-logical theory are derived from it, whether they be the concepts of *Gemeinschaft*, *Ethos* or *Zeitgeist*. As for the majority of concepts in psychoanalysis (introvert or extrovert personality; inferiority complex, etc.) they are a product of the same mental process. Psychoanalysis has also been able to evolve a number of types of matrix construction. Once again, the merits of the analysis are both practical and speculative: on the one hand it brings to light mental processes which transcend the boundaries of particular disciplines while on the other, by making the implicit explicit, it brings a clear awareness of the logical steps used in research. It can thereby contribute to a greater systematisation of scientific work.

These remarks should help the reader to appreciate the fact that Lazarsfeld's article contains the outline of genuine theory of concept formation in the social sciences. The reader will find that other important points are also tackled, like the problem of the relationship between quantitative and qualitative which is analysed, not from an abstract point of view, but by way of a systematic comparison of the selected texts.

Like the majority of Lazarsfeld's articles, this one looks like an *inventory* of problems which at first sight may seem to be rather mixed. However, an attentive *explication de texte* reveals, not just the enumeration and juxtaposition of examples, but an attempt to establish a structural theory of the language of the social sciences which conforms to the fundamental project which we tried to elucidate in the first part of this introduction.

Naturally, as the author himself recognises, this theory is far from complete. Also, it seems necessary to question Lazarsfeld's implicit hypothesis that by and large the qualitative is, if we may be permitted a vulgar but eloquent expression, "the quantitative minus self-awareness". However, it does have the advantage of underlining the urgent need for sociologists to pose the problem of a general theory of induction in those observational situations which are typical of their discipline.

The final article in this second section deals with *Techniques of typology construction in the social sciences.* The *leitmotiv* of typology has appeared so frequently in this introduction and in the articles we have already examined that there is no need to explain it again. Let us simply say that we have included this article because it serves as a kind of summing up and conclusion for reflections on the problem of typology construction presented in the preceding articles. Here, the methodological (and historical) analysis is completed and develops into an exposition of a set of procedures which may appropriately be described as "techniques" because they can be systematically described, taught, learned and applied. What one finds here then, is a definition of certain basic concepts (attribute space, etc.) and operations (reduction, substruction of an attribute space) which formalise the results of the methodological analysis.

Thus the article illustrates one of the functions of methodology which has perhaps been insufficiently stressed until now: that of the extension of the body of techniques available to the researcher once the analysis has attained sufficient systematisation.

Of course this does not mean that methodology becomes transformed into technology as it develops. Even when a methodological analysis does lead to the elaboration of a new technique, the problem of the conditions for the application of that technique, the problem of its relationship to other techniques and many other methodological problems remain.

The last part of this volume presents four articles concerned with "empirical sociology", its definition, its interdisciplinary character and its organisation.

At the outset we have to admit that the term "empirical sociology", which has had general currency since it was used by Lazarsfeld, is not particularly well chosen. It describes *grosso modo* the sociological and sociopsychological tradition of observation by survey. As we saw in the articles in the first section, although sociological surveys have had a very long history, their institutionalisation in university milieux – in fact their institutionalisation *per se* – is recent, and what is more, strongly linked with Lazarsfeld's work and activity. These circumstances explain the origin of the term "empirical sociology" which, when surveys began to be institutionalised, somewhat resembled a *brand image* designed to draw attention to an enterprise, rather than a *concept* with precisely defined contours. In fact it can be said that neither Durkheim's *Suicide* nor even studies like those of de Tocqueville depend on observation. Rather, in both Durkheim and de Tocqueville one finds an inductive procedure which is typical of all the sciences of observation.

There is no escaping the fact that the expression "empirical sociology" is a *historical* concept describing a scientific movement in time and place, rather than a *logical* concept. To make these ideas more concrete we could say that "empirical sociology" as conceived by Lazarsfeld bears the same relationship to philosophical and epistemological empiricism as Destutt de Tracy's "ideology" bore to ideology in Marx's or Mannheim's sense: which is to say practically none.

The last four articles in this volume are about the movement which is associated with Lazarsfeld's name. The first article is a sort of general

introduction to the notion and history of empirical sociology. The two
which follow tackle the problem of the openness of empirical sociology
towards the other sciences, especially history and economics. The last of
them echoes the first article in this collection. Just as the first set out a
kind of programme for the future *history* of the social sciences which
Lazarsfeld says professional historians have still not seriously tackled,
so in the same way, the last outlines the programme for a future
philosophy of the social sciences, a discipline equally neglected by
philosophers of science. At the same time, these two articles – the first
and the last – are more than a programme. They are also like a
declaration of intent and actually describe the programme which
Lazarsfeld himself has implemented, at least in part.

The presidential address on *The Sociology of Empirical Sociology*,
delivered on the occasion of a plenary session of the American
Sociological Association, returns to a number of by now familiar
themes.

Lazarsfeld first of all recalls how the intellectual milieu he experienced
in Vienna led him to pose the problem of the empirical analysis of action.
In particular, his study of occupational choice (*Jugend und Beruf*) was
where he clarified this. It showed the importance of what he was later to
call *methodology* because he had the good fortune to be dealing with an
abundant but unexploitable collection of data. The originators of this
data had attempted to find out why adolescents chose this or that
occupation. But because they had not taken care to isolate the various
dimensions of the question "why?", they obtained conflicting answers:
some made play of earlier experiences, others cited particular aspects of
the chosen occupation, others referred to general orientations towards
occupational values. The same study made clear to Lazarsfeld the
inadequacies of the philosophy of action and the formal theories which
economists had begun to develop on the phenomenon of decision-
making.

This research experience, combined with the intellectual climate
surrounding the Bühlers, thus directed Lazarsfeld simultaneously
towards methodology and towards the elaboration of the empirical
analysis of action. In practice such an analysis could not be carried out
without some training in the art of transcribing abstract questions into
suitable research procedures.

Finally, what Lazarsfeld discovered in Vienna was an original
thought process. He realised that the social sciences could not be content
either with abstract theories or simply with experimentation which was
so fashionable at that time. He discovered that they could take the

middle road of surveys based on a plan of observation congruent with the initial questions and hypotheses. "Empirical sociology" is the name which he gave to this third way, whose origins can be dated quite precisely in retrospect.

In spite of its name, therefore, "empirical sociology" is the opposite of a sociology without theory. For methodology, instead of rejecting theory, is attracted to it. In fact, the operationalisation of abstract questions in the form of research procedures requires detailed reflection on these questions and on their language. The translation of concepts into indices assumes that the dimensions of these concepts can be separated out and the verification of propositions assumes that the relations involved can be precisely spelled out. There is sufficient proof of this complementarily between methodology and theory and hence of the necessity of the relations between "empirical sociology" and theory, in the very fact that Lazarsfeld was led to pose the problem of concept formation in the social sciences – the problem which occupies so much of his work – through reflection on the practical problems of research, like those which he had already encountered in *Jugend und Beruf*.

By virtue of its close links with methodology, "empirical sociology" thus rejoined the European theoretical tradition. But in another sense it rediscovered this tradition. To be precise, it connected up with the European tradition, represented by Booth, Tarde, the "other" Max Weber and the "other" Durkheim.

The last part of the address is a rapid evocation of a problem which was to culminate several years later in a large collective volume: namely, the problem of the uses of sociology.[12] Lazarsfeld gives a balanced reply to this question: the findings of sociology neither can lead to the discovery of the best model of social organisation (in which sense there cannot be a *revolutionary* sociology), nor as a rule can they generate immediate applications (so there cannot be a *technocratic* sociology either). They can, however, by their contribution to the improved understanding of social phenomena, help to alter the perception of social realities and thus indirectly influence the course of decision-making.

The following two articles are specific reworkings of the basic theme of the unity of the social sciences.

In *The Historian and the Pollster*, one can see the convergence of several of Lazarsfeld's major preoccupations. One can also identify the seeds of innovations which were not to become visible on the scientific scene until several years later. This article is first of all an appeal for interdisciplinarity: not an emotional, philosophical or doctrinaire appeal (like those which have been heard recently in numerous university contexts), but a pragmatic appeal highly typical of Lazarsfeld. For, if the vision of a social science transcending the boundaries of present day disciplines is one day to become a reality, it will certainly not be because of incantations which are a prudish modern version of the romantic idea of absolute knowledge. Rather, it will be the result of a sequence of effective methodological and institutional innovations designed to fulfil clearly specified objectives. This does not mean that such innovations will be without implications or that they can be put into effect without difficulty, but only that the necessary, if not sufficient, condition of their realisation is that they be conceived analytically.

Lazarsfeld is making a point here about the cross-fertilisation which could result from a closer connection between the survey specialist on the one hand and the historian on the other. If one examines the writings of past and present essayists or historians, whether they be authors like Goethe or Macaulay, a mediaevalist like La Monte or someone like David Riesman, one can see that they contain numerous propositions which are statements about differentiation , content and changes in opinions and attitudes. Generally speaking, notions like *Zeitgeist*, cultural anthropological descriptions as a whole, and the analysis of social movements and shifts of opinion of course, would have a much more precise content if they could make use of surveys, because in the last analysis all of these approaches involve propositions about opinions and attitudes.

Is this banal? The answer must clearly be no, because although we have seen a development in the past few years in the use of surveys by the historian, they are still far from providing all the help which they could give. Of course, historians of politics and elections in particular are making increasing use of survey techniques. But they are still underused in a number of areas where they could be applied – cultural phenomena, for instance. Ten years after Lazarsfeld's proposals, David Riesman's hypotheses in *The Lonely Crowd*, which continue to be discussed in the sociological literature on change in the nuclear family in industrial societies and the evolution of its structures and role, are still largely speculative in nature. Yet there is nothing to stop their being subjected to verification either by survey or by the secondary analysis of surveys.

However, sociologists, historians and essayists, are not solely responsible for the inadequacies of their relationship with the "pollster". No less frequently, the latter fails to see the advantage of entering into a relationship with the former. Instead of practising a policy of supplying products for current consumption, he could practise a policy of investment for future history and could thus contribute, much better than at present, to the illumination of current history. Just as certain essential phenomena of the past will always remain a mystery to the historian for lack of information about opinions, phenomena of contemporary society will remain opaque for lack of systematic observation of current social realities. There is still time to implement such observations, for example with respect to the effects of industrialisation on family structures or the development of attitudes towards the distribution of income. If we do not do this, we will be depriving ourselves forever of essential tools for the understanding of present-day society at the same time as neglecting our duty towards the historians of tomorrow.

It is doubtless true that survey practices will develop more or less on their own and will spread naturally to new areas. There is little likelihood that the obscurantist reaction of certain sociologists belonging to what the Germans call the group of *Weltverbesserer* or *Soziotheologen* will really amount to anything. It is doubtless also true that surveys cannot be generalised and systematised in all areas in one fell swoop. As Lazarsfeld writes, it is certainly no accident that the Kinsey report was not published until 1948. However, it is by no means certain that complete confidence ought to be placed in this natural development, especially because the objectives of survey research organisations are different from those of today's sociologist or tomorrow's historian and because there is no reason to suppose that the needs of the latter are automatically met by the products of the former.

Since the publication of Lazarsfeld's article, a number of initiatives have been made in several countries with a view to the rationalisation of social accounting (i.e. systematic observations of society in the form of surveys, polls or censuses). The survey has to a certain extent ceased to be product reserved for immediate consumption and has become a document or an investment. The most obvious sign of this preoccupation is the *data banks* which are currently being set up. Today these banks have become one of the key problems in the organisation of the social sciences. Both historians and sociologists are now involved and are making use of them. Nevertheless, the problem of crossfertilisation which Lazarsfeld posed remains unresolved. For, even if it is becoming increasingly possible to retrieve and consult survey data (or statistical data from government sources) in the same way that one retrieves and consults other types of document (for example, books) it still does not automatically mean that the data which are necessary for understanding the basic social phenomena of our time have actually been gathered, nor that they have been gathered in an appropriate form.

The problem posed by Lazarsfeld therefore implies more than the simple establishment of data banks. It also implies that the demands which historians and sociologists make of survey organisations (and government statistical agencies) should combine in such a way that a rational social accounting system will gradually develop and become as indispensable for the contemporary sociologist as for the future historian.

Once again, such an accounting system will not emerge overnight. But it is important to sensitise the community of researchers in the human sciences to this problem, not simply because the progress of knowledge of social phenomena depends on it, but also because it both assumes and implies a rapprochement between the disciplines and thus represents a step in the direction of a general social science. Finally – and here again we meet a preoccupation which criss-crosses the whole of Lazarsfeld's work – the development of a system of social accounting ought to contribute to the rationalisation of social action, just as economic accounting has contributed to the efficiency of economic action.

It is precisely the problem of the potential role of the sociologist in economic analysis which is the subject of *Reflections on business life*. In this article Lazarsfeld puts forward a kind of research programme which has special reference to economic life, although it does not break the continuity of his work on action and decision-making.

This article has an astonishing freshness. The world of economic decision-making is still virtually unknown territory to the sociologist. Yet advances in theory and in the empirical analysis of action provide an intellectual framework into which such an analysis could easily insert itself. The reason for this state of affairs clearly has a lot to do with the fact that many sociologists find the study of "business life" to be more repugnant than other themes which are thought to be more ennobling intellectually. Further, the difficulties of observation are certainly greater in the case of economic decision-making than in the case of voting or consumer decisions. The result is that we remain very ignorant about the mechanisms involved in the making of decisions whose consequences affect our daily life. As Oxenfeldt says, prices do not drop from the sky. But we have to admit to knowing rather little about the decision-making mechanisms which contribute to their formation.

Lazarsfeld's proposed research programme is derived from an assessment of the literature relating to the sociology of business. This assessment brings to light two weaknesses. Firstly, the research in this area is discontinuous, monographic and only rarely allows general propositions to be expressed. Thus the Useems establish that managers who rise up in the hierarchy demonstrate increasingly flexible behaviour, that they "become more and more adapted to the organisational context and as a result their behaviour is more and more predictable".

They tend to regard the obstacles which they encounter as problems to be solved rather than signs of something negative. But these observations, although interesting, are difficult to interpret. In particular, it would be wrong to say that these changes in frameworks of reference are attributable to length of service or career mobility. In short, studies in economic sociology have to take account of advances in methodology.

Moreover, concept formation in studies of business life is characteristically idiosyncratic and imprecise. All studies which are concerned with problems of decision-making and action in a more general sense, must not simply take account of the conceptual and theoretical frameworks proposed by the theory and empirical analysis of action, but must also subject them to a secondary examination. Close scrutiny of the literature relating to business life therefore encourages both a rationalisation of methodology and a conceptual rationalisation which ought to have some bearing on existing theoretical paradigms – paradigms which the work of the Bühlers, Lewin and Lazarsfeld himself gave expression to in various ways.

This is why the reader of this article will find a brilliant digression into the realm of concepts relating to the idea of inclination. This digression is a structural analysis of the dimensions according to which concepts like *preference, opinion, tendency, expectation, plan*, etc. can be differentiated, or in other words the set of concepts used in descriptions of preparations for action. These notions, which are generally applied idiosyncratically and anarchically, can be regarded as corresponding to particular combinations of fundamental dimensions.

As we mentioned earlier, Lazarsfeld's conceptual analysis is carried out using logical procedures (the very same as those described in the article on typology construction) which are formally indistinguishable from those used by Jakobson in his phonological analysis.

The directions contained in "Reflections on business life" are programmatic. But even if a start were made towards the implementation of this programme, it would lead to useful cooperation between sociologists and economists. Of course it must be recognised that Lazarsfeld's programme once again exposes sociology's "psychologis-

tic" character and that the economic analysis of action does not extend
to the whole of the potential field of economic sociology. All the same, it
does represent an essential part of it, in respect of which sociology is well
equipped both conceptually and methodologically, to develop a coherent research tradition.

The Philosophy of Science and Empirical Research in Sociology, the
final chapter in our selection, denounces philosophers of science for their
lack of understanding of the social sciences. But this article goes on to
invite the professional philosopher to take up and systematise the
analysis of the language of the social sciences which Lazarsfeld had
begun in his own work.

Even an author like K. Hempel, who at one time formalised the
problem of classification and typology construction in terms which
Lazarsfeld was to adopt personally, feels a certain amount of re-
pugnance towards using the social sicences to sharpen his epistemological thinking. When he does refer to them it is to extract highly
specific examples which are tailored to the epistemological framework
derived from the natural sciences – the notion of *perfect competition*, for
instance, which bears the same sort of relation to economic reality as the
concepts of natural science bear to nature itself. But this is the exception
rather than the rule. In general, the construction of concepts or of types
follows different procedures in the natural sciences and the social
sciences. On this point there is one piece of evidence that all the treatises
of method in sociology invariably recognise. It is that, although the
social sciences have developed a theory of measurement, the concept of
measurement has a different meaning in physics. In this discipline, using
Meinong's terminology, measurements are divided into *fundamental*
measurements (like measurements of length) and *derivative* measurements constructed out of fundamental measurements (like speed or
acceleration), the former implying an isomorphism between a set of
physical operations and the axioms defining the notion of measurement.[13] In contrast, "measurements" in the social sciences are generally measurements derived from models which rely on particular
hypotheses, like the analysis of latent structures already referred
to.

It is nevertheless surprising to find as Lazarsfeld did, that philosophers continue to use the language of logical inclusion in their
reflections on the notion of class even when, like Black, they refer to
concepts which belong to the social sciences. Of course Black is aware
that these classes cannot be defined exclusively by species attributes and
specific differences: for example, it is hard to see how the notion of

happiness could be defined by the *genus proximum* and the *differentia specifica*. His proposal to replace this idea of class with the idea of "word–sample", which would allow the incorporation of non-identical individuals (intelligent persons, well-managed firms, etc.), is little better. In fact it regards the problem as having been solved. If Black had been more attentive to the work of psychologists and sociologists, he would notice that many procedures have been proposed for the formation of classes in cases where it is impossible to resort to the logic of inclusion. He would also have realised that the theory of concept formation in the social sciences leads to a fruitful questioning of the logical theory of definition.

Lazarsfeld's article is an incentive to reflect on this subject. Why is there such disdain among philosophers of science for the social sciences? Perhaps one of the main reasons for this phenomenon lies in the fact that the spectacular technical achievements of the natural sciences have no equivalent in the social sciences. Is this a result of the relative immaturity of the social sciences or the different characteristics of the subject–object relationship in the two types of discipline? The fact that it is even possible to ask this question shows that philosopher of science could usefully pay attention to the social sciences not only at the epistemological level, but at the level of the theory of knowledge. Whilst the physicist takes the credit for new discoveries, is not the sociologist's main task to differentiate between commonplace but contradictory propositions? It is banal to state that bachelors have a higher suicide rate – banal, because easily explicable. But, as Halbwachs observes it would have been just as banal to state the opposite. Lazarsfeld also took up this theme in an article not reproduced here[14] and his reply to the question would perhaps be that the sociologist's familiarity with his object helps in large measure to deprive his propositions of the spectacular and "esoteric" character which propositions in physics often have. Further, and this is underlined in one of the preceding articles ("Several functions of qualitative methods in sociology"), it is not true that discoveries have been lacking in the social sciences. They are present not in anthropology but even in sociology, when the sociologist is studying his own society. The studies by Roethlisberger and Dickson which provided evidence of the celebrated Hawthorne effect are proof of this. Similarly, discoveries were made by Lazarsfeld himself in *Die Arbeitslosen von Marienthal* and in *Personal Influence*. However, these discoveries tend to become rapidly "trivialised" and merge into the body of received ideas: today for example, it is common sense to acknowledge the influence of personal relationships on occupational satisfaction and output. But it had no place in popular wisdom until Roethlisbergen and Dickson carried out their studies.

A second reason why philosophers of science look down on the social sciences may arise from the fact – which itself leads to a problem in the sociology of knowledge – that the model of science which philosophers generally adopt is derived from the physical and chemical sciences. The "positivism" of the philosophers of science is by no means restricted to the United States. It is striking to find that studies by French philosophers of science typically have a selective perception of the social sciences. Epistemology is oriented more towards economics or structural linguistics than towards sociology. This can probably be attributed to the mathematical (and sometimes pseudo-mathematical) clothing of certain parts of these disciplines together with their apparently esoteric language, which restores epistemology to familiar territory. When the philosopher does take an interest in the apparently less esoteric social sciences like sociology, it is in order to extract examples which are particularly susceptible to incorporation within the epistemological framework derived from the natural sciences. However, this does not prevent the same epistemologist from feeling attracted towards those sociologists whose work is closest to the idea of the great philosophical systems. Indeed, it is more than likely that he will prefer Comte to Quételet and Marx to Durkheim.

The neo-Diltheyan epistemology of the social sciences embraced by some other philosophers is likewise unsatisfying. Starting from general and abstract considerations, they have renewed the attempt to analyse *a priori* the opposition or distance between the social and the natural sciences. Both groups would benefit from taking heed of Lazarsfeld's advice.

This is the common-sense suggestion that a philosopher of the social sciences ought to begin with close observation of the research process and its products – advice which is both provocative and down to earth. But it is worth offering as long as philosophers of science refuse to abandon their selective and apriorist perception of the social sciences.

One could even go further than Lazarsfeld and say that the social sciences, if they are to be taken seriously by philosophers, will have to call into question any epistemology that relies essentially on the natural sciences for its construction and bring about a relativisation of this epistemology. They might thus allow the foundation of a general epistemology to be laid.

Having come to the end of our general presentation, we would in conclusion like to stress briefly Lazarsfeld's concern for what we have somewhat pretentiously called *metasociology*.

As the reader will have realised by now, this metasociology is subdivided into several imaginary chapters which appear here in the form of *leitmotive*: a chapter on the history of the social sciences, a long chapter on methodology, a chapter on the general paradigm of action analysis, a chapter on the organisation of the social sciences and its relationship to this methodology and history and a chapter on the sociology of the social sciences.

The originality of this metasociology has first of all to do with the level of the undertaking itself, or to use a currently fashionable term, its *project*. This originality is clearly evident in at least two aspects of the project. The first is the historical aspect. For, although Lazarsfeld may not have invented the history of the social sciences, he at least demonstrated that the traditionally-based history was to a large extent partial and arbitrary. He showed that the history of sociology can be regarded as completely other than a history of doctrines and ideas, closely following the model of the history of philosophy. Without prejudging either the scientific character of the social sciences or the question of whether the gulf which separates them from the natural sciences should or should not be bridged, he provided evidence of the possibility of studying the history of the social sciences in the same way as one studies the history of the natural sciences. That is, by considering the development of observational methods and analytical techniques, as well as ideas and systems and by studying the development of *concept formation* in the general context of research instead of arbitarily abstracting it. Of course Lazarsfeld does not present us with a complete history but rather the analysis of a number of particular episodes. It is also true of course that his history of sociology is strongly influenced by his own point of view. But his way of looking at historical monographs opens up an unquestionably new perspective in the history of the social sciences.

The second aspect which reveals the originality of the project is obviously that of *methodology*. It is no exaggeration to say that Lazarsfeld was responsible for a profound alteration in the meaning of this word. For him, methodology is neither a collection of particular techniques nor a set of vague and general ideas incapable of influencing the course of research. It differs profoundly from the loosely defined methodology which Leibniz, Comte or Poincaré justifiably attacked. Instead, it is a truly *positive* discipline, having its own methods which Lazarsfeld summed up in the notion of *explication de texte*; a discipline designed to show the structures of the language in actual use in scientific work rather than to lay down impractical general principles or impose particular research techniques. In fact Lazarsfeld's conception of methodological objectives approximates to what could be called a positive *epistemology*.

The originality of Lazarsfeld's project is not simply apparent at the level of intentions, but also in terms of results. A number of the articles published here present discoveries which now belong to the shared stock of social scientific knowledge, whether it be "multivariate analysis", the general idea of which is set out in the article on "The analysis of statistical relationships", techniques of typology construction or historical monographs. Others, such as the article on surveys and history, opens up perspectives which have still to be fully explored. For Lazarsfeld's project has not only produced real and directly tangible results. It has opened up new and previously only partly explored paths, both in the sphere of methodology and the history of the social sciences, and in the sphere of "empirical" research.

It is difficult to analyse the process whereby an innovator comes to create a following. LePlay was the founder of a school; Quételet was not. In the case of Lazarsfeld – one of the few sociologists since the Second World War to have undeniably founded a school – the explanation is not hard to find. Essentially, it has to do with the fact that he pioneered paths which were sufficiently well surveyed for others than himself to conduct new research.

It is true that Lazarsfeld's *Philosophy of the Social Sciences* is open to a number of objections. Whilst the action paradigm is strategically fruitful and integrative, it is also closely linked to the "psychologistic" bias in sociology as conceived by Lazarsfeld. Whilst quantitative methods have an important part to play in sociology and have the advantage of encouraging rigorousness, it is still the case that a large proportion of the questions posed by sociologists are excluded to the extent that a general inductive theory in the social sciences is still lacking. What is the logic of functional or structural methods, or forms of reasoning employed in the realm of macrosociology or historical sociology? These are questions which Lazarsfeld hardly poses. It must also be recognised that he stopped half-way in his reflections on the possibilities of a quantitative macrosociology which would be facilitated by the improved organisation of social observation and better coordination between economic and social observatories on the one hand and university sociology on the other. In short, it is clear that the positive epistemology which he is proposing under the name of *methodology* can be reduced neither to the problem of *concept formation* nor to problems of research design and data analysis. The meaning, or rather meanings, which can be attributed to the notion of *theory* in the social sciences need to be examined and, more generally, attempts need to be made to grasp the *totality* of the mental processes governing their products.

But most importantly, it is Lazarsfeld who provides us with the means to overcome these limitations. There is nothing to prevent a positive epistemology of historical sociology and macrosociology from trying to study work in this area by way of an *explication de texte*. Further, if one wanted to throw some light on the delicate problem of theorisation in the social sciences, the first task would certainly be to determine precisely the *types* of theories which are to be found there and to identify their logical characteristics, not *a priori*, but by close analysis of the products, as recommended. Research of this kind would have profound implications for the future of sociology.

Part Two

Sociological Epistemology

6. Towards a Positive Epistemology[1]

At present, philosophers of science are taking very little interest in the human sciences. Of course this indifference is understandable. The achievements and applications of the natural sciences are incomparably more spectacular than the conquests of the human sciences. The former give the impression of a continuous development, although historians of science show us that the growth or decline of certain branches of even the most rigorous of these disciplines – mathematics – is bound up with events of an anecdotal nature and is determined by the structure of the occupational context. Despite this, it is difficult not to gain the impression that the history of the natural sciences is guided as if by internal necessity.

We are not concerned here with the truth or falsity of this impression. The reverse side is that the human sciences convey an impression of contingency. They seem to proceed by sudden, explosive and often discontinuous movements. It is hard to be convinced of the logic of their development. The explosion and subsequent development of disciplines like psychoanalysis or structural anthropology does not have the linear history which the rational science of mechanics would appear to have. Indeed, scepticism could be taken a stage further in asking whether psychoanalysis and structural anthropology have not been more like "movements" or "tendencies" than disciplines. In fact it seems certain that their specificity derives less from their object or even their method than from the part-scientific and part-philosophical systems with which they are associated.

A discipline like sociology on the other hand still seems to be oscillating between social philosophy and sociography in its search for identity which forces one to admit with Foucault that the human sciences are a passing, though historical, phase with no future. All the same, it is possible that the reputation of the human sciences is the outcome of certain misrepresentations by philosophers of science.

Typically, the work of philosophers of science who take an interest in

135

the human sciences is very general in character. Obsessed by the natural sciences, which are defined once and for all as the model and reference point, they are more inclined to use this model as a yardstick to measure the human sciences than to analyse their progress in detail. This explains why authors such as Granger, Sartre and Foucault believe it is possible to base their philosophy of the human sciences on their understanding of a few major authors and a few fashionable movements. What is more, the problems that philosophers are fond of examining are often *obsolete*. For example, one of the best among them, Karl Popper, addresses himself to the problem of *dialectics*.[2] In a masterly fashion, by giving evidence of the contradictory character of this notion, he demonstrates the impossibility of setting forth historical laws.

However, while it may be true that in Comte or Marx there is a strong desire to demonstrate the existence of historical laws, neither the notion of historical law, nor that of dialectic, belong to the living language of the social sciences. Carl Hempel's recent studies in the problem of typology construction create a similar impression of generality and obsolescence.[3] Hempel's only reference to sociology is a reference to the Weberian notion of *ideal type*. Hempel has no difficulty in showing up its weaknesses. But he seems to be unaware that the problem of typology construction in modern sociology has given rise to a wide range of studies which leave Weber's vague notions far behind.[4] Curiously enough, although concepts like those of dialectic, historical law and ideal type have largely been superseded or forgotten by sociologists, these are the concepts that seem to provide the raw material for the philosophy of the social sciences.

Perhaps the most obvious example of excessive generality is Foucault's essay on the human sciences and, in particular, those already famous pages where, in a brilliant précis, he summarises the *epistemological status* of the human sciences by situating them within a *trihedron* of knowledge. The first dimension of this trihedron is occupied by mathematics and physics, namely the disciplines characterised by "linear and deductive" proofs. The second dimension is occupied by linguistics, the biological sciences and economics. These sciences are characterised by the procedure of "relating discontinuous but analogous elements" in such a way that they are able to "establish causal relations and structural constants between them". The third and last dimension is that of philosophical reflection. According to Foucault, the human sciences occupy the interior of this trihedron. They cannot be located either at the angles of intersection or on the surfaces defined by two of these dimensions. Simply stated, it means that the products of the human sciences are sometimes related to physics or mathematics, sometimes to biology or economics, and sometimes to philosophy or to several of these disciplines at once.

There is an element of truth in these statements by Foucault: Homans's theory of *exchange* certainly attempts to introduce a central concept from economics into sociology.[5] Simon's work on group dynamics uses models with differential equations directly inspired by physics.[6] As for the third dimension there are countless reputedly sociological studies which are strongly permeated by philosophical thinking. Economics and linguistics, not to mention mathematics, obviously do not display the same diversity of orientations and references.

However, it is less certain that Foucault is right to infer, on the grounds of this diversity of inspiration in the social sciences, "their precariousness, their dangerous familiarity with philosophy", etc. All these propositions are so general that their real significance and usefulness is questionable. Foucault even fails to say exactly what he means by the term "human sciences". What is more, his declarations are value judgements, whereas the real problem is to analyse the conditions that explain the special position of the social sciences.

No doubt the experts are partly responsible for this general state of obsolescence in the philosophy of the social sciences. It is unlikely that the wrangle over the opposition between *Naturwissenschaften* and *Geisteswissenschaften* or the opposition between *explanation* and *understanding* would have continued until the Second World War if it had not had the stimulus of Max Weber's epistemological work.[7]

Even some recent publications in sociology echo the old dispute over quantitative and qualitative methods, using very general and *a priori* arguments.[8] For example, they pose the question – it must be for the thousand and first time – of whether the specificity of the human precludes the use of mathematical methods in the human sciences. Which is somewhat surprising when it would be easy to give several dozen examples from sociology, psychology and linguistics of fruitful, not to say indispensable, mathematical applications.

This statement obviously does not get rid of the difficult problem of the relations between mathematics and the human sciences. However, it does show that the difficulties of the relation between the human sciences and mathematics do not arise from the "humanness" of their object. Besides such a hypothesis being suspect and unclear, it is incapable of explaining the very unequal spread of mathematical methods among the disciplines.

In my view, Granger is one of the few philosophers who has appreciated the need to set a new course for epistemology in the social sciences. He quite rightly insists on the need for close observation of research practices to clarify their meaning. Unfortunately, his main discovery in the analysis of the *praxis* of the research is apparently what he himself set out to find, namely a desire for formalism and rigour. Thus, the analysis of latent classes, which was actually designed to solve the practical problems of classification, is presented as a means of "conceptualising" the "qualitative plurality of opinions by means of probabilistic parameters".[9]

Such analyses lead one to suspect that Granger's primary interest lies in the fact that a model like the analysis of latent classes dresses up the old problem of quantity and quality in a new way rather than the sociologist's scientific motives and needs. Granger does not define the *praxis* which he analyses as a function of the sociologist's own goals. At no time does he examine the functions of the instrument he is analysing or the needs to which these functions are supposed to answer. Instead, the sociologist is presented as a sort of double agent who, in the guise of solving problems of no practical importance, is actually serving the highest interests of metaphysics as he unknowingly plays his part in the dialectic of quantity and quality, experiment and concept.

I wish to advocate the idea that a more fruitful epistemology of the social sciences, for the philosopher as well as the social scientist, could be developed if these questions were abandoned once and for all and were replaced by reliance on actual research by sociologists, psychologists or linguists. In other words, a *future* epistemology would be one based, not on general and *a priori* problems, but on which I will call the *flashpoints* or *critical points* of the human sciences.

Some of these *flashpoints* occur at a fundamental level: that of *the vocabulary of the social sciences*. In fact there is a whole series of terms in current use in the language of the social sciences which – as the frequency and breadth of their application shows – are regarded as indispensable but about whose meaning there is far from complete agreement. A contradiction like this between the success of a term and its *polysemic* character seems to provide the philosopher with a much more reliable and promising first line of attack than a general consideration of dialectics, the quality–quantity opposition or the specificity of the human. To make this account more concrete, I will refer briefly to some examples of concepts which seem indispensable yet hard to grasp.

Consider first the notion of *theory* and the uses to which it is put in sociology. A famous passage by the American sociologist Merton lists seven different meanings of the word *theory* in sociology: sometimes it means *methodology*, sometimes *general orientations*, sometimes *analysis of concepts*, sometimes *post factum interpretation*, sometimes *empirical generalisation*, sometimes "*derivation*" (analysis of the consequences of a theory), or "*codification*" (systematisation of empirical generalisations).[10] Lastly, there are occasions when the word theory is employed in something like the conventional sense to designate a set of logically interrelated propositons from which a number of verifiable consequences can be deduced. There is no doubt about the relevance of this analysis and it would be easy to give numerous examples of the polysemy which Merton denounces.

In extending the investigation, one would certainly find still further meanings. Thus, in talk of the *theory of social diffusion*, the *theory of imitation*, the *theory of economic cycles* or *game theory*, for example, the word theory resourds differently in all four cases and in another case, like the expression "the corpuscular theory of light" it conveys yet another meaning. Game theory, which is a group of consequences deduced from a set of primary propositions, has one property of interest to the philosopher, namely that in strict terms it cannot be *verified*: the axioms which it is based on are deliberately idealised. Therefore, the possibility of their consequences being directly tested against reality is excluded by definition. This is not to say that game theory is itself a game, beacause its language and conclusions can be and have been used to good effect in solving certain decision-making problems as they arise in operations research in particular. It is therefore neither an idle game nor a verifiable theory. In this case the word *theory* does not have exactly the same meaning as in the natural sciences.

The *theory* of economic cycles is likewise profoundly different from game theory. The latter is based on a formal and idealised description of human behaviour in competitive situations. The former seeks to explain a well-known fact, namely the existence of economic fluctuations. But the theory of cycles also differs from physical theory to the extent that it involves a set of models related to each other by somewhat loose logical ties, rather than a set of primary propositions together with their inferences. These models represent so many possible explanations of the cyclical phenomena. They may be more or less powerful or more or less realistic. But there are no completely unambiguous criteria for choosing between them.

Similarly, the theory of social diffusion consists of a set of models or small theories, some of which are applicable to ideal situations and others to real but relatively specific situations. In this sense it is as logically different from game theory as it is from the theory of economic cycles.

Finally, in the expression "theory of imitation" (in Tarde's sense), the word theory takes on yet another meaning. Here, the notion of imitation serves simply as a general orientation in the analysis of a whole variety of social phenomena.

For the most part, sociologists, economists and linguists are aware of the polysemy of the word theory. The passage by Merton referred to above is from a classic work familiar to all students of sociology. However, one only has to open the pages of recent sociological "theory" books, such as the *Symposium on Sociological Theory* by L. Gross or H. Becker's *Modern Sociological Theory*, to see quite clearly that the word theory still conceals Merton's seven meanings, not to mention others. Why? Why is the polysemic character of the word so persistent even when all are aware of it? A critical analysis of this situation would almost certainly provide a useful diagnostic instrument for an epistemology of the social sciences.

The word theory, as used in the social sciences, therefore seems to me to be one of those *flashpoints* which could provide a well-defined object for philosophical reflection.

Let us turn now to another example: the word *function*. This is another case of a word which seems to be both indispensable and yet poorly defined. It is certainly indispensable if the regularity of its use is anything to judge by. Explicitly introduced into sociology by Durkheim, it gave birth to an adjective, functional, and then to a noun ending in "ism" – functionalism.[11] Today there is hardly a sociological treatise in which the word does not appear as a *Leitmotiv*. However, every time that someone like Kingsley Davis, Hempel or Nagel has attempted a precise analysis of its meaning, they have encountered stalemate.[12] Hempel asserts that explanations of social phenomena according to their functions are by nature tautological. On the other hand, Kingsley Davis, in a celebrated presidential address to the American Sociological Association, described functionalism as a myth and maintains that the word does not deserve its flexional ending because every sociologist is necessarily a functionalist whether he knows it or not.

I have made my own attempt at a philosophical diagnosis of this word and have tried to demonstrate that there are signs of a slow transformation in the language of sociologists who appeal to functionalism. At one time, it was maintained that the explanation of social practices and institutions necessarily lay in the functions which these practices and institutions assumed in relation to society viewed as a totality. Later, it was realised that certain social practices were either afunctional or dysfunctional. Because this had to be taken into account, a qualified functionalism was devised which consequently lost its explanatory power. If current trends continue, we will arrive at a situation where the word function is all but emptied of its meaning. Indeed, a close inspection of the underlying framework of contemporary "functional" argument often reveals the following from:

$A \rightarrow a, b, c,$
$B \rightarrow a', b', c',$
c is inconsistent with c',
Therefore: A and B cannot appear simultaneously in a society.

The functionalist will then argue that B is dysfunctional in a society which contains A. For example: in an industrial society (A), the persistence of powerful family organisation (B) is dysfunctional, because A and B give rise to contradictory outcomes. The important thing here is that the words function, dysfunction, etc., being implicitly formalised, are thereby decomposed, as it were. Functionalism is no longer a theory for explaining social practices and institutions in terms of their functions, but a certain kind of proof in which – paradoxically – the concept of function can be de-emphasised.

Thus the word function is a second flashpoint which ought attract the attention of the philosopher. There is a third one; namely the word *structure*. Its importance is beyond question, its ambiguity no less. Analysis of this contradiction would appear to be a task of prime importance.[13]

Instead of this, contemporary philosophers are fascinated by structuralism, whether as structuralists or as anti-structuralists, rather as if Socrates, wishing to understand the soldier's gallantry, had made himself a general before questioning Lachès.

There are many other words in the vocabulary of the social sciences that would benefit from a close examination. Especially words which are applied in a general way to frame the social sciences as a whole: theory, function, structure, but also: model, system, type, cause, etc. Then there are those concepts which belong to particular disciplines: culture,[14] attitude, power, etc. The majority of these words could provide the basis for epistemological studies and could act as powerful instruments of observation for anyone wishing to conduct a proper critique of scientific reason as applied to the social sciences.

Thus far we have examined a few flashpoints situated at the basic level of the *vocabulary of the social sciences*. It is possible to identify others, situated at more complex levels.

Take for example the problem of the problem of the *meaning of models* in the human sciences.

Sociology, like most of the human sciences, currently makes use of a well-stocked arsenal of mathematical instruments which are rather loosely termed models. Examining these models closely, one notices that they fulfil extremely diverse functions.[15] They include small-scale mathematical theories, some of which are verifiable and others speculative. Others represent mathematical translations of certain concepts. The remainder have other functions. An important task, therefore, is to construct a typology of mathematical models used in the social sciences, including their functions. A typology of this kind would constitute a powerful instrument for analysing relationships between mathematics and the social sciences. For despite the fact that mathematical models are being more and more widely used in the social sciences, the lack of careful consideration of their function means that their logical status is not clearly defined.

Explorations in the area of models would give philosophers a number of fruitful surprises. What comes to mind, for instance, is the famous example of the classification problem, which is of such importance for the social sciences. In formal terms it can be described as follows: it involves a population of n individuals who may or may not have m characteristics. Thus:

$$\text{Individual 1: } + + - - - + - - \ldots$$
$$\text{Individual 2: } + - - + - - - + \ldots$$

The problem is then to recombine these individuals into groups in such a way that individuals belonging to the same group are as similar as possible to each other and individuals in different groups are as different as possible.

This problem has been formulated mathematically in a variety of ways which help to make the intuitive notions which govern every classificatory operation more precise.

Intuitive methods give different results and more often than not the choice of one method is made in a purely arbitrary fashion. Therefore, current methods of classification are better than the intuitive methods which were used previously. The mathematical formulation introduces more rigour and gives intuitive ideas a controllable form. However, even now there appear to be difficulties in formalising or even giving a precise description of the criteria which would make one classificatory procedure preferable to another. What are the reasons for this situation? Is there a remedy? These are important questions which could possibly be solved by a consideration of the classificatory *practices* that are actually adopted in the social sciences.

To take another example, close observation of the work sociologists do would promote an understanding of the meaning of certain features which distinguish sociology from the natural sciences. No one is likely to disagree with the commonplace that sociological propositions are rarely presented in the form of a theory. They are much more likely to take the form of factual propositions or "empirical generalisations", to use Merton's phrase.

Let us examine the more specific case of the sociological analysis of occupational choice. A whole series of surveys show that the probability of educational achievement and social achievement varies with the status of the family in society. Other studies show that achievement prospects depend on the more or less authoritarian structure of the family. Further studies demonstrate the existence of what might be called *homophilic* phenomena: for example, observers have noted that in the school environment children have a tendency to form themselves into groups definable by their level of aspiration. It would be possible to state a whole range of propositions like this. At present, however, there is no way of integrating them into a single theory showing how these factors combine or interact with each other. The fragmented nature of the research means that even now we cannot be definitely sure whether the function of social background in the inequalities of opportunity of access to various levels of education owes more to cultural or economic factors.

This situation is typical and it is interesting to examine the reasons why. One explanation which is often put forward appeals to the specificity of social phenomena: human phenomena and social phenomena in particular do not lend themselves to analysis so well as physical phenomena; in principle, sociological analysis cannot be as rigorous as physical observation. However, a closer inspection reveals that the characteristic predominance in sociology of empirical generalisations over theories in the strict sense is largely attributable to material constraints.

Imagine, for example, that we wish to analyse the influence of a group of factors on social mobility. First of all, it would be necessary to observe a population of children continuously over a respectable number of years. It would also be necessary to use an enormous sample. Then let us suppose that we isolate, for example, ten factors in two possible states (viz: membership of a family of low/high social status, a family with an authoritarian/non-authoritarian structure, etc.).

An observational design like this would mean that for each observation a child could be classified in $2^{10} = 1024$ different ways. To determine the actual influence of each one of the isolated factors, the 1024 possible combinations would have to be adequately represented in the sample. Supposing there is an average of 100 subjects per combination, the observational design would need a sample population of approximately 100,000 children.

This is the reason why, in practice, it is only possible to take account of a small number of factors at a time. Consider for example a fictitious case like the following, which reveals a negative relationship between the authoritarianism of family relationships and educational achievement, based on a sample of 900 subjects.

		Educational achievement	
		+	−
Authoritarian families	+	130	170
Non-authoritarian families	−	220	80

Once this relationship has been identified it is still necessary to ensure that it is not a spurious one. It is a well known fact that authoritarian families are more numerous in the less privileged classes. We will therefore neutralise this possibly parasitic variable by re-examining the relationship in those groups which are homogeneous in terms of social status. The results obtained look like this:

		Affluent families Educational achievement				Poor families Educational achievement		
		+	−	Total		+	−	Total
Authoritarian	+	50	50	100	+	80	120	200
Families	−	150	50	200	−	70	30	100
Total		200	100	300		150	150	300

This result shows that social circumstances and family have a combined influence on educational achievement.

But could not these factors be concealing others? For example, we know that parents' social relationships have an influence on childrens' social relationships and that these in turn influence achievement and levels of aspiration. However, the purely material difficulty of introducing such a factor is obvious, even supposing that it could be observed. The sample would actually have to be divided yet again, with the result that certain cells would not be large enough for a statistical analysis to be carried out.

These material constraints are even more burdensome when collective factors are introduced. We know, for instance, that children of workers generally achieve better in institutions with an affluent intake than in institutions that recruit from children of less privileged families. We also know that, other things being equal, achievement varies with the provision of institutions. If these factors are to be taken into account, a stratified sample design has to be adopted: samples of types of environment, types of institution, types of classes within institutions and, lastly, samples of pupils within these classes. The costs of a sample survey of this kind are extremely high. This alone is enough to explain why we know rather little about the effects of environment on educational achievement.

In short, examination of this example of sociological research on social mobility leads one to the conclusion that one of the reasons behind its lack of conclusiveness and the tendency for its results to be expressed in collections of separate propositions instead of *theories*, is the extraordinary cost of observational data which would open up the possibility of a genuine theory.

Clearly, these simple remarks are of decisive importance for an epistemology of the social sciences. In fact they show that certain shortcomings of a discipline like sociology depend not on the specificity of its object, but on a set of factors which are sometimes epistemological and sometimes historical in character.

Certainly one of the major reasons behind the special characteristics of epistemology in sociology compared with demography or economic science is historical: the latter two disciplines were "nationalised" both very early and very extensively; in other words, they were placed in the service of the state and accordingly benefited from their support. In contrast, sociology became established almost everywhere within a university framework. This is why the great organisations of social observation, like the Institut National de la Statistique et des Etudes Economiques, are more concerned with economic or demographic phenomena than with other kinds of social phenomena. If more time were available one could comment on the fact that Durkheim's *Suicide* – a book which is generally regarded as a milestone in sociology – only became possible because there were several countries in Europe which had good statistics on suicide.

Pursuing this debate, one could mention a whole series of flashpoints involving relationships between the various social sciences. This is another theme on which the ethereal representations of an author like Foucault could well be replaced by more pertinent philosophical reflections. For example, there is a question to which sociologists are always seeking an answer – the question of the *object of sociology*.

Sociology actually finds itself in a position of detachment from the other social sciences to the extent that its object is not so clearly defined as in the other disciplines. Economics deals with phenomena of production and exchange, linguistics with phenomena of communication, both of which can be isolated relatively easily. Similarly, clinical psychology studies a well-defined class of phenomena. It is more difficult to draw a line around the object of experimental psychology but the specificity of its procedures gives it a unity. In contrast, to say that sociology is the study of social phenomena is to say nothing. Note the difficulties Durkheim encountered when he attempted to separate the social from the individual. To make the specificity of sociology depend on this distinction is actually to give a definition of sociologism rather than sociology.

However, contemporary economists can be heard to say more and more often that, without sociology, they would encounter impenetrable barriers to certain problems. At the same time some linguists would say that certain geographical variations in language cannot be accounted for without resorting to sociological methods.

All these facts are worthy of serious philosophical consideration. What is the function of sociology? Is it destined to fragment into a series of special disciplines? Is its vocation to be the new philosophy of the social sciences? More simply, what does the economist have in mind when he appeals to the sociologist? What does the sociologist have in mind when he declares that this or that product is or is not sociological? Although they cannot be fully answered at the present time, these are important and well-defined questions which could provide further support for an epistemology of the social sciences.

My final example is chosen to represent a family of problems which are likely to be of even more direct interest to the philosopher of science.

The natural sciences provide the philosopher with certain models which can possibly be used to construct a theory of knowledge. To take a specific example, Popper's theory of science contains a certain number of affirmations about scientific knowledge, extracted by induction from observation of the natural sciences. Thus Popper states that a scientific proposition is a proposition which can be proved to be false. This statement rests on the idea that a universal proposition can be proved *false* by the application of a finite and definite criterion, whilst there is no finite and definite, criterion of *truth*.

This criterion is none other than the *modus tollens* of the scholastics:

$$[(p \rightarrow q)\wedge(\bar{q} \rightarrow \bar{p})].$$

The *modus tollens* therefore defines a univocal criterion c from which it is possible to derive

$$c \rightarrow \bar{p}.$$

On the other hand, there is no finite criterion c such that

$$c \rightarrow p.$$

Popper deduces a number of propositions from this observation. He states, for example, that the falsification criterion makes it possible to give a rigorous description of the difference between scientific and non-scientific propositions. In fact the former can be defined as falsifiable, that is as propositions with a structure that allows them to be "falsified".

Another thesis which can be deduced from Popper's remarks is that scientific *progress* (i.e. the choice between a theory T_1 and a theory T_2) always proceeds by applications of the *modus tollens*.

However compelling these propositions may be, they cannot be applied literally to the human sciences. A simple example will illustrate the point: Jakobson's structural phonology. In principle, this theory sets out to determine, on the basis of a number of propositions or axioms (which Jakobson formulates more or less implicitly), the basic sounds or *phonemes* of a language and to describe these phonemes according to a certain number of attributes, properties or distinctive features as they are still called. Thus Jakobson isolated twenty-eight basic sounds or phonemes in the English language. For example, two of these phonemes are the *h* in "hill"–denoted by "h" and "silence", denoted by " # ".

The distinctive features of these phonemes are as follows: "h": voiceless, non-consonantal, fricative; " # " (silence): voiceless, non-consonantal, non-fricative.

The description of "silence" – surprising as it is from the intuitive point of view – is a neat way of showing that insteadof being empirical, it proceeds from the application of a *theory* to the speech – sounds of English.

Strictly speaking, from the Popperian point of view, this theory is neither verifiable nor falsifiable because it does not entail any consequences which could be directly contested by facts. It may of course be regarded as based on reasonable axioms but its results cannot be judged either true or false. However, there are certain facts which lead to a conviction, if not of the theory's truth, then at least of what could be called its *pertinence*.

For example, there is a close correspondence between the structural complexity of phonemes like those described in Jakobson's theory and their order of appearance in children or the order of their disappearance in aphasia.

In formal terms, the situation is therefore as follows: Jakobson puts forward a theory T, based on certain axioms. This theory makes it possible to identify the basic phonemes of a language and to connect them with a structural description. This is all that follows directly from the theory. Therefore the proposition that the order of disappearance of phonemes in aphasia should be related to their structural complexity has nothing to do with the consequences of theory T. This means that if there had been no relationship T would not have been *falsified* either. Nevertheless, the fact that a relationship does appear helps to convince us of its pertinence.

This situation obviously fails to conform to Popper's framework for the theory of science, because in the case of Jakobson's structural phonology we are dealing with a theory which can neither be defined as scientific, because it cannot strictly speaking be falsified, nor as non-scientific, because its concordance with certain classes of facts can be established.

This example shows that a systematic examination of the theories and models used in the social sciences could result in a profound reformulation, not only of the propositions contained in the *Logik der Forschung*, but also of the philosophy of science in general. In this sense the human sciences certainly provide a quarry of materials which could engage the attentions of the philosopher of science.

A word by way of conclusion: it seems to me that a philosophy of the social sciences both needs to be elaborated and yet cannot be elaborated except on the basis of a mass of detailed studies. What I have attempted to do is to present a sample of the perfectly limited and definable problems which arise at certain flashpoints. Despite their limits, these problems will require patient research which has hardly begun.

7. Theories, theory and Theory[1]

The notion of "theory" probably has a more uncertain meaning in the social sciences and sociology in particular than in other disciplines. As far back as the early 1950s, in a passage in *Social Theory and Social Structure*, R. K. Merton[2] pointed out that the word theory was being used by sociologists in seven different ways, only one of which was admissable. These were (1) Methodology; (2) General orientations; (3) Analysis of concepts; (4) *Post factum* sociological interpretations; (5) Empirical generalisations; (6) Theory; (7) Derivations and Codification.

For Merton, it is correct to apply the term *theory* in the strict sense when a proposition: (i) is deduced from a set of more fundamental propositions; (ii) is shown to be consistent with observation. Examples of "theories" in this sense are few and far between in sociology. One of the most famous of all is Durkheim's theory of *Suicide*.

> Thus, it has long been established as a statistical uniformity that in a variety of populations, Catholics have a lower suicide rate than Protestants. In this form the uniformity posed a theoretical problem. It merely constituted an empirical regularity which would become significant for theory only if it could be derived from a set of other propositions, a task which Durkheim set himself.[3]

In the case of *Suicide* the stated proposition derives from a set of primary propositions which Merton summarises in the following way:

(a) Social cohesion provides psychic support to group members subjected to acute stresses and anxieties.
(b) Suicide rates are functions of *unrelieved* anxieties and stresses to which persons are subjected.
(c) Catholics have greater social cohesion than Protestants.
(d) Therefore, lower suicide rates should be anticipated among Catholics than among Protestants.

149

Compared with "empirical generalisations", a theory of this kind has obvious advantages. On the one hand, it can give an *understanding* of the observed relationship. On the other hand, it makes it possible to conceive of this relationship as a particular case which can be subsumed under a more general relationship which provides it with meaning: in fact, if the theory is correct, it should be possible to demonstrate that, in every case, groups with weaker social cohesion have a higher suicide rate. The theory also makes it possible to demonstrate the non-fallacious character of the relationship. Further, it specifies the conditions under which the empirical proposition can be taken as valid: if the Protestants in a particular social situation had greater social cohesion than the Catholics they would have fewer suicides. This is why one actually observes that Protestants have a lesser tendency to commit suicide when they are in a minority situation. For the minority situation is one which tends to reinforce social cohesion.

The distinctions which Merton draws invite a number of questions. Firstly, why does the polysemic character of the notion of theory seem to be especially pronounced in the social sciences? After the publication of Merton's book, several other publications on sociological theory made their appearance, for example those of Howard Becker, Llewelyn Gross, Parsons and Shils.[4] A scrutiny of the contents pages of these different contributions is enough to establish that several years after Merton's critique, the polysemy of the notion of theory remained quite marked. Thus the book by Gross consists of expositions of mathematical models in sociology, functionalism, theory construction and many other subjects.

This question of how the polysemy of the notion of theory in the social sciences came about will be the core element of our article. But other questions have an equal right to be posed. In the first place one can question the pertinence of Merton's classification. The categories are manifestly valid. But are they sufficiently discriminating? Further, one could ask whether there is a need to distinguish between types of theories, a question which leads in turn to the problem of clarifying the *dimensions* used in the construction of this typology. For example, it is clear that the notion of theory presupposes the existence of a set of primary propositions (or axioms) from which verifiable deductions may be made. But such a definition implies that the two key-words involved – "to make deductions" and "verifiable" – are capable of explanation. Now the meaning of these words is hardly specified by Merton. In the example of theory which he borrows from Durkheim's *Suicide*, the expression "to deduce" corresponds to a *syllogistic* type of deduction.

But is this the only meaning which the expression can be given? In particular, these questions pose problems about the verieties of theory and, as we shall see, about levels of verification.

There are many other problems which will emerge as we proceed, like that of the contrast between theory and *post factum* interpretation or the contrast between *a priori* theory and *ad hoc* theory. Although the distinctions that Merton introduced on this point are pertinent, they are inadequately formalised. If the distinction between *post factum* interpretation refers simply to the sequence of discovery (which may go from hypotheses to their verification, or from facts to their interpretation), it is comparatively secondary. If not, what are the logical criteria which could be used to distinguish between the two types?

It must be said that this article makes no pretence either to exhaust the subject or to give an answer to all the problems posed. Instead of producing results, it tries to specify a framework for research, to raise certain problems, to shed light on certain scientific procedures and to make a modest contribution to the epistemology of the social sciences, a discipline which, in our opinion, has hardly come into existence.

THEORIES AND PARADIGMS

One major reason for the *polysemy* of the notion of theory in the social sciences clearly has to do with the common failure to make an important distinction: that is the distinction between *theories* in the strict sense and what we will call *paradigms*.

The notion of theory presumably implies that the propositions which are subjected to verification are *deduced* from a number of primary propositions. In this sense, the example which Merton draws from Durkheim closely corresponds to a theory. Once it is accepted that the frequency of suicides increases with egoism and that egoism is greater among Protestants, it can be deduced by syllogistic reasoning that Protestants have higher suicide rates.

Although theories are not numerous in sociology, it is nonetheless possible to cite a few. For example, there are several theories of this sort to be found in Sorokin's *Social Mobility*. We will simply refer to one of these, which deserves attention, both for its intrinsic interest and for its topicality. The fundamental propositions of this theory can be formulated in the following way:

(a) All societies are stratified.

(b) The persistence of social stratification is assured from one gene-
    ration to another by a number of mechanisms of selection.
(c) In the industrial societies there are two basic selection agencies, the
    family and the school.
(d) If these agencies cease to fulfil their function of selection or
    deteriorate in their fulfilment of this function, it will follow that
    young people will develop social aspirations which society cannot
    satisfy.
(e) When a society engenders needs on a massive scale which it cannot
    satisfy, revolutionary ideologies will develop as a result.
(f) As a consequence, in such cases, one will see the emergence of
    revolutionary movements among youth.

This is certainly a theory. If correct, it does indeed follow that, in the
event of the family or the education system abandoning its selection
function, one will find revolutionary movements emerging among
youth. This proposition is a *necessary* consequence of the earlier
propositions. Moreover, and without prejudice to our subsequent
examination of this distinction, we can say that because the axioms (a) to
(e) entail the possibility of deducing numerous propositions other than
proposition (f), they do not give the impression of an *ad hoc*
explanation. Let us grant, then, that in the two cases we have just
referred to, we are actually talking about a theory in the normal sense of
the term. At the same time, without labouring the point, we should draw
attention to one difference between the two examples: it is evidently
much easier to verify the deductions made from Durkheim's theory than
those that follow from Sorokin's theory. But what we wish to underline
at the present moment is that, given a set of primary propositions, it is
possible to *extract* propositions from them which are testable against
reality, without this "extraction" taking the form of a deduction. In this
case we are referring not to a "theory", but to a "paradigm."

Without claiming to be exhaustive, we will analyse a number of
particularly important types of paradigm. Classification of these
paradigms and an analysis of their functions in scientific language would
presuppose detailed research at which we can only hint here. So the
present classification should only be taken as provisional. A particularly
important form of *paradigm* is characterised by the fact that the
explicanda (the propositions to be explained) instead of being *deduced*
from a theory, are drawn *by analogy* from a body of knowledge
belonging to another domain. The sociology of migration supplies a
good example of the use of an analogical paradigm. For instance, if one

considers the research tradition pioneered by names like those of Zipf, Dodd or Stouffer, one notices that the propositions which are subjected to the test of reality derive less from propositions concerning migratory phenomena themselves than from an analogy with the mechanisms of attraction described by Newtonian mechanics.[5] Paradigms of this type are common in the most mathematised areas of sociology. It is interesting to find that the majority of the mathematical models used in sociology derive from other disciplines.[6] Thus, the sociology of diffusion phenomena (diffusion of rumours, diffusion of innovations) has largely resorted to paradigms from biology and especially from epidemology. For example, Hägerstrand's studies[7] of the diffusion of innovations in a rural environment are variations on the fundamental epidemological model which Verhulst called the logistical model.

But paradigms are not only the product of mathematical sociology. A "theory" such as Homans's theory of exchange also belongs to the class of paradigmatic theories. The basic intuition which Homans explores in his article "Social Behaviour as Exchange" is that the model of interaction of an economic kind can be extended to all the categories of interaction.[8] In exchange, two protagonists X and Y enter into interaction. Further, in the most elementary form of exchange, these protagonists have at their disposal two goods, x and y. For exchange to take place, the costs that X will incur in transmitting the good x to Y must be perceived by him to be less than the benefit which he will receive in obtaining y *in exchange*. Of course, the exchange must also appear to be favourable to Y. This description of the rationality of exchange is commonplace. What is less so, is the *analogical* extension suggested by Homans when he proposes to consider all forms of interaction as an exchange, that is as a system which obeys the same form of rationality as exchange.[9]

In fact Homans gives several examples of studies whose results become more intelligible if they are analysed in the light of the theory, or to be more precise the paradigm, of exchange. One of these studies was concerned with the behaviour of inspectors responsible for scrutinising the administration of private enterprises. These inspectors had to report to a controller. The theory of exchange can be applied easily to the level of interaction between controllers and inspectors. In fact, the inspectors, in cases where they have to give an unfavourable report on the enterprise, run a risk: the risk of being sharply repudiated if the conclusions of their report are poorly founded. Resort to the controller's prior opinion therefore represents for them a benefit commensurate with the risk that they incur when advancing into unknown territory. The cost side is measured in terms of the risk of being judged incompetent. If one now considers the controller, his behaviour is not obviously reducible to that of an exchange partner. However, it can still be explained within the framework of an exchange theory: in order to consolidate his role and to extract the maximum profit from it, he can in fact seek in one way or another to discourage or alternatively to encourage this or that inspector. Let us assume for example that the *cost* that he imposes on his inspectors is too high (for instance because he over-asserts his authority in the course of consultation). In this case, he will discourage consultation, the system of control will lose its effectiveness and he will have to shoulder the responsibility for it. If the cost is too low, he will make himself liable, by other mechanisms which can be easily analysed, to a *loss*. Observation of this system showed that, to reduce the price they had to pay, the inspectors often resorted to consultation with colleagues. There too, the interaction can be analysed in terms of exchange.

This is one example of a case where a set of observations are explained according to a paradigm rather than a theory (i.e. the propositions which correspond to the observational procedure are not *deduced* from other propositions). The paradigm involves taking the mechanisms of social interaction as a whole to be *structurally* similar to the mechanisms of exchange. The epistemological questions that a paradigm of this sort provokes are twofold: firstly, whether – and how – it can lead to an improved explanation or understanding of a situation or a particular social mechanism, and secondly, the *extent* of the class of phenomenon to which it applies or is actually capable of being applied.

Game theory has served in a similar way as a paradigm for a number of sociological studies.[10] As such, this theory rests on a very precise definition of the notion of game. In particular, a game implies that players follow perfectly *defined* and *understood* rules. It also assumes that the stakes are fixed, known in advance, and that their relationship to the outcome of the game is clearly defined. In actual fact, this definition corresponds to a formalisation of the current notion of social games with two or more protagonists. Game theory has served as an analogical paradigm for sociological studies in the sense that it has served to explain observations made in situations which could not be assimilated to games in the strict sense except by virtue of a more or less distant analogy. For example, it has been used in the analysis of international relations or in the analysis of industrial or economic relations. But, in the majority of cases, it is a matter of analogies, because it cannot be said either that the stakes are determined, that they are measurable and comparable, or that the rules of the game are perfectly defined and accepted by the participants.

At this point, we would like to introduce three observations. The first is that the lack of differentiation between theory and paradigm contributes significantly to explaining the uncertainties of the notion of theory in the human sciences. For example, the body of knowledge to which we give the name of economic theory actually consists of both theories in the strict sense and paradigms as well. Thus Cournot's theory of monopoly is not so much a theory resting on the simplification of situations observed in reality as a paradigm. Structurally, it actually bears the same relationship to economic reality as game theory does to international relations. The same is true to the "theory of perfect competition" or the "incrementalist" theory of decision-making. It should also be noted that there is no guarantee that one will always be able to differentiate clearly between theory and paradigm. The second observation is that paradigms can serve as paradigms for paradigms. Hence exchange, which is a paradigm for analysis of social interaction, is dominated by a more general paradigm: that of game theory. Very frequently, theoretical progress consists precisely of generalising a paradigm by subsuming it beneath a more general one. The third observation is that paradigms like those of exchange or game theory have functions which merge to some extent but not entirely with theories in the strict sense. But we will be returning later to this point.

There is no disputing the fact that paradigms play a fundamental role in the development of the social sciences. But they have played an equally significant role in the natural sciences.[11] Moreover, it is interesting to find that the terminological confusion on this point is not restricted to the social sciences. Thus, we find that what has come in practice to be called the "corpuscular theory of light" is, in fact, a paradigm or more precisely, a theory developed according to a paradigm: the Cartesian explanation of the phenomena of refraction and reflection is structurally analogous to the explanation that Homans gives of the behaviour of the inspectors. The explanations are analogical. In the first, the analogy is between light phenomena and impact phenomena; in the second, between economic exchange and social interaction.

The paradigms which we have examined so far can be described as *theoretical* paradigms: in each case, whether it be the sociology of migration or diffusion, the analysis of social interaction or the sociology of international relations, the paradigm has the structure of a set of interconnecting propositions which have some bearing on either another sector of reality or an artificial reality. In the case of the sociology of migration, the paradigm is based on Newtonian mechanics; in the case of the sociology of international relations, it is organised around game theory.[12]

In addition to these theoretical paradigms one finds, among the range of implements which go under the general label of social science *theory*, at least two other important entities which we will call formal paradigms and conceptual paradigms respectively. Like theoretical paradigms they allow the construction of explanatory propositions applicable to this or that segment of social reality. However, these propositions are neither constructed by *analogy* – nor by deduction as in the case of theories in the strict sense – but by *subsumption*. Formal and conceptual paradigms constitute frameworks of reference which provide explanatory propositions with either the elements of a conceptual systems (conceptual paradigms) or syntactic rules (formal paradigms).

We will begin with an example to illustrate the notion of formal paradigm. It involves a functional paradigm of the sort that Merton formulated and that has gained wide acceptance today.[13] It is interesting to note that this formal paradigm comes from the theoretical paradigm of organicist functionalism proposed by Radcliffe-Brown. This latter type of paradigm can be described as theoretical because one result of postulating an analogy between living beings and society is to make biology a paradigm for sociology. It was to be critised by Merton,[14] firstly because social customs, unlike the forms of living organisms, do not invariably have a practical function and secondly, because certain practices or elements in society can be functional for one segment of the society and either afunctional or dysfunctional for others. It was criticised finally and in particular because the idea of smooth functioning or normality is infinitely more difficult to apply in the case of societies than in the case of organisms.

A critique of this kind led to the abandonment of organicist functionalism but not to the abandonment of functionalism *per se*. Merton in fact retains from primitive functionalism the idea that social phenomena cannot generally be explained without taking account of their functions. That said, it is a question of realising that the notion of function no longer has to be defined in relation to society as a whole and that one of the tasks of the sociologist is now to specify the segment or segments in terms of which a function is defined. Further, it is a matter of distinguishing between at least two meanings of the word function. According to the first meaning, an element will be said to be functional in relation to a section of society if it satisfies certain of its *needs*. Thus,

Merton has shown in a celebrated analysis that the American political machine fulfils a function in relation to the minorities and lower classes to the extent that it provides a social welfare service for them. But the notion of function cannot be reduced to this sociopsychological meaning. Thus, the fact that the Ba-Thonga call their cousin on the mother's side grandfather obviously does not correspond to a need, although it fulfils a function. The designation shows the existence of a class of equivalence among Ego's relatives defined by customs and institutions. [15] In effect, Ego has analogous attitudes towards maternally-related kin of different generations; he can, moreover, expect analogous services from them; in contrast, the behaviour, attitudes and expectations that Ego fosters towards his paternally-related kin are totally different and therefore constitute a second class of equivalence in Ego's family relationships. In this case, the terminology associated with *kinship* relations certainly has a *function*. This function cannot however be reduced to the satisfaction of needs. As for the distinction between manifest functions and latent functions, it is sufficiently well known for us not to have to dwell on it here.

Criticism of Radcliffe-Brown's organicist functionalism therefore led Merton to formulate a paradigm of a different logical type. Instead of being a statement of an analogy, this consists of establishing an empty (formal) framework which can lead to the formulation of explanatory propositions by subsumption. Merton's own book incorporates a number of applications of this paradigm, including the analysis of the political machine to which we referred earlier. It is important to analyse the *logical structure* of the explanation which Merton gives the machine phenomenon. This explanation could certainly be expressed in the form of what we earlier called a theory in the strict sense; it could in fact be translated into a set of propositions following from one another and ending up with the necessity of mechanism like the machine in a society with the characteristics of American society. In fact, it is impossible (except in "crime writer's" induction) to infer the existence of the singular. One can *explain* Napoleon's defeat in the Russian campaign but one cannot *deduce* it. Similarly, one can explain the existence of the political machine, but not deduce it, which means that the problem of proof does not have the same form as when one is dealing with a theory in the strict sense. The problem in the present case concerns the *validity* of the explanation rather than the truth of a theory. [16] Now this validity derives from two elements: the validity of the formal paradigm on the one hand, and the validity of subsumptions on the other. In other words, the force of conviction in Merton's explanation comes both from the validity which one can attribute to the paradigm of functional analysis and from the range of facts subsumed beneath this paradigm. What is clear though is that the explanation could not be expressed in the form of a deductive theory in the strict sense.

A research project of great interest, as much for the philosophy as the history of the social sciences, would be firstly to make an inventory of these formal paradigms and secondly to analyse their content as Merton did with respect to functionalism. One important and topical issue would be to find out whether what currently goes under the name of structuralism represents one or several formal paradigms and what the specific content of the paradigm(s) is. The same problem arises *à propos* of Parsons's structural–functionalism. But one also finds paradigms which are not explicit. History seems to be a particularly well-endowed area in this respect because deductive theories are ruled out from the start in historical explanation. This means that the persuasiveness of a historical study, as in the case of the Mertonian analysis we have alluded to, must usually derive from the validity of the formal paradigm which is used, whether this paradigm is implicit or explicit. Of course, a number of historians have tried to make their paradigms explicit. But it is desirable that the question be treated in a systematic way from the point of view of a positive epistemology of the social sciences.

We can be quite precise and say that the *validity* of a formal paradigm must have at least two aspects: *generality* on the one hand, and *heuristic potential* on the other. The criterion of generality obviously refers to the range of questions to which a paradigm can apply. The heuristic criterion refers to a paradigm's capacity for increasing what Lazarsfeld and Barton call the probability of the detection of significant facts concerning a given question.[17]

Just as there is or there can be research at the level of theoretical paradigms (research relating to game theory is one example), so there is, or there can be, research at the level of formal paradigms, as Merton's studies on functionalism show. This research can result in important developments. Thus Merton's paradigm certainly represents a step forward compared with the theoretical paradigm it developed out of, because it is undeniably more powerful in terms of the above two criteria.

Before going on to conceptual paradigms, which are the last class of paradigms, we must make an observation which we will have cause to take up later in this article. Although Merton is right to point out that the word theory is polysemic in the social sciences, he does not tell us clearly how he would classify his own work on the functionalist

paradigm in terms of the seven headings. Is it a question of methodology, general orientations or theory? As far as we are concerned, there
seems to be no problem in using the term theory here. It is true that, from
the strictly logical point of view, formal paradigms are no more theories
than theoretical paradigms. However, from the epistemological point of
view, they play a similar role: they permit the discovery of explanations
and the collection of pertinent facts; they can be evaluated in terms of
similar criteria (generality, heuristic potential, etc.). Moreover, they
sometimes become the *equivalents* of theories in the strict sense when
these are logically inapplicable. The case of functionalism is significant
in this respect: the Mertonian analysis of the political machine shows
that it can be applied to the explanation of cases which, by definition
could not be made the object of a theory in the true sense (hypothetico-
deductive theory). This epistemological equivalence helps to explain
why the same concept of "theory" can be applied to contrasting entities,
in spite of their obvious logical differences. What is more, the
equivalence extends to theoretical paradigms: although from the logical
point of view they are different from theories, they can be equivalent
from an epistemological point of view.

We will now say a word about what we have called *conceptual
paradigms*. In practice, certain explanations derive neither from a theory
in the true sense, nor from a theoretical or formal paradigm but from a
framework of reference whose structure is one of a system of concepts.
This is in contrast to the preceding paradigms which are made up of
systems of propositions: systems of theoretical propositions having an
analogical relationship with the phenomena to be explained in the case
of theoretical paradigms; systems of formal propositions involving a
relationship of subsumption to reality in the case of formal paradigms.
Parsons's *pattern variables* are one explicit example of a conceptual
paradigm (Parsons himself often uses the word paradigm *à propos* of the
different conceptual schemes which he introduces). In this case the
paradigm has a bearing on the *vocabulary* rather than the syntax or any
other structural aspect of the explanation. Moreover, the majority of
studies by Parsons have the same form: they begin by establishing a
conceptual system on which basis explanatory propositions are then
constructed. The history of the case of the *pattern variables* is too
complicated for us to use it here in a swift analysis. Instead, we will refer
to other Parsonian conceptual paradigms, especially those which are
presented in the article on *General Theory in Sociology*.[18]

In the first section of this article, Parsons introduces two conceptual
paradigms. The first differentiates as follows between four levels of

social organisation: the primary or technical level, the managerial level, the institutional level and the societal level. Any "organisation" can actually be analysed in terms of these four levels. Taking the case of a hospital, for example, there are a certain number of tasks of a "primary" or "technical" nature to be fulfilled, namely, deciding which treatments are capable of restoring health to the sick. At the same time, the hospital can only function on condition that management tasks are properly carried out: thus the hospital will normally be provided with an administration. But it is also necessary for the political process, or the goals which an institution sets itself to be simultaneously controlled, approved and facilitated by a board located at the "institutional" level. Finally, because the general goals that determine the hospital's existence are the concern of society as a whole, Parsons introduces an additional level which he calls "the societal level". We are dealing here with a conceptual paradigm, that is, with a system of four concepts. These concepts are sufficiently general to apply to organisations of very different kinds, whether hospitals, schools, scientific laboratories, industrial enterprises or any other type of institution. But, up to this point, they are nothing more than a classificatory system.

However, this hierarchy of organisational levels happens to correlate with a certain set of facts: in particular one can – in part at least – explain the social hierarchy of occupations with the help of this conceptual system. Thus, if the business executive is endowed with a higher status than the engineer, this is because the former is situated at the management level and sometimes at the institutional level, whilst the latter is usually situated at the "primary" level. This is also why the engineer, even if his personal status in income terms is often higher than that of the magistrate, nevertheless has an inferior social status in category terms. For the former is generally situated at the management level, whilst the latter is situated at the societal level. The correlations between the hierarchy of organisational levels on the one hand and the occupational hierarchy on the other therefore enable at least a partial explanation of the phenomenon, which is found in every society, that occupations as such tend to be evaluated in a differential way. If, in category terms the engineer is situated on a lower rung of the occupational status ladder than the business executive, this is not because the former is usually placed below the latter within the hierarchy of a particular organisation. On the contrary, the explanation resides in a much more general process which engenders a hierarchical perception of occupations whose members are not generally speaking found in positions of institutional interaction.

It should be pointed out that we have given an extremely simplified version of the Parsonian explanation – or "theory" – of the differential evaluation of occupations. This "theory" which is partly set out in a fair number of publications, especially in *General Theory in Sociology* and in *A Revised Analytical Approach to the Theory of Social Stratification*,[19] is actually far more complex. It does not derive from a conceptual paradigm, but from an involved set of conceptual paradigms. Thus, in the second of these articles, Parsons sets out a classification of the fundamental values of societies, which is drawn from the *pattern variables*. It is interesting, in the present context, to quote from a passage where Parsons is describing these values, together with the hierarchical order which they acquire in American social perception:

> The broad rank–order of precedence will be, below the paramount value–pattern, the order of relative strategic importance of the exigencies relating to the other three major functional problem–contexts of the system. Thus in our system (American Society) the primary value–focus is universalism–achievement. It may be suggested that the second order precedence goes to the cultural–latent area (universalism–quality) in the maintenance of the strategic cultural patterns on the one hand (e.g. science, education) and the regulation of personal motivation in relation to the basic value system (family, health, etc.). Probably the system–integrative comes next, and except for situations of national emergency, system–goal attainment last; this last is primarily what we mean by our "individualism". Or, to take a contrasting case, in a society where a transcendental religious orientation occupies the paramount position, the first order priority of values will rest in the ascriptive–qualitative norms. Then according to whether it is an actively "proselyting" religion or a more static–traditionalistic type, the next order would tend to be the system–goal attainment or the system–integrative type, with, presumably the adaptive in the last place. In the case of Calvinism, however, system–goal came second (the "kingdom of God on Earth") and because of the nature of this goal, the remaking of secular society in the image of God, adaptive considerations apparently outranked the system–integrative.[20]

This new conceptual paradigm, when combined with the first, leads to a refinement of the "theory" of social stratification and, for example, to an "explanation" of the fact that although the societal level represents the highest organisational level, a career in politics is less prestigious in the United States than in other societies, such as French society, for instance. In fact this occupation is related to a value (social integration) which only belongs to the third level in American society. This hierarchy also explains why, for example, the university profession as such is regarded as inferior in this society compared with the majority of European societies. It results from the fact that the "maintenance of cultural values" in the United States is subordinated to the value "achievement" to a greater extent than in Europe. On the other hand, when a professor displays "achievement", he can attain very high prestige. This possibly explains why American professors – at least if one is to believe the claims that their students have recently been making – sometimes prefer to abandon the "maintenance of cultural values" dimension of their role for the advantages of "achievement" through research. It is impossible to do justice to the richness of Parsons's analysis of the hierarchisation of occupations, especially as this analysis has been taken up many times in different publications without ever having been set out in a fully detailed and clear way.

For our present discussion, it is enough to understand how Parsons, from the departure point of a set of conceptual systems, extracts an "explanation", not only of the existence of occupational hierarchies, but even of the content of these hierarchies and of the differences which can be observed from one society to another in this respect. In the process, one of the phrases of the passage quoted even draws on Weber's famous theory about the origins of capitalism as a particular case of propositions which can be extracted from fundamental conceptual paradigms. And not only do these paradigms lead to an explanation of the phenomenon of occupational hierarchisation; Parsons uses them in a similar way to explain numerous other phenomena of social differentiation (inequality of the sexes with regard to occupational chances, intergenerational persistence of social inequalities, etc.).

The logical connection between paradigms of this type and the explanatory propositions which issue from them is far more difficult to establish and is often far more fluid than in the case of other categories of paradigms. We have used the example of Parsons precisely because he is one of the authors who illustrates most systematically this procedure of the derivation of explanatory propositions from conceptual paradigms. The majority of explanations that he has given of one or other category of social phenomena derive more or less indirectly from one or several paradigms of this type. This is why what he calls "general theory" in sociology largely corresponds to the study of conceptual paradigms which are both general and original.[21]

In no way are we suggesting here that Parsons's approach provides logical models which ought to be imitated or which may have special virtue. In many cases his demonstrations are incomplete, unclear and involve variables which are defined without precision or complete consistency. What we do wish to stress is that Parsons's work, by being a particularly good illustration, helps to identify an intellectual procedure in the human sciences which is often associated with the notion of "theory". It would be interesting, although as far as we are aware nobody has attempted this, to examine systematically the route that Parsons uses to get from his conceptual paradigms to explanatory propositions. What a superficial examination like the present one can show is that the paradigms play an important role in the derivation of explanatory propositions. But the logical connections between the former and the latter deserve to be more fully elaborated than they are by Parsons himself.

The derivation of explanatory propositions from conceptual paradigms which is so clearly illustrated in Parsons is a very common process in sociology. The Durkheimian notion of anomie has given rise to numerous explanatory propositions. The same is true of Tönnies's opposition between *Gemeinschaft* and *Gesellschaft*. Again, one of the important tasks of a positive epistemology would be to determine the logic of the derivation of explanatory propositions from conceptual paradigms of this kind. To that end, it would be necessary to analyse systematically the uses to which they are put. These paradigms probably have at least the following functions:

(a) The function of *detecting* explanatory factors. This can be illustrated by the example we have used from Parsons: it reveals that the hierarchy of "common values" is correlated with observed international differences in the hierarchy of occupations.

(b) The function of *generalisation*. The concept of anomie is a good illustration of the second function. With the help of this concept, Durkheim was able to find a common explanation for the correlation between a large number of factors on the one hand, and variations in suicide rates on the other. Thus both the correlation between the family dimension and the predisposition to commit suicide and the correlation between economic cycles and variations in suicide rates are explained using the same conceptual paradigm. It should also be noted that the introduction of the notion of anomie has a generalising effect in a further sense. This notion makes it possible to conceive of the phenomenon of suicide as a particular manifestation of phenomena of individual dissoluteness that accompany the relaxation of social constraints.

Historically, the "explanation" of the suicide phenomenon given in *Suicide* quite clearly derives from the conceptual paradigm of anomie, because this concept is already present in *The Division of Labour in Society* which was published before Durkheim had developed his theory of suicide.

In general terms, conceptual paradigms, like other kinds of paradigm, have the property of structuring a set of phenomena and uniting apparently different phenomena. It is therefore understandable why they play an important role in the derivation of explanatory propositions. However, we still know very little about the way in which the derivation process occurs.

In passing, it should be noted that conceptual paradigms are not exclusive to sociology. In behaviourist psychology, for example, the importance of the stimulus–response paradigm is well known. It is also known how rapidly Tolman himself abandoned this paradigm to make way for the more genral action paradigm. [22] The difference between the "behaviour" of the behaviourists and the "action" of authors who subsequently used this paradigm consists in the idea that it is impossible to account for conduct if its subjective aspects are ignored. The behaviourists sought to limit themselves to analysing relationships between stimulus and response. Proponents of the action paradigm assumed that in order to understand this relationship – even at the level of animal psychology – it was necessary to introduce intervening variables, like "desires", "inclinations", "dispositions" or "attitudes" of course. The action paradigm itself appears in different forms which require analysis, in sociology no less than in psychology or economics.

There is no shortage of historical examples of conceptual paradigms: for example, notions of absolutism or of feudal society represent a paradigm of this kind. It should also be noted that this type of paradigm is frequently used by sociologists who are close to history, like deTocqueville or Max Weber. The notions of "administrative centralisation" or "bureaucratisation" have led to well known developments. The continuing success of hese notions can doubtless be attributed to the role they still play as a guide to the explanation of a variety of social phenomena.

The following observations can be made to summarise these distinctions:

1. The notion of theory in the social sciences has both a general and a specific meaning In the narrow sense, it corresponds to the notion of the hypothetico–deductive system of propositions. In the broad sense, it goes beyond this to include at least three distinct categories of paradigms, namely theoretical or analogical paradigms, formal paradigms and conceptual paradigms. Theoretical paradigms are theories developed in one sector of reality and applied by analogy to other sectors. The theory of migration belongs to this type to the extent that it is the application by analogy of Newtonian mechanics to migration phenomena. Formal paradigms are systems of propositions which – as their name suggests – do not have reference to any specific content. Mertonian functionalism is a paradigm of this type. Another example of a formal paradigm is represented by the theory of causal analysis.[23] Formal paradigms orientate research and analysis by providing a symbolic representation of the syntactical form which explanatory propositions will take. The relationship between these paradigms and "explanations" of social phenomena is a relationship of subsumption. Finally, conceptual paradigms are systems of concepts which represent the vocabulary in which explanatory propositions will be expressed.

2. To a large extent the categories we have just described cover the distinctions made by Merton at the beginning of *Social Theory and Social Structure*. Thus, conceptual paradigms more or less correspond to his category of the analysis of concepts.

In our view, the classification put forward here has the advantage of providing an explanation of the polysemy of the notion of theory in the social sciences. In fact, it stresses that explanation and generalisation does not necessarily proceed by way of the elaboration of theories in the narrow sense. In a great many cases, a few of which we have mentioned, formal conceptual and analogical paradigms have permitted the discovery of explanations. Thus, Parsons's conceptual paradigm leads to an undeniably interesting explanation of stratification phenomena. Moreover, theoretical paradigms like those of game theory or exchange theory contribute in an important way to the unification of diverse phenomena within a common explanatory system.

There is, therefore, no doubt that these paradigms play an important part in the progress of the social sciences. It is also possible to develop independent research at the level of these paradigms. For instance, it was possible to generalise the analysis of economic behaviour by including it as a particular case within the more general paradigm of games. Subsequently, this paradigm has been developed on its own account and has given rise to an abundnt literature which today comprises "game theory". This theory is not a theory in the sense of physical theories, but in the sense of formal theories, like mathematics, for example. What it involves in fact is a set of deductive systems derived from sets of more or less fundamental axioms which represent different "game" situations. But the theory of games certainly developed, in a long line of descent, from the very ancient paradigm of the *homo oeconomicus*. The game theory example is not the only example of the transformation of a conceptual paradigm into an independent formal paradigm. Linguistics provides numerous examples of this type, like the theory of generative grammar or the Jakobsonian variety of "structuralism" derived from the notion of phoneme.[24]

One of the major tasks for a positive epistemology of the social sciences would be to study the historical transmutation of paradigms. This historical transmutation is possibly one of the important forms in scientific progress.

Another point to note is that the utilisation of this or that type of paradigm is sometimes governed by the logical characteristics of the phenomenon under analysis. Thus, it is difficult to see how hypothetico-deductive theories of the type used in physics could be used – or, at least, could be used *exclusively* – in the analysis of *singular* phenomena; which is why the Mertonian analysis of the American machine could not take the form of a hypothetico–deductive theory.[25] In this case, the "theory" *must* almost inevitably – take a different form from that of "theories in the narrow sense". Formal or conceptual paradigms can therefore be as it were the functional equivalent of theories in the narrow sense, because, like the latter, they give rise to generalisation and explanation. Failure to recognise this functional equivalence is perhaps the greatest weakness of the Mertonian analysis. It possibly derives from the fact that the notion of theory (in the narrow sense) as used by Merton is governed by the epistemology of the natural sciences and the physico–chemical sciences in particular. But it has to be admitted that the characteristic intellectual model of these sciences cannot be applied to the social sciences except in the case where the latter are seeking to explain universal (or quasi-universal) phenomena, like variations in suicide rates, for example. When it is a question of analysing singular phenomena, like the terminology used by the Ba-Thonga to describe kinship relations, the situation is logically quite different. In other words, theoretical activity must, simply by virtue of the context, take another form.

In short, the polysemy of the term theory in the social sciences appears to owe a great deal to the fact that the logical situations which these disciplines encounter whenever they seek to explain this or that social phenomenon, are diverse and cannot always be reduced to the epistemological model sprung from the natural sciences and the physico–chemical sciences in particular. With the result that theoretical activity takes different forms according to the context.

3. It is by no means certain that the notion of theory in the natural sciences is as monolithic as philosophers of science and sociologists tend to assume. We have cited the case of the corpuscular "theory" of light which corresponds logically to a theoretical paradigm rather than to a theory in the strict sense. Even in the physico–chemical sciences, then, it is possible to identify analogical paradigms. It is also possible, although it would need a closer examination, that instruments like cybernetics play the part of formal paradigms in the natural sciences. As for a notion like that of *system*, it is likely that it originally had the status of a conceptual paradigm.[26] Just as Durkheim in *The Division of Labour in Society* subsumed a large number of phenomena beneath the notion of anomie so as subsequently to make this notion a basic element in the explanation of all kinds of phenomena, so it is possible that the Hotion of system in physics originally represented a conceptual paradigm which was later transformed by the introduction of cybernetics and general systems theory, into formal paradigms. We do not intend to give these remarks more weight than they deserve. All that we want to suggest here is that the character of the epistemology of the social sciences which we are dealing with today is probably largely due to a simplified representation of the natural sciences which reduces these to a preferred model, namely Newtonian mechanics.

4. It is our hope that the types of paradigms we have identified could be of use in the history of the social sciences. We have already pointed to the fact that scientific progress often seems to take the form either of the generalisation of a paradigm (as in th case of game theory constructed from the paradigms of "economic theory"), or the transmutation of a conceptual paradigm into a formal paradigm (as in the case of structural phonology), or tꞑe transmutation of an analogical paradigm into a formal paradigm (as in the case of functionalism). Of course it may also take the form of the introduction of new paradigms or criticism of existing paradigms (as in the case of the substitution of the "action" paradigm for the stimulus–response "behaviourist" paradigm).

Another advantage of this typology of paradigms would be to reveal the links between studies of an apparently heterogeneous nature. For example, we have always been astonished to find the structuralist paradigm being traced back to Saussure. For if one analyses a work such as *The Spirit of the Laws* in terms of the paradigm notion, it is clearly apparent that Montesquieu's basic project is to demonstrate that the institutions, customs, etc. in every society constitute a system. The very notion of *spirit of the laws*, translated into contemporary language, is strictly equivalent to that of social structure as employed by authors like Murdock, for example. An investigation of the transmutations and applications of the structuralist paradigm using the perspective described here would certainly lend greater precision to a history and an epistemology of structuralism.

5. We should also emphasise that it is no part of our plan to suggest that sociologists abandon their concern for rigour and verification and be satisfied with hazy derivations from more or less arbitrary conceptual paradigms. For example, we are not suggesting that the Parsonian theory of social stratification is superior to all others. All that we are saying here is that an analysis of the development of the social sciences, and doubtless also of the natural sciences, shows the importance of the different kinds of paradigm which we have been presenting. But detailed epistemological analyses of these paradigms are rare. This is why it would be useful, for example, to study in detail the role of the conceptual and formal paradigms[27] used by an author such as Parsons in order to identify, classify and analyse the procedures which enabled him to move from a particular paradigm to an explanation of this or that set of social phenomena. A study of this kind would not only help to elucidate Parsons's thought but it would also reveal the various methods of proof, including their strengths and weaknesses.

6. At this stage we should stress once again the programmatic character of these "Notes". We are not implying either that the types of paradigm which we have suggested should be distinguished are the only possible ones or that they are defined with perfect clarity. We simply wish to state is that it is important to identify, clarify and codify the types of paradigm that the social sciences employ. The classification that we presented earlier only represents a provisional and hypothetical schema.

7. There is no need to insist on the practical as well as theoretical interest of positive epistemological studies like those we are recommending here. It is common knowledge that substantial methodological progress has been made in the realm of quantitative sociology by a systematic consideration of the reasoning and procedures actually

employed in the research process. However, despite its importance, *quantitative* analysis is only one aspect of the sociologist's approach. This is why it is essential to make an inventory and systematic codification of the mental processes used in sociology. Analysis of the diversity, nature and function of paradigms certainly forms an essential part of this programme of research.

THEORIES IN THE NARROW SENSE IN THE SOCIAL SCIENCES

We now move to an examination of several problems concerning theories in the narrow sense in the social sciences. In particular, we will be asking to what extent one of the most interesting modern attempts at epistemology, Karl Popper's, can provide a useful framework of reference for defining the notion of theory in the social sciences, for establishing and defining the criteria for evaluating these theories, and for classifying the types of theory in the narrow sense which are found in these disciplines. Then, we will deal with the problem of a typology of theories in the social sciences, prior to making a few observations about the notion of verification.

Some aspects of Karl Popper's epistemology

In his famous *Logik der Forschung*[28] Karl Popper takes up the classic problem oi induction and examines the notion of corroboration or verification as applied to the empirical sciences. His answer is that, strictly speaking, the operation of verification has no meaning and that a theory has never been verified. In fact, the notion of verification either does not really correspond to any explicit criterion or is only supported by criteria whose application would correspond to an indefinite or infinite number of operations.

Popper goes on to argue that scientific procedure involves the falsification of theories rather than their verification; never their confirmation, only their invalidation. More exactly, the only means available to the scholar for testing a theory against reality is to construct it in such a way that it can be refuted by nature. Nature can, as it were, give an affirmative answer to the question "is this theory false?" (or a negative answer to the question "is this theory true?"). On the other hand, it cannot give an equally simple "no" to the first question or "yes" to the second.

This observation derives from scholastic logic. Although others had made the same observation, Popper pushed its consequences to the farthest extreme. Let us suppose that we are putting forward a theory T. It will be possible to submit the theory to nature's verdict provided we can make at least one deduction $q*$ expressing the existence in nature of a given state. If the state of nature deduced from T is actually realised, we can draw the conclusion that the theory *is not false*. If, instead, $q*$ fails to correspond with observation q, T can be said to be false. In other words, for Popper, the underlying structure of this scientific discovery is represented by the celebrated *modus tollens* of Aristotelian logic. Formally, the *modus tollens* can be expressed in the following way:

$$(T \rightarrow q*) \wedge \bar{q} \rightarrow \bar{T}.$$

If $q*$ is deduced from T, and if $q*$ contradicts observation q, then T is false. The falsity of a theory can therefore be demonstrated by the application of a simple criterion involving the comparison of $q*$ with q. Now let us suppose that $q*$ and q are congruent. In this case, all that can be said is that one *cannot* conclude $\bar{T}$ (the falsity of T): this is the only proposition which can be derived from the fact of congruence.

In order to demonstrate the truth of a theory it would in fact be necessary:

(a) To know $(q*)$, namely the set of deductions which it is possible to make from T;

(b) To have verified the congruence between $(q*)$ and (q), or in other words to be quite sure that none of the deductions that could be made from T is in contradiction with reality. However, since there is no criterion which makes it possible to be certain that one has deduced all the consequences of a theory, it follows that one can never demonstrate the truth of a theory, only its non-falsity.

These remarks correspond to the commonsense observation that a theory can always be called into question by a new observation. But Popper takes this a stage further: according to him, the application of the *modus tollens* differentiates between two quite distinct types of theory.

He terms them *scientific* theories and *metaphysical* theories respectively. Scientific theories are those whose syntax is such as to allow comparison between $q*$ and q. In other words, scientific theories are those which are refutable or, following Popper's neologism, "falsifiable". In contrast, "metaphysical" theories are those which it is impossible to "falsify" or "invalidate".

It should also be noted that Popper's theory – in principle at least – only applies to theories whose deductions have the form of universal propositions. Indeed, it is obvious that a *singular* proposition such as "Napoleon lost the battle of Waterloo" can be proved either false or true.[29] There is no need either to stress that Popper's reflections apply only to the empirical sciences and not to the formal sciences such as mathematics, in which it is possible to demonstrate the truth of universal propositions.[30]

In short, they only apply to the empirical sciences where statements have the form of universal propositions.

Even if these reservations are taken into account, it seems to us that Popper's analysis, together with his proposed dichotomy between scientific theories and metaphysical theories, provides a logically inadequate framework for the social sciences. We will begin by analysing several examples of *theories* in this realm. The first has already been mentioned in the first part of this article, namely the Parsonian theory of stratification. It can be formulated as follows:

(a) Every social action implies an evaluation;
(b) Every evaluation implies a hierarchical ordering;
(c) Hierarchy implies stratification;
(d) Evaluation of social action is governed by the presence of the value system which pertains to any given society;
(e) In specifying these values, one can deduce a certain number of propositions about the stratification phenomena of this or that particular society or about comparative stratification phenomena in different societies.

We saw earlier how this theory makes it possible, provided the terms are specified, to arrive at an explanation of facts as diverse as the existence of occupational hierarchies or variations in the ordering of these hierarchies in different societies. It can also explain all sorts of "cultural" differences between societies: for example the fact that there is no "political elite" in exactly the European sense in the United States or the fact that the idea of guidance by the educational system appears to be quite generally accepted in the United States, whereas it is a matter of debate in certain European countries.[31]

The 'political elite's" lack of stability, lack of prestige and lack of visibility can be explained by the fact that, in the *instrumental–expressive* dichotomy, the first term is valued much more highly in the United States. American society also gives more weight to achievement than to

the attribution of quality. Similarly, the high evaluation of the instrumental and achievement dimensions means that the development of
scientific activity in the United States is a consequence of technological
development rather than the reverse: "There is a sense in which the
valuation (of science) is derivative rather than primary; the order runs
from technology to science rather than vice versa. But once technology
has attained a certain level of development the connection between it and
science becomes exceedingly close. . . . One may suspect it would take a
real shift of the major value system to displace the 'applied' functions
from their position of priority."[32] Perhaps this passage explains why, for
example, sociology in the United States has never adopted the speculative tone which it sometimes continues to have in Europe, or why the
philosophy of science and logic are much more highly developed there
than metaphysics. Thus we could carry on giving further examples of the
Parsonian theory of social stratification. There is no doubt that this
theory can provide plausible explanations of a large number of social
phenomena that have to do with the differential evaluation of types of
action or status stratification in contemporary societies. In short, the
theory enables numerous deductions to be made which are congruent
with observation.

However, it is by no means certain that Parsons's theory belongs to
either one of the categories in the Popperian dichotomy. For, on the one
hand, it leads to deductions which are directly comparable with
observational data (surveys show that the function of a university
professor is less highly esteemed in the United States than in Germany,[33]
that political functions there are less highly coveted, etc.). In this respect
it is not a "metaphysical" theory. On the other hand, however, it is
difficult to regard it as a refutable theory. In fact, it is scarcely possible to
imagine the fact or the observation which would lead to its rejection. To
a large extent this arises from the fact that the consequences *deduced*
from the theory are not deductions in the strict sense. The consequences
can be "explained" by the theory; but they are not *deduced* in the proper
sense. To be precise, each consequence is derived from the theory by
virtue of a set of *specifications* or supplementary propositions. These
specifications would take on the appearance of an *ad hoc* theory if their
associated primary theory proved to be incapable of explaining a large
number of phenomena and failed to give grounds for its validity and
generality.

In short, it seems that what we have here is a theory expressed in a
syntax such that it is impossible to imagine criteria of refutation.
However, it certainly has scientific validity, firstly because it is *congruent*

with observation and secondly because it explains a large number of social phenomena in the realm of differential evaluation of social action and mechanisms of stratification. We find ourselves in a logically similar situation on examining deTocqueville's *L'Ancien Régime et la Révolution*, for example. In outline, the basic theory contained in this work can be expressed as follows:

"Administrative centralisation" entails a number of consequences concerning:

(a) Evaluation of the political function. This function should be regarded as more important in a State characterised by administrative centralisation than in a State whose functions are decentralised. It follows that political figures will enjoy greater prestige.
(b) Perception of the State by the citizen. The citizen will tend to regard the State as the source of all power and initiative. Individual initiative will be correspondingly reduced.
(c) Political ideologies. Because the passage relating to the third point is fairly concise, we will quote deTocqueville himself:

They [the French *philosophes* of the eighteenth century] did not play an active part in public affairs, as English writers did; on the contrary, never had they kept so steadily aloof from the political arena. In a nation teeming with officials none of the men of letters held posts of any kind, none was invested with authority. . . .
    Though their ways diverged in the course of their researches, their starting point was the same in all cases; and this was the belief that what was wanted was to replace the complex of traditional customs governing the social order of the day by simple, elementary rules deriving from the exercise of the human reason and natural law. When we look closely into it we find that the political philosophy of these writers consists to all intents and purposes in ringing the changes on this one idea.

The first proposition explains the second:

Their very way of living led these writers to indulge in abstract theories and generalisations regarding the nature of government, and to place a blind confidence in these. For living as they did, quite out of touch with practical politics, they lacked the experience which might have tempered their enthusiasms. Thus they completely failed to perceive the very real obstacles in the way of even the most praiseworthy reforms . . ., since as a result of the total absence of any political freedom they had little acquaintance with the realities of public life, which, indeed, was *terra incognita* to them. They took no personal part in it and were unable to see what was being done by others in that field . . . . As a result, our literary men became much bolder in their speculations, more addicted to general ideas and systems.[34]

It is clear that this case is logically similar to the preceding one. The theory is one which explains a large number of facts, probably better than all the theories which had gone before. Nevertheless it is not strictly speaking open to refutation. The only way of refuting it would involve analysing a sample of societies and proving that administrative centralisation is not invariably associated with the characteristics that deTocqueville deduced from it. For the refutation to be convincing, however, the lack of concordance would have to be inexplicable by factors other than the degree of administrative centralisation. Even if the practical difficulties posed by the construction of a sample of this kind could be resolved, there would still remain the logical difficulties arising from international comparisons and especially the application of statistical or quasi-statistical methods to such comparisons. It is true that there are statistical studies that do make use of samples of societies. Indeed we will be examining one of them later. But it is clearly evident that there is a limit (determined by the nature of the question asked and by the state of information available) beyond which the use of statistical methods is unlikely to lead to greater rigour than the methods used by deTocqueville. To express the same idea in Popper's language, one could say that the use of statistical comparison does not necessarily endow a theory with the quality of falsifiability.

Logically, the structure of deTocqueville's theory can be characterised in the following manner:

(a) It consists of the statement of a number of correlations between the degree of administrative centralisation and certain other factors (degree of individual initiative, the more or less abstract character of political philosophy, etc.).

(b) The "correlations" are of neither a statistical nor quasi-statistical kind. In actual fact, they rest on comparisons between a very small number of units (France on the one hand, Britain and the United States on the other).

(c) The convincing character of the theory is due to the fact that it is possible to extract from these basic propositions, by a sequence of what can conveniently be called psychological rather than logical deductions,[35] an explanation for *a large number* of the peculiar features of French society. By "psychological" deduction we mean a sequence of propositions: for example "Decisions are more often taken at the level of central administration. Since political figures have greater power, the political function will *consequently* have greater prestige." The consequence is not a logical conclusion, but a conclusion which derives from our social experience. This is why we use the term psychological deduction.[36]

(d) *Strictly speaking, the theory is not refutable.* This is because, given the nature of the procedure which leads from premises to inferences, one cannot conceive of an observation to contradict the theory. Given that this theory explains a large number of facts, one would tend rather to introduce *ad hoc* hypotheses to incorporate an apparently incompatible fact. It is this, much more than the psychological character of deduction which makes the definition of a fact to contradict the theory practically impossible.

To finally convince the reader of the inadequacy of the Popperian dichotomy, we will take a third example borrowed from the realm of structural phonology. This example will be different in kind from the earlier ones to the extent that the point of departure is not a theory, but a classification. It is well known that one of the major problems of phonology was to determine the basic sounds or phonemes of languages. Most prominent linguists, whether Troubetzkoy, Jakobson or Harris, subscribed to a particular solution to this problem. Consider, for example, Jakobson's phonology. Using a succession of complex procedures, Jakobson identifies a certain number of phonemes in the English language, which he described in terms of a number of "distinctive features" or as sociologists would say, classificatory dimensions. Thus the phoneme *i* in *pit* is described as "voiced", "non-consonantal", "diffuse", "acute", the phoneme *h* in *hill* as "voiceless", "non-consonantal", "fricative", the phoneme # , which is the linguistic equivalent of "silences" in music, as "voiceless", "non-consonantal", "non-fricative". The surprising character of these descriptions itself shows that they are the outcome of a theory, or that they are deduced from a set of primary propositions or axioms.[37] But Jakobson's proposed objective is not to construct an empirically verifiable theory. In other words, no empirical propositions can be deduced from this "theory", which is therefore a theory in the formal sense of the term (like mathematical theories for example). However, the descriptions of phonemes which can be derived from this theory allows them to be ranked according to their degree of complexity. One then discovers that this order of complexity coincides with the order of occurrence of certain empirical processes such as the appearance of phonemes in children or their disappearance in aphasia. The correspondence between the ordering of phonemes which derives from the formal classification and these empirical processes therefore leads to an explanation of the latter by the former. This is an interesting example because it illustrates the case of a theory which can explain certain phenomena even though its correspondence with these empirical phenomena cannot strictly be deduced from the theory. In practice, the order of complexity described by the theory does match the development of certain empirical processes. However, in the event that this match did not occur, it would not be legitimate to interpret this as a refutation of the theory. Jakobson's phonology therefore shows that theories do exist which do not embody criteria of falsifiability but which nevertheless can contribute to explaining certain empirical phenomena.

These observations should be sufficient to demonstrate that the criterion of falsifiability, though seductively simple, is quite inadequate to characterise the notion of scientific theory. Because, in the realm of the social sciences at least, there are non-refutable theories that lead to convincing explanations of certain phenomena. We have to admit that the notion of "conviction" (a subjective correlate of the notion of "verification") deserves more detailed analysis. This is why we will devote several of the pages which follow to the subject. First, however, we wish to make some general remarks which should serve to remove a doubt which might have crept into the reader's mind. Even if the Popperian scheme is relativised, we do not believe that one is forced to accept simply any theory. In other words, we do not believe that the *modus tollens* is the only criterion for accepting or rejecting a theory. More specifically, although the application of the *modus tollens* translates basic logic into scientific procedure in a number of areas it is only one of the basic structures of induction.

The *modus tollens* is actually characterised by an opposition or a state of confrontation between a theory T and nature. In such a case, the only possible outcome of this confrontation is the one described by the *modus tollens*. But scientific progress can also result from a confrontation between theories. Thus, it is possible to imagine a situation in which a theory T_1 would explain phenomena $q_1, \ldots, q_n$, whilst a theory T_2 would explain phenomena $q_1 \ldots, q_n \ldots, q_m$. In this case, T_2 would be preferred to T_1 because of the criterion of *generality*, even when T_1 is not refuted. This formal presentation allows one to codify the logical correlate of the subjective conviction which theories such as those of Parsons or deTocqueville convey. Strictly speaking they cannot be refuted, because their syntax is such that it is difficult to conceive of facts that would refute them. However, their force of conviction comes from the fact that they explain a large number of facts.

Of course we are not suggesting anything particularly new in referring to the criterion of generality. It is as old as the criterion of refutability itself. We simply wish to stress that the criterion of refutability, contrary to what Popper maintains, is not the primary condition of scientificity. In other words the criterion of refutability does not have to be met before the criterion of generality can be applied. On the contrary, in our opinion, verification or validation of a theory should be seen as the result of the simultaneous application of these two criteria as well as others which we will now examine.

The criterion of generality is not in fact the only one which it is possible to place alongside the criterion of refutability. Thus, if one is dealing with two theories of stratification the one which is capable of accounting for not only the greatest numbers of phenomena but also the most detailed phenomena will certainly be preferred. This is the feature of Parsonian theory which makes it such an important contribution to the analysis of stratification. For it provides an account of a whole range of quite specific differences in empirical systems of stratification. The same is true of deTocqueville's theory, which makes it possible to account simultaneously for phenomena as specific and as different as French political philosophy, the distribution of conurbations throughout France and the prestige accorded to political figures. One could refer here to a criterion of specificity.

In a general way Popper can be reproached for having neglected the fact that the first parenthesis of the *modus tollens* $(T \rightarrow q)$ requires a detailed analysis. The three terms included in this parenthesis (T, q, and the relation $\rightarrow$) can conceal logically distinct realities. In the first section of this article we saw that T could take various forms. In the pages which follow, we will have occasion to analyse other logical distinctions between the theories which are found in the realm of the social sciences. Further, we have seen that the relation "$\rightarrow$" can have several quite separate meanings. Clearly Popper's interpretation is one of logical implication. But it must be noted that depending on the nature of T, but also on various other factors, the relation can have other interpretations. It is possible that, from the *normative* point of view, the only one worthy of consideration is that of implication. However, the *positive* point of view which we are adopting here obliges us to state that in practice (in the natural sciences no less than the human sciences) the relation has more varied interpretations. We have distinguished between "logical" deduction and "psychological" deduction which usually corresponds to the statement of a causal relationship between two elements (like deTocqueville's conclusion that power entails prestige). We also saw in the first part that, depending on the nature of T, the relationship of implication could take on different meanings (analogy, subsumption, etc.).

Lastly, it remains to consider the characteristics of q. Although for analytical purposes it can be useful to regard q as a single proposition, it should not be forgotten that in practice q is nearly always a *set* of propositions which would be better denoted by q. Now the characteristics of this set are of considerable importance. As we have seen, one of the characteristics is $N(q)$, namely the number of propositions contained in q. If $T_1 \to (q_1)$ and $T_2 \to (q_2)$ and, other things being equal, $N(q_1) > N(q_2)$, T_1 will clearly be preferred to T_2. Moreover, the *specificity* of the propositions contained in (q_1) and (q_2) should be taken into consideration. If the statements of (q_1) are more specific than those in (q_2), all other things being equal T_1 will be preferred to T_2.

In general, the structure of q exerts a considerable influence over the degree of conviction which a theory carries. It is in any case unlikely that the two criteria which we have mentioned exhaust this notion. Clearly the "distance" between the elements of q will alter the strength of conviction a theory has. If a theory provides an explanation of phenomena from very different domains, one will be more easily inclined to accept it. If the Durkheimian theory of suicide is regarded as a kind of model in sociology, this is probably because it simultaneously satisfies this whole range of criteria. Firstly, it satisfies Popper's criterion of refutability: where social cohesion is weaker, the likelihood of suicide increases in every case. There are more suicides among Protestants than Catholics, but the rates of suicide among Protestants decrease when their cohesion is reinforced by the fact that they are members of a minority. When anomie increases, suicide rates increase similarly in every case: suicides increase in societies where the institution of the family is under greater threat from divorce; they also increase during economic boom periods; they decrease with the enhancement of the family dimension etc. In short, all the correlations that can be derived from the theory of social cohesion and anomie are confirmed.

But the Durkeimian theory does not satisfy this criterion alone. It also satisfies the criterion of generality: it is possible to derive from the theory numerous consequences about variations in suicide rates (variations in the function of family structure, regional variations, variations connected with economic cycles, seasonal variations, variations in the function of religious denominations, etc.). Given that it can be demonstrated quantitatively, the theory also satisfies the criterion of specificity. These points, which we cannot elaborate further without leaving the framework of our discussion, show that the scientific modernity of *suicide* is far from being exclusively dependent on the fact that it prefigures modern statistical techniques.[38]

In summary, it seems clear that Popper's criterion of falsifiability is inadequate to account for the *reality* of scientific work or scientific discovery. For when one examines the processes of theorisation that occur in the social sciences, one is forced to conclude that they conform to a far more complex logic than the one described by the *modus tollens*. However, we are quite prepared to admit that whereas the *modus tollens* provides a criterion which is easily seen to be satisfied or not, at least when the particular theories which Popper has in mind are being considered, the criteria which we have defined are less easily applicable. Thus, in practice it is no simple matter to enumerate $N(q)$ and thence to make a simple decision on this basis between two theories. However, there is no denying that when we "evaluate" a particular theory in the realm of the social sciences, we have to rely not only on the falsifiability criterion but on a host of other criteria. If, from the point of view of an *a priori* epistemology Popper's criterion has the advantage of simplicity, it has the drawback of only taking into account very specific kinds of scientific procedure. In comparison with the other criteria it is more of an abstraction than a formalisation. For instance, it would be possible to conceive of a statistical form of verification for the various propositions of *positive* epistemology that we have introduced here. Because, difficult though it may be to apply the criteria suggested above to a specific theory, they do explain the intersubjective hierarchisations which patently exist. For example, they explain why deTocqueville is still highly regarded although he did not produce a verifiable (falsifiable) theory in the strict sense. They similarly account for the importance of Durkheim as well as Parsons.

There is one final point which needs to be underlined. If, like Popper, one reduces the *modus tollens* to its most elementary form and one interprets q as a single proposition, the notion of the *truth* of a theory is deprived of meaning. In fact it then becomes impossible to define a finite and definite criterion of truth, since the falsity criterion is immediately applicable. However, it must be acknowledged – as we have pointed out – that in practice, q is a complex whole. This observation is important because it revitalises the meaning of the notion of truth. Formally, the notion of truth is stripped of meaning in Popper's theory because the relation between T and q is asymmetrical. One can have $T \to q$, but never $q \to T$. Logically, it must follow that if one interprets the relationship in terms of implication, one has to acknowledge the asymmetry. It also follows that when q is an isolated proposition, nothing about T can be deduced from $(T \to q) \wedge q$. The reason for this is that it is impossible to show that q can be deduced only from theory T alone. In fact, there could easily be a set of theories T', T'' . . . from which q could also be inferred. But let us now consider q as a set of statements (q) rather than as a single proposition. To the extent that the *structure* of (q) is rendered complex by the list of criteria whose elements we have partly described (generality, specificity, distanciation), the *subjective* probability that (q) can be deduced from an alternative theory T' is reduced. If we explain this subjective probability by $P(T')$, $1 - P(T')$ is an ideal measurement of the subjective probability of T being true. Naturally, it is difficult to measure $1 - P(T')$ properly.[39] But this formalisation has the advantage of showing that the notion of *truth* is not without meaning. In fact, although it is never possible to state that a theory is true, one can compare two theories in terms of the subjective probability of their being true because this subjective probability depends on a multidimensional variable which is difficult but not impossible to define, namely the structural complexity of (q).

This formalisation would seem to provide a better account of the nature of scientific work in the social sciences than Popper's criterion of falsifiability. But it can also be asked – and this is a question which we will leave to the philosopher of science – whether it may not apply equally to the natural sciences. It is true that certain scientific *discoveries* can be described as products of the *modus tollens*. The discovery of the phenomenon of interferences which was to call in question the corpuscular theory of light, or the Michelson–Morley experiment which had implications for the theory of relativity, are classic examples which neatly confirm Popper's thesis. However, does scientific progress always follows this path? Is it not rather the case that this type of scientific "revolution" is unusually spectacular and therefore has a better chance of being incorporated within the spontaneous history of science? In the present context we can only pose this question for both the philosopher and the sociologist of science.

As far as the social sciences are concerned, we can certainly give several examples of scientific "revolutions" which correspond, not to Popper's model, but to the one which we outlined above. A particularly illuminating example in this respect is the Durkheimian theory of suicide. If, as it seems, this theory effectively banished the theories that came before it, like those of Italian positivism, this is not so much because it demonstrated their falsity but because it led to a set of inferences (q) of incomparably greater structural complexity. It is true that at various points, Durkheim demonstrated the falsity of a specific theory. Thus he demonstrated that the theory of matrimonial selection put forward by Bertillon was false, because it led to inferences which observation showed to be contradictory.[40] However, strictly speaking, he did not demonstrate the falsity of the "psychopathic" or "mechanistic" theories of suicide which he aimed to discredit. If his readers find his theory more persuasive than those of his predecessors, this has to be because it leads to a set of inferences which is structurally more complex. To take a very specific example: it is impossible to choose between the interpretation of seasonal variations in suicide given by the Italian positivists and Durkheim by applying the falsifiability criterion. The existence of these variations can actually be deduced from both types of theory, which are thus both in accordance with observation. If Durkheim's criticism is convincing, it is because his theory simultaneously explains seasonal variations and variations in suicide on a function of the level of divorce rates, for example. In short, the structural complexity of (q) in Durkheim means that the value of $1 - P(T')$ is much greater than among his predecessors. We should be clear about the significance of this: it does not simply mean that Durkheim's theory is *better* because it is more general, but also that it is seen as having a higher probability of being true.

We would have no difficulty providing examples of this type of scientific revolution in the social sciences. Levi-Strauss's theory of incest taboos, which treats this phenomenon as a consequence of the need to regulate the circulation of women in primitive societies, certainly corresponds to this model.[41] It has become accepted, at least in part, not because it could explain a fact which contradicted this or that previous theory but rather because it provides an explanation of matrimonial rules in a number of societies and leads to a set (q) of much greater structural complexity than in previous theories.

The above formalisation also makes it possible to distinguish between the *ad hoc* or *post factum* interpretations which Merton speaks of and theories in the strict sense. An example of *post factum* interpretation which verges on caricature is one of the theories criticised by Durkheim, which attributes the universal increase in suicide rates in spring and summer to a heat-induced physiological and psychological agitation which is responsible for the rise in the propensity to commit suicide. If one holds to Popper's criterion, this theory is acceptable. It actually leads to an inference which is in accordance with observation. If it scarcely seems satisfying, it must be because the reason lies elsewhere than in the criterion of refutability. This reason is not hard to state: if the theory is unconvincing, it is because the subjective probability that the same inference could be drawn from another entirely distinct theory is very great. But this subjective probability is in turn a result of the lack of structural complexity of (q).[42]

In short, the subjective difference which is expressed linguistically in the distinction between "theory" and "*ad hoc* theory" or "*post factum* theory" corresponds in our formalisation to a threshhold (difficult to locate with precision) in the "structural complexity" of (q), a threshhold beneath which the quantity $1 - P(T')$ is regarded as low and above which it is regarded as high.

Once again, the main weakness in our formalisation compared with Popper's is at the level of operationalisation. Whereas the criterion of falsifiability is immediately applicable, the variables we are introducing (structural "complexity" of (q), subjective probability $1 - P(T')$, etc.) are hard to manipulate in practice. However, this formalisation appears to us to provide a more efficient conductor for a positive epistemology.[43] It leads to a more serious analysis of scientific progress and at the same time accounts better for certain semantic distinctions ("theory" and "*ad hoc* theory", for example). Further, it makes it possible to tackle the problem of verification in the social sciences. In terms of the theory of knowledge, it has the advantage of reintroducing the notion of "truth" in a precise form. Finally, it generalises Popper's analysis which one cannot help but interpret as the formalisation of several privileged examples of "scientific discoveries" which are perhaps used more for their spectacular qualities than for their ability to really typify scientific discovery.

It is true that our criticism of Popper rests on examples taken from the social sciences. One fundamental question would be to discover whether it also applies to the natural sciences. Obviously there is no question of our reaching a conclusion on this. But the simple fact that the question can be asked indicates that a general epistemology would benefit from consideration of this still barely developed discipline of "positive epistemology" in the social sciences.

What matters now is to see not only that the logical structure of the theories which can be constructed in the social sciences is, as we have been suggesting throughout this article, highly variable (which is why Popper's epistemology derived from a highly specific type of scientific procedure is inadequate) but also that this variatio is very frequently a consequence of the logical context in which these theories are situated.[44]

Types of theory as a function of their logical context

The foregoing considerations led us to introduce the notion of *degree of verification* in relation to the theories which are encountered in the social sciences. Sometimes the criterion of falsifiability is applicable (Durkheim), sometimes it is not (deTocqueville). Obviously, other things being equal, the degree of verification of a theory varies according to whether this criterion is or is not applicable. But the validity of a theory also depends on other factors such as the "structural complexity" of the set of inferences which can be made from it. This "structural complexity" of (q) is itself the product of a number of criteria (generality, specificity, distanciation, etc.).

What we wish to suggest here is that the "level of verification" which a theory can attain is often determined by the external circumstances which characterise the logical context of the investigation. This variation in the "verification level" of theories in terms of their logical context clearly helps in large measure to explain the polysemy of the notion of "theory" in the social sciences. In fact, when the level of verification does vary, this circumstance is often attributable to the context and not to intrinsic differences in the nature of the theories: hence the impression of equivalence between theories from the point of view of the degree of validity when, from the logical point of view, these theories are characterised by very different levels of verification.[45]

In order to illustrate this idea, we will begin in our customary manner by presenting a few examples. The first is taken from linguistics: it concerns the structural analysis of stress in English, the elements of which are presented in some of the work of Chomsky and Miller.[46] Their basic intuition is that the rules of grammar are not arbitrary conventions but systems of signals which make it possible to translate and clearly understand spoken messages. They therefore set out to analyse different linguistic phenomena in this perspective and especially the rules of stress in English. The fragments of this still unfinished theory which they have presented are enough to illustrate the procedure. Suppose that we start with the following axioms:

(a) A simple or compound noun is generally stressed in an initial position.
(b) When a segment can be decomposed into a system of interlocking elements and these elements are of the same grammatical kind, the first stress is dominant and to some extent lowers the others. Thus the segment *black board eraser* can be decomposed into two interlocking elements: [*black board* (*eraser*)]. Also, the elements are of the same kind (substantive).
(c) When the interlocking elements are grammatically different in kind, the last main stress is dominant and to some extent lowers the others.

If one applied these propositions, one obtains a series of transformations which reconstruct the stress pattern of a number of spoken segments. Take the segment *John's blackboard eraser* as an example. It leads to the following transformations (the figures placed above the words indicate the intensity of the stress):

$$
(1) \quad \left\{ \begin{matrix} 1 \\ John's \end{matrix} \quad \left[\begin{matrix} 1 & 2 & 1 \\ black & board & (eraser) \end{matrix} \right] \right\}
$$

$$
(2) \quad \begin{matrix} 1 & 1 & 3 & 2 \\ John's & (black & board & eraser) \end{matrix}
$$

$$
(3) \quad \begin{matrix} 1 & 2 & 4 & 3 \\ (John's & black & board & eraser). \end{matrix}
$$

The hierarchical ordering of stress derived from the theory is actually the same as that employed by an English language speaker. Notice, too that this "theory" is not an *ad hoc* or *post factum* theory, because it is capable of correctly deducing the stress pattern of numerous segments.

This theory (which we have presented here in a highly condensed form)[47] is especially interesting because there is a sense in which it corresponds to the ideal type of the notion of theory. In fact it is possible to deduce from the limited number of propositions involved a large number of consequences which are in accordance with observation: it makes it possible to *deduce* the stress pattern actually used by English language speakers. Moreover, it confirms the basic intuition of Chomsky and Miller that the rules of grammar constitute systems. Lastly, it explains certain phenomena which appeared to be a mystery until the advent of structural linguistics: namely the ease with which apparently highly complex and anarchic rules are normally learned by young children, and the assurance with which they are normally applied.[48]

But the point which we wish to stress here is that the "level of verification" attained by this theory is to a large extent a consequence of the logical context in which it is situated. The characteristics of this context are as follows:

1. The class of *facts* which the theory should account for in principle is perfectly defined: it is concerned with the hierarchy of stress characteristic of any segment of the English language. One of these facts is:

1   2   4   3

John's black board eraser. Naturally, one can formulate an indefinite number of segments. But it is clear that a theory capable of correctly deducing the stress patterns of a sufficient number of segments could be taken as valid since the structural complexity of (q) would then be regarded as sufficient.

2. The observational situation in the case of Chomsky and Miller can be characterised as an *experimental* situation: on the one hand, the *data* they are using are inexhaustable; on the other hand, they have complete freedom of choice as far as these data are concerned. One imagines in fact that they first sought to formulate their axioms in terms of a small number of segments and that they went on to verify them in relation to other segments. The inexhaustible character of the data, the perfectly defined character of the facts to be explained and the complete freedom of choice of data combine in their effects to make possible the formulation of a falsifiable and general theory. In short, the logical context has a structure close to that which is frequently (but not exclusively) encountered in the natural sciences.

But the logical context can be and generally *is* less favourable in the social sciences. Thus, it is rare that the class of facts to be explained by a particular theory is as well defined as this. This reason alone would be enough to explain why a theory of stratification, for example, can never be as logically satisfying. For the class of facts relating to the phenomena of stratification clearly cannot be defined in so precise a manner as the class of facts relating to the phenomena of stress.[49] Perhaps therefore one of the sources of scientific progress will be those reformulations which provide access to classes of precisely defined facts. An example of a reformulation of this kind can be found, once again, in Durkheim's *Suicide*: ideally, the class of facts which Durkheim proposes to explain consists of the entire range of quantitative variation in suicide rates, this being a function of the variables used for observing them. The passages where, in somewhat academic fashion, he seeks to define the notion of suicide and those where he decides to exclude certain quantitative information like the subdivision of suicides in terms of the way they were carried out, can be regarded as an attempt to reach an unequivocal definition of the class of facts to be explained.[50]

In other respects, however, Durkheim found himself in a logically much less favourable situation than Chomsky or Miller. In fact, the logical context in *Suicide* is *quasi experimental* rather than experimental in character. The methodological difficulties which result from this are well known and have been described many times over.[51] Thus, despite his precautions, Durkheim did not successfully eliminate all ambiguity in the interpretation of the statistical relationships which he observed. For exaple, Selvin observes how much care he took to demonstrate the existence of a non-spuriou relationship between religious denomination (Protestants–Catholics) and suicide rates.[52] What he actually does, after presenting the correlation in a very general form (comparison of suicide rates in various countries with protestant and catholic majorities respectively) is to re-examine it controlling for the possible effects of non-religious variables which could explain the first correlation. Thus he compares suicide rates among the Swiss cantons and the German states. Still not satisfied, he eventually gives a table in which the relation between denomination and propensity to commit suicide is established, not at the collective level (cantons, states, etc.) but at the individual level. The different tables logically complement one another and mutually exclude the ambiguity of interpretation. In spite of these precautions, it is nonetheless true, as Halbwachs pointed out, that a certain ambiguity remains.[53] No amount of effort can alter the fact that the majority of protestants live in cities whilst the proportion of Catholics living in the country is much higher. In short it would be necessary to have access to information which would enable certain possible parasitic effects to be deliberately excluded. But this type of difficulty is precisely what characterises, in varying degrees, every *quasi experimental* situation: by definition, it is impossible in this situation to make the explanatory factors independent of all the possible parasitic effects.

Moreover, the difficulties may not only stem from the quasi-experimental situation itself but from the characteristics of the available data. In the case of a quasi-experimental situation, the interpretation implies the use of a statistical method (so-called ' multivariate'' analysis) which involves the *logical* separation of those factors which cannot, as in the case of experimentation, be separated *physically*. But the logic of this method makes the elimination of *ambiguity* strictly dependent on the *scale* of the observed sample. We will illustrate this point with an example borrowed from Murdock.[54] In *Social structure* Murdock puts forward a general theory designed to explain a perfectly defined class of facts, namely the differentiation or lack of differentiation between the terms used to designate kinship relations. Thus, in our society, the term "father" designates a class comprising a single kinship relation, whilst the term "grandmother" assimilates two distinct relationships and the term "cousin" a still greater number. Ethnologists had long since been aware that the connections between terms describing kinship relations and quite distinct types of relationship varied appreciably from one society to another. Murdock's theory aimed to explain these variations. To do this, he made use of the information available in the Yale archives on 250 primitive societies. One of the "theorems" deduced from his theory is the following: "in the presence of non-sororal polygyny, collateral relatives outside of the polygynous family tend to be terminologically differentiated from primary relatives of the same sex and generation". To demonstrate this theorem, Murdock set out the following table, in which he examines the frequency with which "relatives outside of the polygynous family" are designated by similar or different terms, according to whether or not the societies accept non-sororal polygyny.

TABLE 7.1 Terminological differentiation of relatives as a function of the form of marriage; the figures refer to cases

Pairs of relatives	Non-sororal polygyny		Other forms of marriage	
	Different terms	*Same term*	*Different terms*	*Same term*
Mother's sister/mother	53	58	48	70
Father's brother's wife/mother	36	46	37	45
Father's brother's daughter/sister	28	84	23	95
Mother's sister's daughter/sister	30	78	23	90
Brother's daughter/daughter	38	61	39	73
Wife's sister's daughter/daughter	22	28	16	24

Source: Murdock, *The Social Structure* (Glencoe, Ill.: The Free Press, 1965) p. 144.

As can be seen, the attempt at proof ends in stalemate: if one considers the second line of the table, one notices for example that contrary to the predictions of the theorem, the father's brother's wife and the mother are designated by different terms with the same frequency, whether one is dealing with a non-sororal polygynous system or any other system. In the other cases, the differences do occur as predicted but they are weak and scarcely significant. However, there is little doubt that the theorem is true. The fact that it is not proven is because non-sororal polygyny is frequently combined with a patrilocal form of residence and a patrilineal type of descent.

As other results show, these factors exert an inverse influence on terminological differentiation. In fact, if one removes the influence of certain of these factors by leaving out part of the sample, one can establish a new correlation table in which, this time, the predictions derived from the theorem are better satisfied.[55] It is significant however that Murdock only controlled one of the parasitic factors and not both because the size of the available sample would then have been too small for a statistical analysis.

These examples show clearly that the logical characteristics of a theory, and especially the level of verification which it can attain, depend largely on the logical context in which it is situated. Describing this context is not a simple task because it has multiple characteristics. The relatively well-defined character of the class of facts relating to the theory is one aspect. Another aspect is represented by the experimental, quasi-experimental or non-experimental character of the context. Within each of these categories, it is possible to introduce further distinctions. Thus Murdock's theory is quasi-experimental but the conditions of observation are such that it is possible to combine it with a statistical form of verification. In other cases, where the available sample is extremely restricted, one can still resort to *quasi-statistical* verification. This is the case for example in Lipset's study of contextual variations in political participation in North America:[56] impressed by the high level of political participation in the rural areas of Saskatchewan, he put forward the hypothesis that this remarkable phenomenon was due to a combination of factors (weak social stratification, administrative density, presence of strong economic fluctuations, etc.). In order to demonstrate that these were indeed the factors responsible for the observed phenomenon, he set out to examine the relation between the presence (or absence) of these factors and the evel of political participation. However, given the *extent* of the unit of observation (provinces) it is obvious that the sample *population* comprised only a very small number of cases; which is why this can be called a "quasi-statistical" analysis.

But the universe of observation can consist of an even smaller number of units. This is especially the case when the analysis is concerned with a singular phenomenon, as was Max Weber when he investigated the singular phenomenon which we know as the capitalist type of economy. In this case, the range of comparitive mthods from statistics to quasi-statistics is unusable. This is why, to meet this specific but not unusual logical situation, anthropologists and sociologists have developed a series of formal paradigms such as functionalism, which we had occasion to use in the first part of this article, or like the method of structural homologies which is illustrated with particular brilliance in the work of Panovsky on Gothic architecture and scholastic thought. Because we have paid some attention elsewhere to paradigms of this kind we will refrain from analysing them here.[57]

There are, however, still further characteristics which come to modify the logical context in which a theory is situated. At this juncture, we have to reintroduce certain distinctions which were made previously. Thus, when the derivation of propostions from a theory is *deductive* (logical implication), the level of verification attained is higher than when it is *psychological* in nature. To be more precise, psychological derivations presuppose emirical confirmation which cannot always be produced. This distinction can be understood by comparing the example of Chomsky and Miller's theory of stress in English with Durkheim's *Suicide* or with deTocqueville's *L'Ancien Régime*. In the first case, the derivation which proceeds from primary statements to the determination of the stress in a specific segment is purely *deductive* in nature: it would not be difficult to do it mechanically. In the second case, the derivation which leads from the basic propositions to the statement of a relationship between a variable and the rate of suicide is obtained by the introduction of a set of intermediate propositions which do not follow logically from the former. Here, the deduction is not mechanical. A proposition can only be extracted from what goes before if its *semantic* content is taken into consideration. As we said earlier, the derivation here takes the form of a sequence of statements which affirm the existence of relationships of causality between certain phenomena. In other words, it involves a pseudo-deduction.

The quality, validity or, if preferred, the truth of a theory depends on all of these factors. Which is the same as saying that they are the subjective correlates of two types of logical characteristics which theories have:

(a) *Internal* characteristics (falsifiability, structural complexity of sets of inferences (*q*) which derive from the theory, etc.).
(b) *External* characteristics or characteristics of the logical context (the more or less well defined character of the class of facts relating to the theory; experimental, quasi-experimental or non-experimental situation; characteristics of the available data, etc.).

It is probable that the differences between the natural sciences and the social sciences are less marked with respect to the first type of characteristic than with respect to the second. In actual fact, the formal paradigms used in the analysis of singular objects (functionalism, analysis of homologous structues) are more typical of the social sciences. The same is true of psychological derivations, which are made possible by the observer's familiarity with his object. This is characteristic of the social sciences and since Max Weber it has been customary to refer to it as *Verstehen*. In this connection it is still necessary to point out that, as the foregoing discussion demonstrates and as Weber himself affirmed on several occasions, *Verstehen* and *Erklären* are not in opposition. The specific relation between the observer and the observed explains certain peculiarities of the explanatory process in the social sciences. But it does not replace *explanation*.

On the other hand, it is probable that the list of *internal* characteristics which we elaborated (or outlined, to be more precise) applies to every explanatory process regardless of which part of reality is involved. Indeed, there is no reason why the notion of *truth* in the precise sense in which we have expressed it here or the notion of *structural complexity* should only be applied to specific classes of theory. In fact, these notions are defined in a formal way, i.e. independently of all content (although they derive from a *positive* analysis of scientific procedure in the social sciences. To give a direct answer to this question, however, it would be necessary to verify empirically whether the epistemological schemas introduced here are exclusive to the social sciences.

We set ourselves a number of objectives in these "notes". We will now attempt to review the main points which havebeen made and set out some guidlines to enable the present observations to be transformed into concrete research. The first objective was an attempt to understand the polysemic nature of the notion of "theory" in the social sciences. As Merton showed in the observations with which we began, the notion of "theory" is used in very diverse ways in sociology and in the social sciences in general. In spite of Merton's diagnosis, however, the polysemy remains, as a quick glance through any book dealing with sociological theory will show. Why? Firstly, because the social sciences, and perhaps the natural sciences as well, include within the notion of "theory" not only "theories" in the strict sense, namely hypothetico–deductive systems of propositions capable of being verified (or refuted or falsified, to use Popper's language) but also what can be called "paradigms". The divergence of the natural sciences at this point possibly arises from the fact that transformations from elementary paradigms (conceptual paradigms) into more complex paradigms (formal and analogical paradigms) and thence into theories in the proper sense are certainly less easy in the social sciences. This is why conceptual paradigms in the natural sciences are generally relegated to the level of histoy whilst, very frequently, they continue to form an integral part of the social sciences.[58]

Another reason for the polysemy of the notion of theory in the social sciences is perhaps to be found in the greater complexity of the *logical contexts* in which social science theories are situated. At least, this is so when one compares them with the ideal models which the epistemology of the natural sciences puts forward (although it remains to be verified whether this is actually the case). For example, it is this diversity of logical contexts which explains why sociology uses formal paradigms like functionalism, the analysis of structural homologies or "quasi-statistical" induction alongside statistical analysis of an econometric type. As we have shown, the use of these paradigms which may be rather uncertainly defined is a consequence of the logical situation which the researcher sometimes encounters – a situation which could be described as "degenerate comparative analysis". This is the situation, for example, that characterises Max Weber's investigations into the origins of capitalism, deTocqueville's into French society, Lucien Goldmann's into the origin of the novel, Merton's or Parsons's into the characteristics of American society or a great many ethnological studies of one particular society or another. We use the phrase "degenerate comparative analysis" because, on close examination, it can be seen that these studies always rely more or less directly on a comparison with objects other than those being analysed. This is perfectly clear in the case of deTocqueville, whose theory concerning French society depends throughout on an implicit comparison with the Anglo–Saxon societies. It could also be said that deTocqueville's theory reduced to its essential logical structure, consists of a set of pseudo-correlations between the variable "degree of administrative centralisation" and a number of dependent variables (value attributed to the political function, more or less abstract character of political ideologies, etc.). But the "verification" is obviously not statistical in nature (nor even pseudo statistical). As we have seen, it depends rather on the structural complexity of (q). In spite of this, it should be noted that deTocqueville's theory makes implicit use of the language of *variables* which is used in an explicit way in studies of a statistical kind.

This variety of logical contexts means that the notion of the validity or truth of a theory, although it is capable of being defined in a formal way, is probably more complex in the social sciences than in the natural sciences, at least if current epistemology is to be believed. The result is that the "theories" put forward by the social sciences convey a marked impression of heterogeneity.

Our second objective was to conduct an exercise in positive *epistemology*. By and large, what is currently called epistemology in the social sciences appears to consist either of paraphrases of current epistemology in the natural sciences more or less adapted to the social sciences, or of abstract theses which echo the philosophical discussions of the nineteenth century on the status of the *Geisteswissenschaften*, or even of methodological polemics which make appeal to one or other of the possible dogmas. However, the production of the social sciences is now copious enough for their epistemology to be able to go beyond the form of abstract or *a priori* discussion based at best on instances. The state of epistemology somewhat resembles the state of the philosophy of causality which always trailed one generation behind the state of scientific thinking. When Hume undertook to carry Galileo's scepticism about causality to its absolute limit, this notion was on the verge of being reintroduced through developments in biology. But some time had to elapse before it was re-installed in philosophy by Stuart Mill. Wittgenstein, for his part, was influenced by the principle of indeterminacy in physics at the time when economics and sociology were giving new life to the idea of causality. The same goes for the epistemology of the social sciences: it retains a neo-Diltheyan flavour and shows little concern for a systematic analysis of the products of these disciplines. In our view, the rise of the social sciences makes an epistemology of the social sciences all the more necessary because this rise has been accompanied by an undeniable dispersal and fragmentation coupled with great vulnerability to fashionable phenomena.

A positive epistemology is one which sets out to analyse a well-defined class of objects (the products of the social sciences) and which poses equally well-defined questions about these objects. (Why should one theory seem to be more convincing than another? What is meant by verification? What kinds of structure does the notion of theory designate? What are the objective correlates of the subjectively incontestable distinction between theory in the strict sense and *post factum* explanation? How did Durkheim refute Ferri?). In short, it involves a kind of grammatical analysis of those specific discourses which are the products of the human sciences so as to disentangle their implicit rules and structures as well as to identify their limitations and sources of objection.

One point which we chose to dwell on at some length was the "logic of scientific discovery", to use Popper's expression, in which the structure of scientific progress is summarised in its essentials by the *modus tollens* of scholasticism and which can be applied to the social sciences. We then ascertained the need to formulate a more general theory and to set up hypotheses concerning the major modalities of scientific progress in the social sciences. At this juncture we will simply list them as a reminder:

(a) *Modus tollens*;
(b) Formulation and transformation of paradigms;
(c) Formulation of more powerful theories from the point of view of the internal criteria summarised in the notion of "structural complexity";
(d) Action upon the external factors (by an appropriate modification of observational procedures or by a stricter definition of the class of objects covered by a theory, for example).

Although imperfect, this schema would certainly provide a better understanding of the actual development of the social sciences than Popper's which seems to rely on an idealised view of the sciences. It should also be noted that we are only preoccupied here with the problem of "theorisation" in the social sciences. Obviously a logic of scientific discovery would presuppose that equal attention had been paid to the development of observation (observational techniques and instruments, the organisation of observation, etc.) and to analytical techniques.

Similarly, it seems essential, without falling into a psychologistic epistemology, to consider the psychological processes that accompany scientific phenomena. Scientific theories are made by individuals and are the object of collective opinions. Therefore, one important task for the positive epistemology which we have tried to illustrate here is to determine the logical correlates of these subjective phenomena. This is what we attempted to do for example when we analysed the notion of the *validity* of a theory.

Our third objective was of a *methodological* kind. In fact it appears that a systematic analysis of the actual products of the social sciences can clarify the scientific procedures used and thence be useful for future research. The simple fact of isolating certain of the processes which contribute to scientific progress can have its usefulness from this point of view. For instance, it is useful to recognise that the *validity* of a theory has an important logical correlate ("structural complexity" of (q)), which can itself be analysed according to a number of dimensions. Awareness of this proposition can lead to the conception of new observational procedures to improve the value of this variable. Moreover, the same propositions shows that the quality of the statistical verification to which numerous investigations attach great importance, especially in sociology, is only one of the *dimensions* of the validity of a theory. The analysis in *Suicide* is directly pertinent in this respect: the strength of the validation in Durkheim's theory depends as much on the structural complexity of the propositions which he draws from it as on the statistical elaboration. For a sophisticated statistical elaboration is not incompatible with an *ad hoc* theory if the structural complexity of T is low. The abundance of *post factum* theories which is to be found in contemporary sociology – as Merton pointed out – possibly derives from the Popperian epistemology and from the privileged status which it accords to the criterion of falsifiability.

Our fourth and final objective was to foster systematic research in the realm of social science epistemology which we could only outline in the present essay. The processes of scientific development which we have described can perhaps serve as schemas for a history of the social sciences. For instance, the analysis of the logical dimensions of the notion of "validity" could issue in research of an experimental or at least empirical kind which would make it possible to define the subjective correlates whose reality we have postulated. The notion of "structural complexity" could be elaborated on the basis of an enumeration and systematic analysis of a number of theories. The processes by which paradigms are transformed could be studied using concrete examples. Finally, a systematic comparison between the processes of scientific development in the natural sciences and the social sciences would be extremely useful in furthering the construction of a general epistemology or a "logic of scientific discovery". This epistemology could not be elaborated until a considerable number of specific studies had been carried out; which is perhaps the best excuse we can make in defence of the rough, provisional and disorderly character of these "notes". They were designed to raise and identify certain problems rather than to solve them.

8. The Notion of Function[1]

In this note, we are proposing neither to perpetuate the lengthy debate which had developed around the notions of structure and function nor even to give a detailed analysis of the notion of structural–functionalism. The reader will be familiar with Hempel's[2] and Davis's[3] famous articles on functionalism which seek to demonstrate the tautological character of the supposed functionalist method. And so much has been written about the notion of structure that we could not possibly review it here.

What we wish to suggest is that the notion of *function* could be experiencing a process of relativisation similar to that which a certain number of concepts, like the concept *truth* or the concept *evidence* and many others, have undergone.

Firstly, let us examine the concept of *truth*. It is at the heart of Greek philosophy. In the sixteenth century, with the work of Galileo and the founding of the experimental sciences, it seemed indispensable to the scholar. However, at the same time, it was regarded as ambiguous. For it gradually came to be realised that a scientific theory is essentially a theory which can be called into question by new facts or new observations. In short, a scientific theory is a set of propositions which one can never be sure are true. Put another way, the predicate *true* can never be attributed to a scientific theory without betraying a dogmatism which is utterly contrary to the spirit of science. That is, a scientific theory is never true or false; it can only be false or not false.

It is generally agreed that, to some extent, the entire epistemology of the seventeenth century represents an attempt to resolve this problem. Descartes's theory of evidence and the *mathesis universalis* of Leibniz attempted to reveal the sign of truth in the positive sciences. But these enterprises met with failure. The notion of evidence put forward by Descartes is no less ambiguous than that of truth.

In fact, one only has to observe scientific thinking in practice to realise that the scientist is never demonstrating the truth of a theory (here we are only considering theories in the empirical sciences, not formal theories like mathematics and logic). All he can do, by using appropriate criteria, is decide whether a theory is false or not false. A theory is judged to be false if, for example, one of its inferences fails to correspond with reality. In the opposite case it is judged to be not false. But it is not judged to be true. This is the basis of Popper's statement, central to the *Logik der Forschung*,[4] that a scientific theory is essentially a theory expressed in such a way that it is capable of being proved false. In other words, a scientific theory is one which is *falsifiable*, not verifiable.

What is gained by replacing the concepts of truth or verifiability – which come from a sort of spontaneous epistemology – with concepts of falsity and falsifiability? Nothing more and nothing less than the removal of the ambiguities of the notion of truth as applied to the empirical sciences. It is impossible to convince anyone that a theory is true (which is why Descartes resorted to the obscure and intuitive notion of evidence). On the other hand, it is possible to be convinced, without ambiguity and by the deductive method, that a theory is false. To be precise, the proof of falsity takes the form of reasoning which the scholastics called the *modus tollens*:

$$[(p \rightarrow q) \wedge \bar{q}] \rightarrow \bar{p}$$

In words: if proposition p implies proposition q and if proposition q is false (if $\bar{q} = $ non-q), then proposition p is false ($\bar{p} = $ non-p). Thus, although the non-truth of p can be proved by perfectly explicit logical reasoning, it is not possible to conceive of an equally definite and practicable argument which could demonstrate the truth of an empirical proposition. It can be shown that this argument would have to be either indefinite or infinite.

The answer to the problems and ambiguities of the notion of truth as applied to empirical scientific theories is therefore obtained by the removal of this notion and its replacement by the notion of falsity. In other words, whereas the notion of falsity is fully admissable within scientific discourse (to the extent that it can be defined *formally* and unambiguously), the same cannot be said of the notion of truth. This latter notion cannot be formalised. To be specific, there is no form of reasoning R, finite and definite, which could establish the truth of an empirical proposition p, in the way that the *modus tollens* makes it possible to establish the falsity of p.

Once again it should be stressed that these observations only apply to the empirical sciences and, more specifically, to the sciences whose propositions are universal statements about nature. They do not apply to the formal sciences (like mathematics or logic), whose propositions can be proved to be *true* by finite procedures. Neither do they apply to the sciences which contain singular statements. Thus, although the proposition "all storks have red feet" can be falsified but not verified, the proposition "some storks have red feet" can be verified, but not falsified. Similarly, there are some propositions, like historical propositions ("Napoleon lost the battle of Waterloo"), that can be both falsified and verified. The important thing to realise is that contemporary logical reflection on the sciences is helping to relativise and formalise the notion of truth. In other words, as soon as one analyses the form of scientific proofs or whenever these proofs are brought to bear on the logical form of propositions, it has to be admitted that the notion of truth takes on different meanings depending on the context. In the empirical sciences, with their universal propositions, the concept has been banished from the research process. In contrast, there are still useful criteria of truth in the formal sciences.

We will now briefly consider the notion of *evidence*. There is no need to stress the importance which scientists and epistemologists, at least from Descartes to Cantor, attributed to this concept. However, from the start, this notion caused considerable controversy both because of its obscurity and resistance to formalisation. It has a twofold origin in a spontaneous conceptualisation of certain psychological phenomena (like the flash of inspiration which suddenly reveals the solution to an enigma or a problem) and a regular philosophical sleight of hand. Because if a proposition is self-evident, it implies or at least seems to suggest that there is no need to examine the criteria for this evidence. From which it is possible to conclude that the evidence is undefinable and is recognisable simply by the demands it makes.

We are well aware that the notion of evidence was taken seriously in epistemological thinking until the late nineteenth century. The difficulties involved were certainly appreciated from the time of Descartes onwards. But was it not the case that the notion formed an indispensable part of the foundations of science and especially of the mathematical sciences? In fact, just as every mathematical theory is a set of inferences drawn from propositions which cannot actually be demonstrated, those propositions need to be true for the edifice as a whole to be of any value. Because their truth cannot be maintained by rational proof, it must be supportable for intuitive reasons.

Of course none of these reasons was sufficient to solve the problems of the notion of evidence. What is certain though is that they kept the notion alive for centuries despite the obvious difficulties it entails.

How the history of the notion of evidence came to an end is well known. The axioms which now serve as the point of departure for the development of mathematical theories are no longer defined in terms of putative evidence. They are simply defined as propositions posed *a priori*, possessing certain properties which we hardly need to point out here, like the property of non-contradiction.[5] In short, the notion of evidence is extinct and has been replaced by formalised notions.[6] Instead of being a self-evident proposition beyond proof (an obscure and in principle undefinable property), an axiom is a proposition which, as far as it forms the point of departure for an argument, is deliberately left unproven. This proposition possesses other well-defined properties, such as compatability with other axioms.

Before analysing the way in which these antecedent notions of truth and evidence can be applied to the present problem, it is worth repeating that their psychological importance is perfectly understandable. The analysis of errors of meaning and the spontaneous epistemology which captured so much of the attention of seventeenth century philosophers, invoked the idea of truth. Similarly, the sudden psychological enlightenment which may be experienced when looking for the solution to a problem invokes the idea of evidence. These observations correspond to incontrovertible facts. Further, it is clear that the language of science is permeated with notions borrowed from the spontaneous epistemology we referred to earlier. But it should be recognised that scientific procedure entails the progressive elimination of notions which cannot be formalised, or at least their translation into formalisable notions which contain no ambiguity.

The notion of *function*, to which we can now turn, is comparable at several points with the two notions we have just analysed. What is more, it relies on a spontaneous psychology and epistemology which seem hard to avoid. To quote Radcliffe-Brown: "The concept of function as applied to human societies rests on an analogy between social life and organic life. Recognition of this analogy and some of its implications can be traced back at least as far as Protagoras and Plato. In the nineteenth century, the analogy, the concept of function, and the word itself, appeared frequently in social philosophy and sociology."[7] Thus, we are dealing with a notion which, from Protogoras to the present day, has seemed to be indispenable in that it suggests itself immediately whenever one examines a social system, however superficially.

However, like the notions which derive from the spontaneous epistemology we analysed earlier, this notion raises certain difficulties. In the first place, as Radcliffe-Brown himself recognised, it elicits explanations of a teleological kind. More importantly, it is obscure and non-formalisable. We do not intend to review the detailed criticisms which authors like Merton have made of Radcliffe-Brown.[8] What we do wish to point out is that the development of functionalism appears to indicate a reformulation of the notion of function but a reformulation which spells the end of the notion as such. In other words, we are arguing that the notion of function like the notion of evidence, is undergoing decomposition because of the very progress of research. Coming as it does from a spontaneous epistemology it cannot be incorporated within a scientific language without fundamental reformulation.

To show this, we will quickly recall the debate between what could be called the *absolute* functionalism of authors like Radcliffe-Brown and Malinowski and the relativised functionalism of sociologists like Parsons, who is sometimes associated with the expression "structural–functionalism".

The fundamental hypothesis of absolute functionalism is that the notion of function has an intuitively obvious meaning. Thus it is assumed that the functions of elements within a culture, for example social customs, can be analysed. To quote again from Radcliffe-Brown's article to which we have already referred: "The function of a particular social custom is the contribution it makes to the total social life."[9] Incidentally, Radcliffe-Brown prudently adds that "the hypothesis does not require the dogmatic assertion that everything in the life of every community has a function. It only requires the assumption that it *may* have one."[10] Whatever its outcome, functionalist analysis presupposes that the notion of function has a specific meaning, that functions can be clearly identified and that it is possible to state the function of this or that social custom. The difficulty is the impossibility of defining and formalising the notion of function without ambiguity.

To show how that notion of function is disintegrating in contemporary structural-functionalism, we will limit ourselves to a single, straightforward example taken from Parsons:

First let us discuss some of the problems of the modern type of "industrial" occupational structure. Its primary characteristic is a system of universalistic–specific–affectively neutral achievement-oriented roles. There must not only be particular roles of this type but they must fit together into complex systems both within the same organization and within the ecological complexes linking individuals and organizations together. It is out of the question for such a role system, to be directly homologous with a kinship structure, so that it should be essentially a network of interlocking kinship units, as many other social structures, like the feudal, tend to be.[11]

Before analysing the implicit conception of the notion of function behind this sample of structural–functional analysis, we will clarify certain points of vocabulary for the reader's benefit. A simple example will help to show what Parsons means by "universalistic–specific–affectively neutral achievement-oriented roles". Consider the "role" that is described by the expression "bank clerk" in contemporary industrial societies. In the exercise of his functions – in the performance of his "role" – this individual has to deal with customers. His role requires that he treat them all in the same fashion: the role is therefore "universalistic". In contrast, he behaves with "filial respect" towards particular individuals (*Ego's* parents). Further, our clerk will only discuss a distinct set of problems with his customers: his role is "specific". In contrast, the father–son relationship colours all the exchanges which take place within these complementary roles. It is understood that exchanges between the clerk and his customers take place in the realm of "affective neutrality". In addition, a bank clerk becomes a bank clerk in order to achieve certain ambitions. The role is therefore "achievement oriented." On the other hand, certain roles like that of "son" are *ascribed*.

Having explained these points of vocabulary, the meaning of Parsons's analysis is quite clear. It turns on a contrast made between the industrial societies and certain non-industrial societies. In the latter, occupations and employment are – if not actually determined by the individual's location in the kinship system – at least *homologous* with this system. In contrast, the majority of occupations and employment in the industrial societies are independent of the individual's location within the family system.

But Parsons goes further. He is not simply content to state the relationship between two facts: the "industrial structure of occupations" and the lack of homology between occupational and family roles. He uses this relationship to deduce the proposition that the "industrial structure" of occupations implies a society in which family ties are reduced to the nuclear or "conjugal" family: "we may say with considerable confidence to those whose values lead them to prefer for kinship organization the system of mediaeval Europe or of Classical China to our own, that they must choose. It is possible to have either the latter type of kinship system or a highly industrialized economy, but not both in the same society."[12] Later on, Parsons expresses it even more

succinctly: "One could say that the conjugal type of family system is the
one which least interferes with an industrial economy."[13]

This passage provides a specimen of functionalist analysis in the
modern sense of the term. For instance, Parsons is declaring that an
industrial society cannot *function* unless kinship relations are defined in
a certain way. Reversing the terms, it could be said that the "conjugal"
character of the family in industrial societies has a positive *function*
within the social system: the nuclear family appears to be the kind of
family organisation which best fulfils the requirements of industrial
societies.

At first sight, therefore, this would seem to relate closely to the
functionalism of Radcliffe-Brown or Malinowski. However, let us look
more closely at the *form* of Parsons's argument. It runs as follows: if
a society requires that its individual members generally play roles
defined as "universalistic", "specific", "affectively neutral" and
"achievement oriented", this *implies* certain consequences, like the fact
that an individual's place of residence cannot be compulsorily fixed.
Now freedom of choice in where to live is limited in a society where
family organisation is highly complex and constricting. The role
required by societies of the industrial kind also imply that individuals
have great freedom in choosing their occupational activities; they
presuppose that individuals can relate to other people within the same
society and that in principle these relationship can be neutral and
limited. The opposite and limiting case, a society in which the "others"
were all kin, would have a system of "particular", "diffuse", "affectively
non-neutral" and "ascribed" roles.

Formally, the argument is therefore as follows:

(a) A feature A implies circumstances *a, b . . . n.*
(b) A feature B implies circumstances *a', b' . . . m.*
(c) Circumstances *a* and *a'*, for example, are incompatible.
(d) Hence: features A and B cannot be present simultaneously within a
    society.

In the example, feature A would correspond to the notion of
"industrial society" and feature B to "extended" family systems.
Similarly, circumstances *a, b, . . . n* would correspond to the phrase
"playing "universal"", "specific", etc. roles towards *Alter*" and circumstances *a', b', . . . m* would correspond to the phrase "playing"
particular", "diffuse", etc. roles towards *Alter*."[14]

The most striking feature of this argument, which is formally analogous to most of the accounts which are given by Parsons himself, Merton[15] or Max Weber, whom contemporary structural–functionalists regard as their precursor, is that the word *function* does not appear at all. Briefly, if what we are saying is correct, defences of structural–functionalism put forward by authors such as Merton or Parsons are characterised by their lack of explicit reference to the notion of function or at least by the fact that their statements can be formalised in such a way as to exclude the term function. The formal schema above which we used to summarise Parsons's argument does not contain the word function. The same point could be made using many other examples.

Thus the notion of function seems to be no more essential to accounts of structual–functionalism than the notions of truth or evidence are to accounts of scientific procedure. Just as physics has dispensed with, and has an interest in dispensing with, the obscure notions of truth and evidence, sociology can dispense with the notion of function. Given the difficulty of breaking with the concepts of a spontaneous epistemology, it may even do this while calling itself "functionalist".

There is an exact parallel in the way in which the notions of *truth* and *evidence*, which also stem from a spontaneous epistemology, have had to be fundamentally reformulated into equivalent, unambiguous notions. The research process itself is producing a reformulation of the notion of function which is making it superfluous. Because the notion of function is obscure and undefinable, contemporary functionalism is not characterised by studies of the functions fulfilled by the elements of social systems. Instead, what authors like Parsons and Merton are tending towards is the definition of certain rigorous mental processes by which to analyse social systems *qua* systems. Explicitly or implicitly, a structural–functionalist analysis is one which demonstrates, or seeks to demonstrate by rigorous methods, either the necessity or the impossibility of the co-occurence of certain elements within a social system. Rejection of the notion of function is precisely that condition which will lend the analysis greater rigour.[16]

Part Three

Questions of Method

9. The Functions of Formalisation in Sociology[1]

The importance of formalisation in sociology is frequently challenged. The most forthright indictment comes from Sorokin,[2] whose criticisms are well enough known not to require repetition in detail. To summarise them briefly, formalisation is either simply a shorthand, or unnecessary or absurd. The first charge, though sometimes justified, overlooks the importance which parsimony of explanation and the identifiability of the variables can have in the development of a theory or hypothesis; thus there are certain studies which, despite their incapacity for deductive reasoning beyond the form of syllogism, are sufficiently clear and coherent for a more powerful language to be applied to them eventually. The second charge – that formalisation is unnecessary – is hardly worth dwelling on: once a logical system has been constructed, one can find out whether it is useful or necessary but one cannot determine whether it is useless or unnecessary; a paradox which is not uncommon in the history of science. As for the third charge of absurdity, it derives from the questionable proposition that things are by nature necessarily either qualitative or quantitative.

We will be providing illustrations of some of the functions of formalisation in sociology which in our opinion help to refute the charges of uselessness and absurdity. We will stick to a number of straightforward applications in which the value of formalism can be simply shown. We will deliberately exclude the important and controversial function which is represented by completely formalised theories (models); it is obvious that a discussion of these cannot be limited to the framework of one article. We are concerned with three functions in particular: metric, critical and conceptual.

I

There would be no need to dwell on formal measurement, which is so

205

widely diffused in the form of Thurstone, Guttman and other scales, if its meaning were not so commonly misunderstood. The first thing to be said is that it cannot be defined either as a way of making measurable that which cannot be measured, or making measurable that which can be. The fact is that there are no quantitative objects or qualitative objects in social nature; all that can be said is that language or observation describe a gradation or at least a categorisation in every attribute characterising a social object (an organisation is more or less centralised, more or less bureaucratised; a society is more or less hierarchical or differentiated; a party of the right or left, etc.) but that they are unable to classify a given set of objects unequivocally, except in particular cases. Because every social theory involves disclosing the causal structure of a set of attributes, this means that one of the conditions for the possibility of verification is intersubjective agreement about the classification of a set of objects within a set of attribute categories.

In many cases, the classifying can be done intuitively or by a simple and scarcely debatable operation. In other cases, especially when it is a question of ordering as well as identifying, the concept that corresponds to a given attribute implicitly defines the relationship of inequality between the two objects needed to make the measurement in terms of conditions which are so complex that one has to construct an instrument of formal measurement. Once the requirements involved in the concept have been made explicit, any measurement which satisfies these conditions can be taken as equivalent. Let us suppose, for example, that one decides to classify the members of a group of organisations or the departments of an organisation participating in joint decisions in terms of their respective power: to make this more concrete, imagine a group of five organisations (or departments) which have to make frequent decisions on a majority basis in decision-making situation which are comparable and in which each one has a vote. In such a situation, it is natural to define power in terms of conflict situations; indeed, no one would doubt that if A_1's motions are always passed in preference to the motions of A_2 when the two associations hold opposing views in a set of comparable situations, one has to accept the relationship: the power of A_1 > power of A_2 or simply, $p(A_1) > p(A_2)$. Note that, as far as the evidence goes, the situation described here is quite specific: in no way does it cover the totality of the problems of measurement posed by power relationships. However, regardless of the concrete situation in question, the sociologist is always faced with the following alternative: he can either formally translate the conditions implied by the concept into operational measures or he can engage in an "intuitive" appreciation and reduce the probability of reaching intersubjective agreement on the stated propositions – the inability to define the measure being related to the inability to define the concept. The problem involved here is specific but its solution reflects a general research strategy.

In our example, one procedure would be to analyse a series of comparable decisions and examine the conflicts between two organisations in order to determine the meaning of the relationship of inequality for each pair. The relationship $p(A_i) > p(A_j)$ could then have the explicit meaning: in the majority (or totality) of conflicts between A_i and A_j, A_i succeeds in gaining more votes for its point of view than A_j. Two possibilities are then open depending on whether the relationship ">" is transitive or not. In the first case, the measure of power is satisfactory because one invariably finds that $p(A_i) > p(A_j)$ whenever one observes $p(A_i) > p(A_k)$ and $p(A_k) > p(A_j)$. However, the hypothetical situation analysed here is certainly too complex for the transitive case to be taken as the norm: in reality it is highly probable that situations will occur where simultaneously $p(A_j) > p(A_i), p(A_i) > p(A_k), p(A_k) > p(A_j)$. When this does happen, it is clear that p does not allow the organisations to be ordered, hence it cannot be used as a measure.

However, a situation like this is no proof that the attribute involved in the ordering exercise is not measurable: it simply proves that the relationship of inequality thus defined is intransitive, and no more. Because numbers constitute an ordered set, one way to guard against the appearance of phenomena of intransitivity is to associate a number with each object, ensuring that this application satisfies the conditions laid down in the analysis of the concept. In the present case, one could imagine simply enumerating the victories obtained by each one of the organisations. To make this more specific, let us suppose that each pair of organisation is observed in four "singular" conflicts and that the results are presented in the form of a matrix like the following, in which the number situated in the intersection of the ith row and the jth column indicates the number of victories won by A_i over A_j. This matrix we will call M.

	A_1	A_2	A_3	A_4	A_5
A_1	2	3	3	4	1
A_2	1	2	4	3	4
A_3	1	0	2	2	3
A_4	0	1	2	2	3
A_5	3	0	1	1	2

In this example, A_1 wins 3 victories over A_2, 3 over A_3, 4 over A_4 and 1 over A_5; the total of these numbers gives a measure of the power of A_1. For formal reasons, we will also assume that each organisation is opposed to itself. The number 2 which appears in the diagonal cells simply expresses the identity of the power of a given organisation and therefore does not introduce any specific hypothesis. Taking account of this convention, one has a new definition of power P:

$$P(A_1) = 13; \; P(A_2) = 14; \; P(A_3) = 8; \; P(A_4) = 8; \; P(A_5) = 7.$$

However, it is clear that such a definition does not correspond perfectly with the analytical conditions of the concept, because the relative power of an organisation does not depend solely on the number of victories which it is capable of winning but also on the power of the losing organisations. To this extent, it is important to take account of the fact that in three out of four cases, A_1 was beaten by A_5, which is nevertheless a "weak" organisation. This hypothetical situation could occur in a social reality where a coalition in favour of a weak organisation tended to form when this latter entered into conflict with a powerful organisation; it would correspond to a sort of regulatory mechanism with the function of avoiding to great a disparity of forces, whilst at the same time taking account of their relationships.

The concept of power therefore implies that the power of each element is weighted according to the power of the elements over which it appears to have superiority. In our example, where A_1 wins 3, 3, 4 and 1 victories over A_2, A_3, A_4 and A_5 respectively who themselves win a total of 14, 8, 8 and 7 victories respectively, a simple system involves weighting the number of victories obtained by A_1 with each of the organisations in term of their score or number of victories. Proceeding in the same way for each of the five organisations, one obtains

$$P'(A_1) = 131; \; P'(A_2) = 125; \; P'(A_3) = 66;$$
$$P'(A_4) = 67; \; P'(A_5) = 69.$$

The effect of this weighting is instantly obvious: the ranking according to power is altered. However, one objection immediately springs to mind: the power of A_1 has been weighted according to the power of A_2, A_3, A_4, A_5, but the power of these organisations themselves has not been weighted – and so the argument could continue indefinitely. One finds therefore that the analysis of the concept ends in a series of operations which have the form of a *regressio ad infinitum*. Is it possible, in these conditions, to find a satisfactory measure for the concept?[3]

The quantities P are obtained by finding the sum of the elements in each row of the matrix M. It is easy to see that the quantities P′ are similarly obtained by summing the square M^2 of the matrix M row by row.[4] To take the next step of weighting the power of organisations A_2, A_3, A_4, A_5 in order to calculate the power of A_1 it is necessary, as we have seen, to take account of the power of the organisations over which they were victorious and not simply their victories; in other words, the quantites P″ have to be calculated on the basis of the quantities P′ in exactly the same way as one calculated the quantities P′ on the basis of P: by finding the sum of the rows in M^3. One obtains:

$$P''(A_1) = 1172; \ P''(A_2) = 1122; \ P''(A_3) = 604;$$
$$P''(A_4) = 598; \ P''(A_5) = 664.$$

Once again, the power ranking is altered. However, it is easy to show that if the operation is repeated and P^3, P^4 . . . , are calculated in turn, the order is eventually stabilised after a small number of iterations. In the present case, for example, one would have:

$$P^3(A_1) = 10,578; \ P^3(A_2) = 10,282; \ P^3(A_3) = 5568;$$
$$P^3(A_4) = 5518; \quad P^3(A_5) = 6046.$$
$$P^4(A_1) = 96,824; \ P^4(A_2) = 94,152; \ P^4(A_3) = 50,888;$$
$$P^4(A_4) = 50,592; \ P^4(A_5) = 54,912.$$

Thus after the successive iterations, the order of the five organisations becomes:

	A_1	A_2	A_3	A_4	A_5
P:	2	1	3	3	5
P′:	1	2	5	4	3
P″:	1	2	4	5	3
P^3	1	2	4	5	3
P^4	1	2	4	5	3

One can see that the order which is finally obtained is appreciably different from the initial order, and that it is definitive after the second iteration.

How are we to evaluate this operation? It is obvious that P is an extremely crude measurement. It does not take account of the fact that as well as simply counting the situations of domination one should take into consideration the power of the dominated organisations; a condition like this can be disclosed analytically by applying the concept of power in the present context. Thus the ordering obtained by the weighting procedure undoubtedly corresponds more closely to the concept. Moreover, in certain cases, one could check the superior quality of the final measurement by examining its "external validity": if one knows from theory or from experience that the power of an organisation is, in certain conditions, tied to a variable V or to a set of variables (V), the links ought to be more clearly revealed by the use of the final measure rather than the initial measure to estimate power. In other words the measure P should on average give rise to less coherent and more dubious results than measure P^∞. It is easy to see that P does not constitute a satisfactory measure except in the simple but clearly unrealistic case examined at the outset which allows a relationship of transitive inequality to be constructed.

Another advantage of the measure P^∞ is that it immediately furnishes not only a power ranking but also a quantitative measure of the relative power of each organisation in the society constituted by the five elements. Using P* to describe this measure, one would find

$$P^*(A_1) = 0.28; \; P^*(A_2) = 0.27; \; P^*(A_3) = 0.15;$$
$$P^*(A_4) = 0.14; \; P^*(A_5) = 0.16.$$

Such a measure has no importance in its own right; but it can become extremely useful if one wishes to compare, for example, a group of societies in terms of the distribution of power between their elements.[5]

The effect of introducing metric formalisation is therefore to enforce the scruitiny of the complex character of sociological concepts. It is true that the present example is a specific one; however, the situation that it illustrates is far from exceptional. The moment one wishes to analyse relationships between attributes linked to concepts that cannot be defined by a simple measure, it is necessary, if ambiguity or very crude results are to be avoided, to make a formal translation of the conditions involved in the analysis of the concepts. It is only by taking these conditions into account that one can arrive at intersubjective agreement on the measurement used. Although formalism obviously does not allow one to determine *the* best measure of a concept, at least it allows in certain cases, as the foregoing illustration shows, the construction of a measure which is *closer* to the connotations of the concept than any which could be obtained intuitively or by more rudimentary methods.

This example also shows the impossibility distinguishing between the measurable and the non-measurable at the level of things themselves: one only has to examine the relationship of inequality defined at the outset to see clearly that it fails to satisfy the condition of transitivity, which has to be checked in every operation defining an ordering; one might deduce from this that relative power is not measurable in such a case. However, this would be a blinkered view: a formal analysis of the concept shows how it is possible to define an order between the elements in spite of the intransitivity of the original relationship.

Without going into further examples, we can note that all the general models of measurement share the same logic as the above measurement: if one looks at a Guttman scaling of a group of items which clearly belong to a single conceptual category one cannot logically disallow the ordering which it defines among the classes of individuals. Similarly, a Spearman structure corresponds to a situation in which a set of intercorrelations can be cancelled out by the introduction of a single unobservable variable, so that the value which an individual has according to this variable can replace the whole set of values corresponding to the observable items: if a structure of this kind is found and one acknowledges the conceptual unity of the set of items, one must likewise accept the measurement which derives from it. Thus these general measurement techniques have a common outcome; intersubjective agreement which becomes necessary once certain postulates are admitted.

In each case, the function of formalism is to translate the analytical conditions of a given concept, to derive from it categorisations, orderings or quantitative measures that are in accordance with these conditions, to ensure intersubjective agreement on the measurement and to characterise complex structures. On this last point, it is worth noting that the idea of a matrix associated with a graph which we used in our example has very broad implications for the analysis and characterisation of a great many social objects (groups, oganisations, etc.)[6].

II

(*a*) A second function of formalisation has to do with activities of a *critical* nature applied to various aspects of research. Once again, we will proceed by way of a detailed analysis of specific examples which illustrate a general situation.

A significant proportion of sociological output depends on the use of data supplied by administrative accounting systems. This being so, one generally knows the distribution of certain attributes within a population of geographical areas, not individuals. However, one is usually interested in relationships between attributes at the individual level: the question therefore is to know how far it is possible to get from one level to the other; in a broad sense it is the problem of the "critique" – in the Kantian sense of the term – of ecological analysis. Without entering into the details of a problem which we have analysed elsewhere,[7] we will simply examine one particular point which firstly has the advantage of showing the usefulness of formalisation compared with verbal reflection, and which secondly presents a quite interesting example in which formalisation has to be applied for general empirical facts to have meaning. The problem is the following: having observed a very strong correlation between two group characteristics, what can be said about their relationship at the individual level? To answer this question, one has to explain the coefficient r between groups as a function of coefficient ϕ between individuals (assuming dichotomous attributes). We know that a coefficient of correlation can be defined as the ratio of the covariance of two variables to the product of their standard deviations; for n geographical areas $k(k = 1 \ldots n)$ which are assumed, for simplicity's sake, to be of equal size, one therefore has

(2a.1)

$$r\sigma_1\sigma_2 = \frac{1}{n}\sum_{k-1}^{n} (p_{1,k} - p_1)(p_{2,k} - p_2) = \frac{1}{n}\sum_{k=1}^{n} p_{1,k}p_{2,k} - p_1p_2$$

where $p_{1,k}$ is the frequency of characteristic 1 in group k, $p_{2,k}$ the frequency of characteristic 2 in the same group; and

(2a.2)
$$\phi e_1 e_2 = \frac{1}{n}\sum_{k-1}^{n} p_{12,k} - \frac{1}{n}\sum_{k-1}^{n} p_{1,k} \cdot \frac{1}{n}\sum_{k-1}^{n} p_{2,k}$$

$$= \frac{1}{n}\sum_{k-1}^{n} p_{12,k} - p_1p_2$$

where e_1 and e_2 represent the deviations of variables 1 and 2 at the individual level in the population group ($e_1 = \sqrt{p_1p_{\bar{1}}}$; $e_2 = \sqrt{p_2p_{\bar{2}}}$). It is easy to express r as a function of ϕ, using [2a.1] and [2a.2]

(2a.3)
$$r\sigma_1\sigma_2 = \frac{1}{n}\left(\sum_{k-1}^{n} p_{1,k}p_{2,k} - \sum_{k-1}^{n} p_{12,k}\right) + \phi e_1 e_2$$

$$= \phi e_1 e_2 - \frac{1}{n}\sum_{k-1}^{n} (p_{12,k} - p_{1,k}p_{2,k}).$$

The quantity in parentheses in (2a.3) has an interesting form: it represents the numerator of the individual correlation coefficient in group k, that is to say ϕ_k. One can then express r as a function of the general individual coefficient and the individual coefficients characterising each group k.[8]

(2a.4)
$$r\sigma_1\sigma_2 = \phi e_1 e_2 - \frac{1}{n}\sum \phi_k e_{1k} e_{2k}$$

It is this formula which provides the opportunity for an original application of formal method. In fact it does not mean very much in isolation; in particular, it does not allow the calculation of the interesting value ϕ, since it is an equation with $n+1$ unknowns ($\phi; \phi_1, \phi_2, \ldots, \phi_n$). But it provides a useful instrument for analysing the outcome of general empirical facts in the situations examined by the methods of ecological analysis: where in practice, the effect of one individual attribute on another often depends largely on the environment in which it is observed. In other words, if one examines the correlation between two attributes in an area small enough to be considered as the common environment for all its members, it will be found to be much weaker than in a population drawn from different ecological contexts: in other words, in many of the situations encountered in this type of analysis, control of the variable "environment" must show ϕ_k on average to be less than ϕ. Further, because of the heterogeneous distribution of characteristics within areas, which is entailed in the application of ecological analysis, the quantities e_{1k} and e_{2k} will, on average, be very much smaller than e_1 and e_2. This means that if the environment does have a marked effect, the second term in the right hand part of (2a.4) will be negligible compared with the first. Because e_1 and e_2 will be smaller than σ_1 and σ_2, as can easily be verified, r will be greater than ϕ. In short, calculation of the individual relationship between two characteristics on the basis of the observed relationship between geographical areas depends on the effect of the environment. If this is very intense, the correlation coefficient r calculated for groups will be associated with a much weaker individual correlation coefficient. But it is also possible for the environment to have a minimal effect, in which case the second term in the right hand part of (2a.2) will not be negligible. In this case, it is very difficult, knowing r, to assess the individual effect. Thus the *interpretation* of a relationship between variables observed at the level of geographical or administrative units ("schizophrenia is more common in poor areas", for example) assumes that one knows the effects of the environment. Using ecological results of this type, it is therefore impossible to determine either the individual effect of one variable on another; or the effect of the environment. This formal analysis has a critical function: it shows that the value of ecological analysis often derives from information from other sources, thus making it possible to distinguish what one knows from what one can actually deduce. It also has a heuristic function: it shows in the present case that it is necessary, both for theory and prediction, to distinguish between those parts of an explanation of a specific form of social conduct (vote, suicide, crime, etc.) which refer to the environment, individual attributes and the interaction between these factors respectively. If it is not possible to determine the importance of these various types of effect with the help of formal or empirical analysis, an ecological result is difficult to use or even interpret.

(b) A general problem with verbal language is that it typically runs the risk of arguing according to the principle of contiguity or, in other words, admitting without discussion the equivalence of contiguous notions or propositions. The paradox described above is one example of this; it shows that one cannot risk translating a proposition that is true at the collective level into a proposition at the individual level, without taking care to express the operation of "translation" formally, in such a way as to determine its logical consequences.

The dangers of this kind of reasoning are often apparent: for example, when one unguardedly infers causality from a correlation, or the absence of causality from a lack of correlation; or in the range of problems involved when one tries to move from the collective to the individual level, as in the example just given; and also in the process of deduction from the microsociological to the macrosociological, namely the very common situation in which, from a knowledge of the way in which elements within a system behave, one tries to determine the behaviour of the system itself. Such a danger can be seen in practically all of the attempts that have been made to formalise a descriptive theory of the functioning of a system. The formalisation developed by Simon from certain theories of Homans,[9] by Festinger[10] from group dynamics, and the formal model constructed by Barton[11] relating to a case study of the functioning of a prison, all show that when a verbal theory is precise enough to justify a translation of its propositions into a formal language – that is, when the variables used are, if not precisely defined, then at least specified in some detail and their connections made clearly explicit – the inferences which can be drawn from them with the help of formalism are sometimes unanticipated and are generally more numerous than those which can be obtained by a syllogistic approach. Whilst contiguous reasoning tends to extrapolate from the behaviour of elements to the behaviour of the system, experience proves that even very simple systems can behave in a paradoxical way. This point is important because it sheds light on a key aspect of the critical function of formalism, applied this time to sociological theory and not simply to the interpretation of statistical results.

Let us take as an illustration an "elementary" problem in the sociology of organisation:[12] one department in an organisation has responsibility for taking either/or decisions (aptitude/non-aptitude–guilt/

innocence – acceptance/rejection). This department has two levels: a level of pre-selection where negative decisions are taken and a second level where positive decisions are re-examined. The two stages comprise a rudimentary form of division of labour, with the category of decisions taken at the lower level controlling the upper level.

We will deliberately make this more concrete: at a preliminary stage it is better to argue at the level of types rather than at the level of specific objects; it may facilitate the introduction of formalism and the results obtained are more general. The present ideal type corresponds to an important subset of organisations or departments or organisation which are complex (having several levels) and which have responsibility for classificatory decisions concerning a set of objects. To simplify matters, we will assume that the characteristics of the external population which provide for "entry" to the system are stable through time.

Once this ideal type is given, the problem is one of describing the behaviour of the two components in the simplest way possible: given that the objectives of the organisation itself do not vary through time, the second stage S_2 will take a constant proportion of the positive decisions if the quality of the elements passed on to it by S_1 remains constant. Because the characteristics of the external population are assumed to be stable, the proportion D_2 of negative decisions (and obviously the proportion $1 - D_2$ of positive decisions) depends entirely on the proportion D_1 of negative decisions taken by the first stage S_1. However, one can regard S_1 as trying to attain two contradictory objectives: the first (O_1) being to enhance its efficiency in pre-selection by increasing the proportion of negative decisions and the second (O_2) being to avoid conflict with the objectives of the organisation as a whole by allowing "valid" elements to pass through.[13] One can then pose a number of questions about the behaviour of the system subsequent to its being set in motion.

1. Supposing that S_1 gives strong preference to O_1 compared with O_2, i.e. that it attaches more importance to its efficiency in relation to the upper level, will one see the decline and rapid disappearance of negative decisions from S_2?

2. Supposing that S_1 does not give special preference to either one of its objectives compared to the other, will D_1 and D_2 oscillate through time?

3. Supposing that S_1 does not give special preference to either one of its objectives, will the system reach equilibrium?

The same questions could be translated into another language: one could inquire as to the conditions under which this type of twin-level organisation would exhibit a functional equilibrium; whether it is necessary for the lower level to allow a certain amount of divergence between its own elevations and those of the upper level, etc. But regardless of whether these questions are formulated in a specific sociological language or in a formal language, they are difficult to answer if one is forced to depend on "intuition" or experience. In contrast, their formalised expression leads to unequivocal answers.

In the broadest terms, the axioms of the system can be translated into two equations:

(2b.1) $$D_{1,t} = f(D_{2,t-1}, D_{1,t-1})$$
$$D_{2,t} = g(D_{1,t})$$

$D_{1,t}$ and $D_{1,t-1}$ are the proportions of negative decisions taken by S_1 in the course of period t and the previous period; $D_{2,t}$ and $D_{2,t-1}$ are a comparable notation for S_2; f and g are the indeterminate functions. In order to translate the functioning of the system into the easily manipulable form of the equation with finite differences,[14] we have assumed that the decisions are made at discontinuous intervals in time. S_1's objective O_2 (not to overlook the "desirable" elements) has been translated in an indirect way; the first equation can be expressed verbally in the following manner: "The proportion of negative decisions taken by S_1 clearly depends on the proportion of negative decisions taken by S_2 in the previous period $[D_1 = f(D_{2,t-1}, \ldots)]$; however, since S_1's adaptability to S_2's decisions is not absolute, S_1 tends to adhere to its former criteria of classification $[D_1, t = f(\ldots, D_{1,t-1})]$." At the same time, the function g is obviously a decreasing function of $D_{1,t}$: in a given period, the negative decisions of S_2 are inversely proportional to the negative decisions taken by S_1 at the beginning of the period.

Thus far, our translation of the sociological theory has been pure shorthand. It becomes something else entirely if g and f are given determinate forms. At this level of abstraction, the simplest being the most general, we will select the most elementary possible forms:

(2b.2) $$D_{1,t} = aD_{2,t-1} + bD_{1,t-1}$$
$$D_{2,t} = \frac{c}{D_{1,t}}$$

Bringing the value of $D_{2,t-1}$ taken from the second equation into the first, the system can be expressed thus

$$(2b.3) \qquad D_{1,t} = \frac{a'}{D_{1,t-1}} + bD_{1,t-1}$$

or $a' = ac$. The quantities a', b are the structural parameters[15] of the system. Once the theory has been translated into this form, it is possible to confront it with a number of questions and get unequivocal answers. First of all, the equilibrium point of the system can be expressed as a function of these parameters, namely as the point at which, if it exists, proportions D_1 and D_2 will cease to vary from one period to another. All it requires is to write $D_{1,t}$ as equal to $D_{1,t-1}$.

$$(2b.4) \qquad D_1{}^* = \frac{a'}{D_1{}^*} + bD_1{}^*$$

The asterisk symbolises the proportion D_1 of negative decisions which, when reached, will cease to vary. On solving this equation, one finds

$$(2b.5) \qquad D_1{}^* = \sqrt{\frac{a'}{1-b}}$$

In other words, if the proportion D_1 of negative decisions by S_1 during the period t attains the value expressed by the right hand function of the above equation, one obtains $D_{1,t+1} = D_{1,t} = D_{1,t-1}$, etc. Similarly, by using the second equation $(2b.2)$, one obtains:

$$D_{2,t} = D_{2,t+1} = D_{2,t+2} = \cdots$$

For this equilibrium, the quantity beneath the root symbol must be positive: it is easy to see that $a' = ac$, for formal or theoretical reasons which we need not go into here, must be positive; similarly, b must normally be less than 1. In addition the equilibrium value has to come between 0 and 1, because D_1 is a proportion: it can be seen that this condition will remain unsatisfied if the objective O_2 is too heavily stressed; in this case, the denominator becomes weak and may be less than the numerator.

But the most important question is this: supposing that the value of the structural parameters is not inconsistent with the existence of an equilibrium point, will the system on reaching a state which approximates to this point, have a tendency to draw closer to it or move away from it instead? In the former case, one would be dealing with a stable equilibrium; in the latter case, with an unstable equilibrium, the system having a tendency to depart from its equilibrium state.

One way to answer this question is to examine the behaviour of the system in the neighbourhood of its equilibrium position. Let us assume, for the purposes of analysis, that the proportion of negative decisions at $t - 1$ is slightly less than the equilibrium position:

(2b.6)					$D_{1, t-1} = D_1{}^* - \varepsilon \qquad (\varepsilon > 0)$

In the following period, the proportion of negative decisions made by S_1 will be

$$D_{1, t} = \frac{a'}{D_1{}^* - \varepsilon} + b(D_1{}^* - \varepsilon)$$

or again

$$D_{1, t} = a'\left(\frac{1}{D_1{}^*} + \varepsilon'\right) + b(D_1{}^* - \varepsilon) \qquad (\varepsilon' > 0)$$

$$= \frac{a'}{D_1{}^*} + bD_1{}^* + a'\varepsilon' - b\varepsilon$$

Following the definition of equilibrium $D_1{}^*$ (2b.4), one now has

$$\frac{a'}{D_1{}^*} + bD_1{}^* = D_1{}^*$$

Hence

(2b.7)					$D_{1, t} = D_1{}^* - (b\varepsilon - a'\varepsilon').$

Thus the question of knowing whether the system does or does not tend to approach the equilibrium between $t - 1$ and t is simply a question of finding whether the quantity $b\varepsilon - a'\varepsilon'$ is or is not smaller than ε, which is evident from a comparison between (2b.6) and (2b.7).

Without analysing the behaviour of the system in detail, one can see what happens using a single starting point for different values of the parameter a' and b. First of all, there is a group of values for these parameters which give the system a regular equilibrium tendency. Suppose, for example, that $a' = 0.2$ and $b = 0.6$ and that at the beginning of the observation 60 per cent of the decisions made by S_1 are negative. It is easy to see, applying the above equations, that equilibrium is equal to 71 per cent and that the system moves consistently and rapidly towards it: 60 per cent of negative decisions at t_1, 70 per cent at t_2, slightly less than 71 per cent at t_3, and a percentage closer and closer to 71 in the following periods. Now if S_1's propensity b to persist in its previous behaviour (to emphasise its goal O_1), is weaker, and its propensity

$a = a'/c$ (to emphasise objective O_2) is stronger than in the previous case, the movement towards equilibrium is slower. Finally, if the tendency to prefer O_2 instead of O_1 becomes more marked, one encounters phenomena of *oscillation*. Thus, when the importance attributed to O_1 is half as great and the importance attributed to O_2 is twice as great as in the above example, one obviously finds an increase in the equilibrium value, now at 77 instead of 71 per cent: this is natural because the importance attributed by S_1 to its pre-selective function is greater in the second case than in the former; but more specifically, one finds that the system, while approaching its equilibrium, varies from one period to the next in its placing around this equilibrium point. If one continues to assume that the initial state of the system corresponds to a percentage of 60 negative decisions out of a 100, then one will actually observe 87 in period t_2, 74 in period t_3, 78 in period t_4 . . . with this percentage continuing, in the subsequent periods, to oscillate more and more weakly around the equilibrium value.

Note that a comprehensive examination of the behaviour of the system is made difficult especially by the limits imposed on the parameters and variables and because of the non-linear character of the model; but the important thing to notice is how a variation in the theoretical hypotheses about the functioning of a system can relate to a scarcely foreseeable distinction in the types of possible behaviour.

Thus, formalism makes it possible to give an explicit answer to the questions posed on page 215: the tendency towards equilibrium is consistent, only if S_1 does not give excessive preference to its goal of efficiency in relation to S_2 and ignore the danger of excluding "valid" elements; in cases where S_1 does ignore this danger and is preoccupied with anticipating the decisions of S_2, one finds instead, evidence of jolts (oscillations) in the system: thus, *the condition for the functional harmony of the system is that* S_1 *simultaneously acknowledges its two contradictory goals*. Finally, when the equilibrium position is reached, the fact that S_1 continues to embrace the goal of improving its efficiency with respect to S_2 does not actually entail a decrease in the negative decisions of the latter.[16]

We have been at some pains to develop this example because it seems to us to be highly instructive. Although the social system described here is relatively simple, it is difficult to determine its real behaviour in terms of functioning if one relies on simple intuition: we have had to proceed by way of a laboratory model[17] which gives sometimes paradoxical answers to the questions posed. It seems fair to suggest that attempts to describe the functioning of complex social systems which involve numerous variables are based on illusion unless they are alerted to the very strict limits of "intuition" and deduction of the syllogistic type.

The example we have been using illustrates once again the critical and heuristic role of formalism: criticism of the hasty conclusions which one might be tempted to draw from a system of propositions, and criticism of implicit hypotheses introduced during analysis; as an example of its heuristic role, the proposition that the stability of an organisational system can coincide with the existence of an objective which is not opposed to change shows that in the analysis of social systems, one must guard against the adoption of axioms which are valid at the individual level but not at the level of the system.

III

Finally, we wish to make mention of a third function of formalism. For reasons of space, we will refer to it here as the conceptual function. In fact, it is more generally concerned with sociological language in all its aspects and theorisation.

In sociology, concept formation is largely free of formalism; in other words, it contains few concepts that are formally defined. It is inevitable that this should be so at least in the present state of affairs; in fact, sociological concepts, like those of every science, derive from lived reality and cannot acquire a formal definition until they become part of theoretical systems which are themselves formalised. However, concepts which are close to their everyday meaning have the obvious disadvantage of being open to challenge as to their definition, and indeed their usefulness. At this level, it is often difficult to decide whether one concept is better than another.

It is quite a different matter when a concept, issuing from everyday experience, finally emerges from the research process to coincide with a specific formal structure or set of structures: in this case, the term with which it corresponds becomes a pure symbol, serving simply to designate these structures, and it is ultimately of little importance, except for practical reasons, whether this sign is borrowed from this or that *notion* in everyday language. We are not assuming that, in the present situation, every sociological concept should be tied to a formal structure or set of structures; even less that sociology should imitate the more developed sciences, and furnish itself with a limited stock of formal concepts. However, it is obvious that conceptual disputes cannot be settled either by the introduction of conceptual systems or by systematic examination of semantic usage: these methods fail to provide a way of reaching genuine intersubjective agreement. In other words, a concept can only lead to this kind of agreement if it ceases to be part of the metalanguage and is defined strictly within the terms of sociological language itself.

It is not difficult to illustrate this point. Certain Durkheimian notions – the notion of social fact, *conscience collective* etc., – have given rise to complex debates and they continue to do so: does the thing called "conscience collective" actually exist? Is it a metaphysical entity?[18] Can it be salvaged by taking it to be imminent in individual consciousness (*Wirbewusstsein*)?[19] One could go on posing such questions but to little effect, for they are certainly unanswerable. Durkheim himself is partly responsible for these questions; there are certain passages on the "conscience collective" which make them quite explicit.[20] However, if one abstracts Durkheim's ontological statements and limits oneself to an examination of the epistemological meaning of the notion of conscience collective, as it appears in *Suicide* for example, one can see that it reduces quite simply to the hardly contestable fact that groups can be characterised as units of analysis and that group characteristics can be seen to have an effect on individual characteristics: for example, the difference between the sexes in the propensity to commit suicide changes sign with the spread of divorce throughout the global society.

Should the concept of "conscience collective" be kept to refer the specific class of phenomena defined in this way? As a matter of fact, there is no reason why not. However, this does not mean that there is no need to carry out a "critique" of the concept: to clearly define the structure of a social fact or phenomenon of conscience collective; to identify it and classify its sub-types if possible in terms of a formal principle, so as to ensure the identity of types and the exhautiveness of the classifications; to confront the formal structures with their real equivalents. It is a "critique" of this kind which we intend to outline below.

On examining the structure of the effects of group characteristics, one will observe quite distinct varieties, corresponding as it were to species of the genus "conscience collective". It is useful to distinguish between these in order to form new concepts.

Doubtless such a "critique" could be conducted verbally; however, verbal analysis directly encounters a limitation because it is forced to select in an arbitrary and therefore unconvincing way, a certain number of criteria which experience provides. In contrast, in formal translation, the concept can be tied – as we shall see – to a group of identifiable and rigorously defined structures. Many of these structures correspond to concepts which can be discovered by verbal analysis but many of them correspond to entities which might not be recognised as such in everyday language and sociological theory but which are still empirically observable. A concern for "structural" definitions, or definitions which combine in a single word a set of rigorously defined formal conditions, rather than descriptive definitions is a feature of all the sciences: there is no doubt that the notions of speed and acceleration correspond to distinct entities within experience. However, no one today would dream of denying either the difficulties involved in the formalisation of these notions or the benefits. This same is true in biology: the equations of cybernetics are often no more than translations of notions which have been current ever since the first speculations on living phenomena. In sociology, there are fewer examples of the formal translation of familiar notions – which is hardly surprising – but they are becoming more and more frequent. The one we have chosen here is the notion of "conscience collective" both because it provides a simple illustration and because it shows how a somewhat outdated notion may still be demonstrably fruitful when expressed in a formal language. With due allowance being made, this is rather like the old notion of finality as applied to living phenomena: in simple terms, its content is that of the concept of homeostasis; its form is obviously something else.

Let us define a society in terms of a set of characteristics S_1, $S_2, \ldots$, which we will assume are obtained from the properties of members: thus S_1 could represent the proportion of workers, S_2 the proportion of Protestants.[21] Formally, a comparative study across societies such as *Suicide* consists of describing each society in terms of its location along the continuum $S_1, S_2, \ldots$, and comparing the sub-type of individuals in terms of a dependent dimension. It is easy to see that this idea precisely formalises the notion of "conscience collective" or "beliefs and sentiments common to average citizens of the same society".[22] One will also notice that a great many sociological problems, although they appear in different forms, have a logical framework analogous to this formalisation. Thus the Durkheimian proposition which links the proportion of suicides to religion and to the situation of religion within the society as a whole is the simplest possible structure which corresponds to the present definition: the total society is defined by one characteristic (the proportion of Protestants) and the individuals similarly by a single attribute (religious persuasion).

What have we gained by such a formalisation which merely generalises certain types of propositions to be found in *Suicide* and reveals their logical framework? In order to see, let us examine this basic structure and ask ourselves how, at this very simple level where society and its members are defined by a single dimension, "conscience collective" manifests itself.

The variable characterising society (for example, the proportion of people possessing quality s) we will call S; individuals for their part are divided into two classes $\bar{s}$ and s. The dependent variable is designated D. We will assume that it is continuous (proportion, percentage of people possessing characteristic d). The existence of something like a conscience collective can then be symbolised by the two following expressions:

(3.1) $$D_s = f(S) \qquad D_{\bar{s}} = g(S)$$

which imply that the proportion of people classified positively according to the dependent criterion in the two population sub-groups s and $\bar{s}$ is a function of the variable characterising group S; as a general rule, the function must be assumed to be separate for the two sub-populations. Again, thus far we are dealing with a simple shorthand expressing the structure of propositions analogous to the previously quoted proposition from *Suicide*. However, as with the example from the previous section, we shall see that formalism becomes a useful instrument immediately one gives a general form to the indeterminate elements, which in the present case are the function f and g:

$$D_s = a_s S + b_s \qquad D_{\bar{s}} = a_{\bar{s}} S + b_{\bar{s}}$$

a_s and b_s ($a_{\bar{s}}$ and $b_{\bar{s}}$) are the parameters which describe the influence of attribute S on the sub-population s($\bar{s}$).

Immediately, the formal translation reveals the existence of a multiplicity of effects of S: they are numerous enough to be able to identify interesting combinations in the values of the parameters. Without attempting to list them all, we will give several examples but without concrete illustrations so as not to negate the generality of the analysis.

1. $a_s = a_{\bar{s}} > 0$; $b_s = b_{\bar{s}}$ in this case, the proportion of s in the group determines the proportion of D, although characteristic s has no individual influence on characteristic d: in fact, in a given society characterised by a value S_i of S, the two sub-populations s and $\bar{s}$ have an equal tendency to display characteristic d because the functions f and g are not clearly defined. This type of effect can be produced by certain mechanisms of identification, reference groups or, in Tarde's language, imitation; it can also happen when the frequency of an individual attribute affects the group climate and when characteristic d depends on this latter variable to the exclusion of the individual characteristic s itself.

2. $a_s > a_{\bar{s}} > 0$; $b_s > b_{\bar{s}}$. In this case, the relative susceptibility of two sub-populations ($dD_s/ = a_s$, $dD_{\bar{s}}/dS = a_{\bar{s}}$) to the frequency of a charac-

teristic S is unequal, as is total susceptibility: this kind of social environmental effect is frequently observed in the analysis of electoral behaviour; in a general sense, structure 2 is typical of the effect of an ecological type environment, whilst structure 1 is clearly more observable among groups of individuals comprising a functional system. This distinction is a simple hypothesis which could only be taken into consideration if the studies described by structure (3.1) were sufficiently numerous. Obviously this is not actually the case, because they presuppose a particularly costly type of sample design.

3. $a_s > 0$, $a_{\bar{s}} < 0$; $b_s < b_{\bar{s}}$. This type of effect is characteristic of certain situations of competition between social units (s and $\bar{s}$), when the intensity of an opinion, behaviour, etc. varies according to the minority or majority position of the group.

We will limit ourselves to these three specific structures, bearing in mind that they are a sub-set of the typology which can be constructed in terms of system (3.1), when f and g are given a linear form. It is obvious that system (3.1) can be generalised without difficulty: if (s) designates a specific combination of dichotomous attribute categories, (3.1) can be generalised in the form of 2^n equations, such that

$$(3.2) \qquad\qquad D(s) = f(s)\,(S_1, S_2, \ldots, S_n)$$

However, as soon as the number of variables S_i which are implied exceeds 2, system (3.2) becomes purely speculative, at least at the current stage of research. We simply mention this here to show how formalism provides a framework within which it is possible to register some progress in research.

The important thing is this: the current sociological language and tradition use a large number of concepts and notions which correspond to the generic idea of the "conscience collective": social climate, imitation, identification, group reference, effects of the ecological environment, etc. on definition and identity, about which there seems to be some difficulty in arriving at intersubjective agreement. In contrast, as soon as one makes a formal translation of the effects of societal characteristics on individual behaviour, one can perceive a number of perfectly defined and distinct structures; if one or other of these structures seems to correspond closely to the meaning which the theoretical tradition or current language gives to this or that specific notion, it can be used to designate that notion. However, the above example shows that there is a greater number of possible formal structures than those which are found in the verbal tradition: obviously one cannot find a concept there for every structure which can be defined formally and observed empirically. Moreover, phenomena which are considered at the verbal level to belong to distinct, well-defined and unrelated headings can be seen to be formally identical, with closely similar structural parameters.

The above example is illustrative of a general situation in the sciences as a whole and in sociology in particular, where a concept coming from a metalanguage, from observation, from "intuition", and defined at the outset at the ontological level, is introduced into scientific language with the status of a formal structure: the debate over "conscience collective" is not without its analogy with the debate in physics over "life forces" which today clearly seems to have little meaning. In general, a concept is without foundation until it is defined in the context of a scientific language; as long as it derives from experience alone, it can only fuel controversy, even if care is taken to introduce it within the framework of an *a priori* conceptual system.

We must now give a reminder that we have far from exhausted the list of the functions of formalisations in sociology: in particular, we have not dealt with its role in theorisation, except indirectly. However, the above examples should suffice to show that intersubjective agreement on the meaning of concepts, the definition of variables, the interpretation of results, and even deduction from verbal theoretical propositions, depends to a large extent on the level of formalisation of the language. The same examples also show that the development of formalisation depends on the accumulation of empirical research: we have seen that the analytical constructions of the measure of organisational power ought to be based on comparison with external variables; the theory relating to the ideal type in section IIb should be verified by a comparative study of a group of organisations; each argument in the last section presupposes a sample design with two levels (sample of societies, groups; sample of individual members of these societies, groups, etc.); as a result they call for costly investigations which until now have been few and far between: the typology of structures involved in the general notion of conscience collective can scarcely be satisfying whilst studies of this kind are not widely available. At present, formalism (3.2) remains a partially empty framework at this point, although heuristically useful. Finally, empirical research and formalism appear to be in a situation of mutual dependency. Their reciprocity tends to introduce into sociology, as into every science, a language which is complex and farther and farther removed from direct experience of social facts.

One can also see how formalisation helps to provide bearings for an epistemology of the social sciences. Indeed, the few illustrations given above make it possible to advance a number of epistemological propositions:

(a) Social objects are measurable, not by virtue of intrinsic quantitative properties, but whenever one is capable of defining a measure which corresponds to a set of analytical conditions derived from the connotation of a concept.

(b) Concepts which correspond to verbally-defined entities can, under certian complex conditions, be combined with certain rigorously defined and identifiable formal structures, thus implying a necessarily nominalist position.

(c) Finally, empirical sociology tends to involve an *a priori* consideration of social phenomena, which is distinct from conceptual or theoretical thinking in the traditional sense: the above development of ecological analysis, the analysis of the ideal type of organisation in section IIb, and the formal expressions (3.1) and (3.2) represent a consideration of social phenomena which is independent of any specific content.

10. The French University Crisis: An Essay in Sociological Diagnosis[1]

There is no shortage of books, articles and other publications on the May–June 1968 university crisis. Quite the contrary, they can be numbered in tens if not hundreds. Yet the striking thing about them is that, even among those written by sociologists, there are scarcely any which make systematic reference to information about the functioning of the university system whether the course of this information is sociological research itself or studies carried out in an administrative context.

Indeed, there are hardly any direct studies of the May–June events. A number of sociologists attempted to gather information or indulged in "participant" observation of the general meetings which were held in the universities and elsewhere at the time. But these investigations were improvised, restricted in scope and very localised. What is more, their results were unpublished. And without the means of systematic comparison between one study and another they certainly could not contribute significantly to our knowledge of the "events".

Generally speaking, sociologists were not only caught unaware by the May–June events, they were also seized with a kind of panic when they discovered the inappropriateness of the methods and techniques they were in the habit of using. What was the good of questionnaires or interviews in trying to grasp the reasons behind such an important crisis? Even if it had been physically possible to plan and carry out instant surveys on a large scale, would they have supplied the sought after explanations? Participant observation also had its limitations: to observe a meeting does not give a full understanding of the behaviour of the participants. This does not simply depend on observable conditions in the here and now, but on factors which are not directly observable. One cannot grasp the causes of a revolt by observing the behaviour of those in revolt.

227

This panic response to the inadequacy of sociological methods meant· that sociologists often resorted either to *a priori* explanations or to attempts at instant history.

But why should the meaning of the May–June events in the universities be looked for in the events themselves? It is true that these events cannot be understood fully without unravelling the train of events which followed the troubles at Nanterre. It is true that the general mobilisation of students after the police intervention in the Sorbonne has a partly historical explanation. But it can also be explained by the students' "situation" in the university system and in the social system. There is actually a considerable amount of information both about the functioning of the university system and the place of young people in the social system.

In short, sociologists seem to be better equipped to produce an explanation of the May–June crisis than some of them claim or even believe. They can certainly not make use of contemporary studies of the events but they can work with a considerable body of data gathered prior to this period. In combination, these sources provide a means of understanding why the university conflict was much more widespread than in other countries, why university departments of sociology were more conflict-prone than others, why levels of electoral participation varied from one discipline or faculty to another, and many other differential features of the university crisis.

In the following analysis of the dysfunctions of the French university system prior to May 1968, I have attempted to show that these dysfunctions gave rise to a new "student condition" which made the student in 1965 and the years which followed a completely different social entity from his 1950 predecessor: a marginal being in a situation of anomie and suspension from social participation.

I

Let us begin with the most familiar and straightforward data. The number of French students has risen considerably over the last twenty years (Table 10.1).

At the same time, participation rates in tertiary education are noticeably higher in France than in neighbouring countries, with the exception of Belgium (Table 10.2). The American rates are not comparable with European rates because they include junior college students who are closer to the upper secondary level in Europe than to the beginning of the university level.

TABLE 10.1 Number of French students: growth from 1954/55 to 1966

1954/55	150631
1955/56	152246
1956/57	165169
1957/58	175500
1958/59	186101
1959/60	194763
1960/61	214672
1961/62	244814
1962/63	282222
1963/64	326311
1964/65	367701
1965/66	413756
1966/67	459466
1967/68	499442

Source: *Informations statistiques*, Bulletin published by the Ministère de l'Education Nationale, December 1967, p. 675.

A number of things follow from this situation. Firstly, in spite of investment initiatives by the state, teaching conditions remain poor. In all disciplines, the environment is less satisfactory than in England or Germany (Table 10.3). It is similarly unsatisfactory compared with Belgium where there was a student–teacher ratio of 11.3 in 1961/62 and the Netherlands where it was 8 in 1960/61. In France in 1962/63 the overall ratio for institutions of higher education was 23.[2]
This ratio has improved, since it was 29 in 1956/57 and 21.6 in 1963/64. However, it is still abnormally high compared with neighbouring countries and it must have necessarily serious consequences for teaching.

It should also be noted that the explosion in participation rates has been contained by increasing the number of assistant and senior assistant posts instead of professorships. Thus the proportion of teachers in the assistant category has grown in a way which is without parallel in adjacent countries (Table 10.4).

In fact, the recruitment of assistants and senior assistants was to prove insufficient and greater and greater reliance had to be placed on a system of "complementary hours" taught either by existing personnel or, as is increasingly the case, by people whose main sphere of activity lies outside higher education (secondary school teachers etc.). This system

TABLE 10.2 Rates of access to higher education in several countries (relationship between the number of registrations in the first year and corresponding age groups)

	%
United States (1963)	34
England (1961):	
University	4
Further education	2
Training colleges	2.5
	8.5
Federal Republic of Germany (1963)	
University	5.8
Teachers' colleges	1.7
	7.5
Belgium (1963)	17.4
France (1963)	13.8
Italy (1960)	6
Netherlands (1961)	4.6

Source: R. Poignant, *L'enseignement dans les pays du Marché Commun* (Institut Pédagogique National, 1965), p. 185.

TABLE 10.3 Number of students per teacher by discipline, for several countries

Disciplines	Germany	Great Britain	France		Italy	
	(1961)	*(1962)*	*(1958)*	*(1963)*	*(1952)*	*(1962–3)*
Humanities and philosophy	15	8.5	58	53[a]	46.8	59.5
Law, economics and social sciences	27.5	9.3	60	50[a]	68	66
Natural and exact sciences	10	7	27	17	24	12.8
Medicine and pharmacy	6	6	17	10	11.6	6.3

Source: Poignant, *L'enseignement dans le pays du Marché Commun* (Institut Pédagogique National, 1965), p. 233.

[a] The value of these figures is too high: no account is taken of part-time personnel.

TABLE 10.4 Structure of the university teaching staff in different countries

France	1956/57	1963/64
Professors and lecturers	3152 (56 %)	4903 (33 %)
Senior assistants & assistants	2479 (44 %)	10195 (67 %)
Italy	1951/52	1962/63
Professors and lecturers	2197 (29.5 %)	5375 (38.2 %)
Assistants and other personnel	5265 (71.5 %)	8497 (61.7 %)
Germany	1960	1961
Titular professors	2098 (21.5 %)	4312 (16.8 %)
Extraordinary professors, personal chairs	2058 (14.5 %)	5232 (20.4 %)
Emeritus professors with teaching responsibilities	—	—
Assistants	9268 (64.2 %)	16113 (62.8 %)

Source: Poignant, *L'enseignement dans le pays du Marché Commun* (Institut Pédagogique National, 1965), p. 231.

has the obvious advantage of reducing costs. However, it has serious disadvantages the moment it is used extensively. When more than nine out of every ten hours teaching consists of "complementary hours", as is sometimes the case, the control, programming and harmonisation of teaching becomes virtually impossible.

The poor state and qualitative deterioration of the educational environment, combined with the probable decline in the quality of students which follows from the increased rates of participation and the decline in teachers' qualification at the secondary level, must be partly responsible (together with other factors which we will be analysing later) for the extremely high failure rates.

To begin with there is a survey which gives a measure of the proportion of failures in humanities faculties.[3] It comes from a study of the cohort of students who enrolled in the Faculté des Lettres in Paris in 1962 (Table 10.5).

Provided there are no interruptions or failures, degrees are awarded three years after entry into higher education. It can be seen that the proportion of students who obtain degrees after four years of study in higher education is never greater than 50 per cent and is on average 30 per cent. The proportion of students who obtain no certificate at all after four years is 41 per cent.

TABLE 10.5 Pass rates (%) in several disciplines after three years of degree study (Faculté des Lettres de Paris)

Disciplines	Degrees awarded	No certificate after 3 years	Failure Withdrew after 2 years	Withdrew after 1 years	Total	Partial success
Classics	47	11	7	3	21	32
Philosophy	41	11	14	2	27	32
Geography	37	10	12	10	32	31
Spanish	33	8	14	11	33	34
Contemporary literature	29	10	18	14	42	29
Psychology	29	5	30	12	47	24
History	26	11	22	18	51	23
English	26	12	22	11	45	29
German	25	13	17	10	40	35
Sociology	17	15	26	18	59	24
Total	30	11	19	11	41	39

Source: Bisseret "Carrière scolaire d'une cohorte d'étudiants inscrits en 1962 à la faculté des Lettres de Paris: les filières d'orientation et les facteurs de réussite", *Rapport Convention Ministère Education Nationale*, June 1968, mimeo.

Another survey conducted in the University of Orléans gives a similar idea of the proportion of failures. In the population involved, 23 per cent of the first cycle students failed their examinations at least once (Humanities, Sciences, Law). In the second cycle (Sciences) 67 per cent of students failed once. It should be pointed out that these percentages do not take into account those students who *withdrew* because they are based on the population of students *still present* at the university at the time of the study. Thus the percentage of enrolled students who reached the second cycle in the sciences without having failed is in all probability very low at 33 per cent.[4]

It is possible to get a more general idea of the extent of failures (and withdrawals) by comparing the number of newly enrolled students (as a proportion of the corresponding age group) with the number of diplomas granted four or five years later (also expressed as a proportion of the corresponding age group). (Table 10.6).

TABLE 10.6 Pass rates in higher education in several countries

Country	New admissions as a percentage of corresponding age groups	Diplomas awarded as percentage corresponding age groups	Relation between the two percent- ages (pass-rate)
Germany	4.2 (1957/58)	2.5 (1963)	60
France	6.7 (1956/57)	3.8 (1960/61)	57
Italy	4.4 (1954/55)	2.8 (1958/59)	63
Netherlands	3.4 (1956/57)	2.0 (1962/63)	58

Source: Poignant *L'enseignement dans les pays du Marché Commun* (Institut Pédagogique National, 1965), p. 196.

The value for the pass-rate in France is too high because it is based on a calculation which includes not only the universities but also the *Grandes Écoles*, where the pass-rate is close to 100 per cent. A simple calculation, correcting for the number of students in the *Grandes Écoles* as a proportion of all students, shows that the success rate for France should be reduced from 57 per cent to slightly over 50 per cent.

It can also be seen from a comparison with Table 10.2 that the admission rate for French universities doubled between 1956/57 and 1963, whilst it rose less than 50 per cent in Germany, Italy and the Netherlands. It remains to be seen whether this difference in the rate of educational expansion led to a fall in "pass-rates". To get a precise idea of this it would be necessary to generalise, both in time and space, Bisseret's type of longitudinal analysis.

The above figures are actually very imprecise and are no substitute for a detailed picture of failure rates. Nevertheless they do give an impression of the importance of these rates.

Another, even rougher estimate is gained by relating the total number of diplomas obtained to the number of students. Obviously it does not provide a measure of failure rates but it does suggest national differences. Table 10.7 suggests that, other things being equal, the "productivity" of higher education is considerably lower in France than in the two other countries.

It could be that the difference between France and Germany is due partly to the differing rates of educational expansion and partly to differences in institutional structures. Failure rates in the German humanities faculties (Philosophische Fakultäten) are apprently very high and of the same order of magnitude as the French rates. But the

234   *The Crisis in Sociology*

TABLE 10.7 University diplomas awarded and number of students in several countries

	France (1964)	Germany (1963)	Italy (1963)
Number of students	367701	263100[a]	273000
Diplomas awarded[b]	27877	37899	23019

Source: Poignant, *L'enseignement dans les pays du Marché Commun* (Institut Pédagogique National, 1965), pp. 187 and 297. *Informations statistiques*, Bulletin published by the Ministère de l'Education Nationale, December 1967, p. 675.

[a] Including teachers' colleges.

[b] Degrees, engineering and medical diplomas, etc. on admission to more advanced diplomas.

number of students enrolled in humanities is far lower in Germany than in France. This is a result both of the disparity between rates of educational expansion and the fact that in Germany, future teachers are educated in specialised institutions (Pädagogische Institute) instead of in faculties of humanities, as in France.[5]

However, the frequency of failure and withdrawal are not the only characteristics of the French university system. The student who obtains a diploma is still, in many cases, exposed to intellectual unemployment. In a predictive study Vermot-Gauchy estimated in 1965 that by 1975 French universities would be turning out 65,000 graduates every year.[6] At that time the economy would be able to provide something in the order of 40–45,000 jobs for graduates from higher education, of which 20,000 would be taken up by graduates of the *Grandes Écoles* who would be given preference. In total, therefore, only one out of every three university graduates would be successful in finding employment in the market for jobs.

In psychology P. Oléron estimated in 1967 that 20 per cent of the students enrolled in this discipline could expect to find employment.[7]

In Paris, in the Faculté des Lettres alone, more than 400 students are enrolled in sociology for 1968/69. Since sociology teaching has still hardly become a specialised occupation in France because of the lack of methodological instruction and research training, sociology graduates tend to seek jobs primarily in the public sector (university-type teaching and research jobs sponsored by the Centre National de la Recherche Scientifique). Employment in the private sector (applied sociology) is still very limited. Overall, the number of jobs requiring four or five years of higher education is probably no more than one hundred every year in the whole of France.

It seems paradoxical that the problem of opportunities hardly surfaced in the themes of the student conflict in May–June 1968. The students attacked the "mandarins", the lack of communication between professors and students, the examination system and, more generally, the consumer society. Up to a point, those who raised the problem of opportunities were regarded with contempt.[8]

This displacement possibly occurred because the majority of the "revolutionary" students, in France as elsewhere, came from affluent social backgrounds and were less aware of the problem of opportunities because of this. These are the students who created and propagated the ideological themes of conflict.

As we shall see below, the main threat to the student from an affluent background comes from the problem of social downgrading rather than the problem of opportunity. Social downgrading is a condition of shame which is difficult to complain about in public and which has to be explained by those who suffer this fate with the help of an ideological "transposition".

With the enthusiasm and romanticism of May–June in the background, an I.F.O.P. poll conducted between 12 and 23 September 1968 showed that student anxiety, in a situation where it could be expressed directly (without transposition), had its origins primarily in the problem of the social evaluation of university studies (Table 10.8).

TABLE 10.8 Reasons for anxiety among students

Here are three reasons which could explain the student troubles in the months of May and June. Please classify them in order of importance, placing the one which played the most important role first	1st (%)	2nd (%)	3rd (%)
Concern about the possibilities of finding opportunities to correspond with the chosen course of study	56	33	8
Opposition towards the consumer society.	7	10	8
The university's lack of adaptation (curricula, teaching methods, material resources) to current needs.	35	54	8

Source: Institut Français d'Opinion Publique, "Sondage étudiants, septembre 1968", *Réalités*, November 1968, no. 254.

A number of hypotheses about the causes of the May–June student revolt can be drawn from the above data. The considerable growth in numbers has had the following consequences:

1. In quantitative terms, the teaching environment has scarcely improved (the number of students per teacher has scarcely fallen) and it has deteriorated in qualitative terms (the average level of qualification of students having decreased considerably). At the same time it should be noted that the change in the structure of the teaching body is related to a pedagogical change (an increase in the proportion of practical work entrusted to assistants and senior assistants compared with the theoretical instruction given by professors and lecturers). This transformation in the composition of the teaching personnel represents a move away from a mode of instruction which placed great importance on the student's own work, towards a more directive style of teaching. In other words, it represents an attempt to substitute the pedagogy of 'training" for a pedagogy of "education" in its original sense and higher vocational training for general culture. However, within faculties of humanities and law especially, both the traditions of the teaching staff and the resource limitations mean that teaching wavers between the two poles of "education" and "training". At the present time, intensive instruction is the monopoly of the *Grandes Écoles*. The case of sociology is typical in this respect: by and large the consumers of applied sociology prefer to use engineers who are products of the elite scientific colleges than sociology graduates who are less than fully professionalised.
2. The complete freedom for anyone to enter university and the complete lack of guidance means that the system encourages a negative orientation, through failure in examinations and through withdrawal in mid-course.
3. The number of students means that they have to compete for jobs which, in many disciplines, are certainly far fewer than the number of graduates. They are also forced to accept jobs which they could have obtained after a shorter period of training.

II

The problem of competition for jobs is not the only cause of the student revolt. If students have attacked the university system and if, as the I.F.O.P. poll we referred to above suggests, many of them blame it for being poorly adapted, this is because it has become contradictory and *unstable* in consequence of the pressure of numbers combined with changes in the social composition of the student population.

In broad outline, the recent history of French universities, from 1900 to the present day, can be described in terms of two ideal types, the first corresponding to the period up to about 1950 and the second becoming increasingly well established after that date.

Until about 1950, French universities recruited essentially from the "bourgeoisie". Children of managers or fathers in the liberal professions represented 35 per cent of the total number of students in 1939 and only slightly less in 1950 (33 per cent). The proportion of sons of clerical workers, artisans and small businessmen is small and does not vary between 1939 and 1950. Children of industrial and agricultural workers are hardly represented at all. There again, the proportion remains stable for the duration of the period (Table 10.9).

TABLE 10.9 Social composition of the French student population: its evolution through time (1939–60)

			Distribution		
Parents' occupation	*1939*	*1945*	*1950*	*1956*	*1960*
Liberal professions	188	180	174	118	125
Managerial (commerce and industry	160	165	154	75	57
Officials (government and forces)	257	250	281	286	283
Clerical (commerce and industry)	126	131	121	150	190
Artisans and small businessmen	38	47	51	125	122
Agricultural landowners	40	37	51	52	50
Industrial workers	16	15	19	34	34
Agricultural workers	9	7	9	8	7
Rentiers without occupation	98	78	62	39	45
Unknown occupations	68	90	78	113	87
Total	1000	1000	1000	1000	1000
N	52014	81205	122003	135197	174150

Source: *Informations statistiques*, Bulletin published by the Ministère de l'Education Nationale, 32–33, October–November 1961, p. 268.

After 1950, the situation developed more and more rapidly in the direction of a decline in "bourgeois" or upper class recruitment and a sharp rise in "middle class" recruitment. The share of the liberal professions fell between 1950 and 1960 from 17.4 to 12.5 per cent and it had declined to 9.6 per cent in 1965 (Table 10.10). Conversely, the share of artisans and small businessmen rose from 17.2 per cent in 1950 to 31.2 per cent in 1960. The result was that *the proportion of middle class students compared with upper class students quadrupled in fifteen years.* Meanwhile, although the proportion from industrial working class backgrounds doubled during this period, the number remained very small.

These statistics are well known and have been used many times by French sociologists. However, in a curious way, they have fastened on to the idea that higher education has resisted democratisation and have focused primarily on the under-representation of workers.[9]

TABLE 10.10 Social Composition of the student population in 1965/66

Farmers	Agricultural workers	Industrial and commercial business owners	Liberal professions, upper management	Middle Management	Clerical workers	Manual workers	Others
58/1000	6/1000	148/1000	289/1000	167/1000	86/1000	94/1000	152/1000

Source: *Informations statistiques*, Bulletin published by the Ministère de l'Education Nationale.

Without ignoring the genuine and profound inequality in university recruitment, these statistics can be read otherwise to argue that, whilst *social recruitment* to universities (the probability of an individual from a given social class studying for a degree) has hardly changed, the *social composition* of the university has become highly democratised because the share taken up by the upper strata has been reduced considerably when compared with the middle strata. Such is the extent of this transformation that one could say that between 1950 and 1960 the "bourgeois" university became a university dominated by the middle classes. An observation like this is hardly likely to produce a significant ideological echo. All the same, from the sociological point of view it is important if one seeks to understand the student phenomena of May–June 1968.

Thus, French university institutions were firmly based on recruitment from the bourgeoisie and functioned smoothly as long as this recruitment remained essentially bourgeois, that is until about 1950.

In fact, the complete absence of a system of guidance hardly presented any problems. The limited number of students reduced competition in the job market whilst the secondary school and then university student's bourgeois background automatically provided him with typical models of desirable occupations within his family surroundings, which also provided help and support. In any case, there were rather few of these occupational models. The majority of students in faculties of humanities and sciences could at least be confident of an opening in teaching. (For example, the 1954 census shows that 7600 or half of the 15,200 total population of graduates in pure science were employed as teachers in secondary or higher education). But it was more usual for upper class students to enroll in faculties of medicine and law which were a preparation for high status occupations. The university was a guarantee of social promotion and held the promise of occupational security for students from the middle and lower classes. For students from the upper classes, examinations in the faculties of humanities and sciences (agrégation) and the faculties of law and medicine guaranteed their place in the existing social hierarchy. Whilst the family—through its position in this hierarchy—formed the main system of selection and guidance, the university was able to exercise *a posteriori* control by examination.

In addition to this negative system of guidance (total freedom for any individual possessing the baccalaureat to enter university, complete freedom of initiative, *a posteriori* control) the ideal type of the bourgeois university has another feature: its exclusive concentration on "education" in the broad cultural sense and its lack of awareness of "training". Once again, the limited number of students and the limited range of occupational models which faced the student on completion of his studies (as shown by the concentration of graduate qualifications in the 1954 census) made it possible to postpone the vocational adaptation of these qualification until the post-university period. Society and the economy required graduates rather than specialists. The disciplines were largely mapped out. Essentially, teaching took the form of reconstituting the parts. Students enjoyed the maximum possible liberty in organising their work and were subject to only one sanction, the examinations. The curriculum changed slowly, if at all. It was not difficult to discover what had to be learned to pass the examinations.

On the whole, the universities before 1950 still closely resembled the ones which were described in the novels of the nineteenth century. In

Flaubert's *L'Éducation Sentimentale*, Frédéric Moreau decides to enroll in the Faculté de Droit in Paris (called the *École* de Droit at that time). He and his friends see entry into the École de Droit as the beginning of a great career in politics, law or business. Because rank is determined by family and endorsed by the university, success in social terms must be a product of personality and character. Frédéric Moreau prepares for his exams without an enormous amount of effort but passes them without much difficulty.

The main features of this ideal type of the bourgeois university survived until 1950. Neither its liberal orientation nor the principle of freedom of access to higher education were called into question by any of the subsequent reforms, including that of Fouchet and Edgar Faure's reforms which followed the May–June 1968 events. Students are still completely free to enter university and they alone are responsible for their progress. At the very most, some faculties have decided to introduce restrictions on secondary school leaving qualifications (the requirement of "mathematics" for entry into science faculties). But these restrictions are very recent and quite exceptional. In faculties of humanities and law in particular, the broad "cultural" orientation remains predominant.

In May–June 1968 the students protested strongly against the two main features of the ideal type. "Culture" and the examination system constituted two of the main targets in the "troubles". They were clearly not proposing to replace the system of negative guidance with a system of positive guidance. Quite the contrary, they were opposed to any kind of "selection" system and there are obvious reasons for this process of transposition.

But why the conflict? Because the harmony which prevailed between the social system and the university system and characterised by an exclusive focus on culture and liberal guidance mechanisms has been progressively destroyed. There are two main causes for this: the change which has occurred in the social composition of the student population and certain changes which have taken place in the social system itself.

Studies which have investigated the mechanisms of educational guidance show that they vary to a large extent according to social class. The lower one descends in terms of social categories, the less guidance a child receives from the family model. At the secondary school level, most fathers of high social status will have completed their own secondary education and will be in more or less direct contact with members of occupations requiring a certain amount of further education. This is why at the age of fourteen or fifteen, as a recent survey carried out in the

Bordeaux region confirms, the expression of occupational preferences increases as one climbs the social scale (Table 10.11).

The relationship is much more clearly pronounced among boys than among girls (Table 10.12), almost certainly because occupational models are transmitted more easily from father to son than from father to daughter. A further reason is that the girl's social role is more conducive to decisions governed by internal factors (girls make more "idealistic" decisions; the "idealism" of their choices depends much less on their socio-economic level). As numerous studies have shown, they are in a sense less subject to social determination.

TABLE 10.11 Percentage of pupils having "chosen" an occupation, in terms of socio-economic status

	Socio-economic status				
	Low				High
	1	*2*	*3*	*4*	*5*
% of choices	53	58.2	60.7	65.5	61.4
N	492	534	303	203	277

Source: R. Boudon, F. Bourricaud et al., "Le choix professionnel des lycéens", *Convention D.G.R.S.T.*, July 1968, mimeo.

TABLE 10.12 Occupational choice as a function of sex and socio-economic status

	Low		Status		High
	1	*2*	*3*	*4*	*5*
% of choices					
Boys	44.7	51.6	53.7	60.9	61.9
	(257)	(271)	(145)	(110)	(147)
Girls	62.1	65.0	67.0	70.9	60.7
	(89)	(92)	(52)	(27)	(51)

Source: R. Boudon, F. Bourricaud et al., "Le choix professionnel des lycéens", *Convention D.G.R.S.T.*, July 1968, mimeo.

From the age of 14 or 15 onwards, this uncertainty about the future depends on social status (Table 10.13), it increases as social status decreases.

242 *The Crisis in Sociology*

TABLE 10.13 Confidence in the future in terms of social status

	Confidence in the future		
Social status	Confident	Anxious	Neither confident nor anxious
Low	20.9% (213)	45% (459)	34.1% (347)
High	31.7% (150)	39.1% (185)	29% (138)

Source: R. Boudon, F. Bourricaud et al., "Le choix professionnel des lycéens", *Convention D.G.R.S.T.*, July 1968, mimeo.

This anxiety or uncertainty is largely determined by the fact that attendance at secondary school reduces the family's influence over the child from the lower classes: it seems that this loss of influence is even greater when the cultural level of the family is low (Table 10.14).

TABLE 10.14 Family influence as perceived by the child, in terms of the cultural level of the family

	Cultural level of the family			
	Low			High
Perceived influence	1	2	3	4
Strong or average	37.1%	38%	43%	61%
Weak	62.9%	62%	57%	39%
N	248	192	244	179

Source: R. Boudon, F. Bourricaud et al., "Le choix professionnel des lycéens", *Convention D.G.R.S.T.*, July 1968, mimeo.

There is a tendency for the school to compensate partly for this lack of family influence: the perceived influence of teachers decreases with status (Table 10.15). However, this influence is only rarely perceived to be important. Consequently, the gap left by the family is only partly filled by the school system. This explains another finding of the Bordeaux study which suggests that lower class children tend to rely more heavily on the media of mass communication as sources of vocational information.

TABLE 10.15 Teachers' influence as perceived by pupils, in terms of the cultural level of the family

| | Cultural level of the family | | | |
| | Low | | | High |
Perceived influence	1	2	3	4
Strong	14.8 %	14.6 %	11.7 %	8.3 %
Average	24.4 %	22 %	26.4 %	24.9 %
Weak	60.8 %	63.4 %	61.9 %	66.8 %
N	250	213	265	217

Source: R. Boudon, F. Bourricaud et al., "Le choix professionnel des lycéens", *Convention D.G.R.S.T.*, July 1968, mimeo.

Generally speaking, the relative lack of family influence means that the lower class pupil perceives his future more in terms of the here and now of his achievement in the school environment than in terms of models provided by the family. Whereas the ambitions of upper class pupils are essentially governed by the family's social level, those of the pupil from a more modest background are established by a process of trial and error based on his academic achievement. In fact there is a very close relationship between the prestige of the chosen occupation and academic achievement when the family's cultural level is low and a very weak relationship when the cultural level is high (Table 10.16). When it is low, the proportion of those who choose a low status job varies between 27.7 and 64 per cent according to academic achievement. When it is high, there is practically no variation.

A further point to note (last line of Table 10.16) is that the differences in levels of academic achievement in terms of the cultural level of the family appear too much less pronounced at this stage (fourth and fifth form) than the differences among younger children like those studied by A. Girard, for example.[10] This is because informal guidance mechanisms make progress in school much more dependent on academic success for pupils of modest background. As a result of this process, students from lower class backgrounds are more thoroughly selected and, because of the lack of family influence, are more subject to the implicit guidance system of academic achievement.

The populations that enter the universities have distinct features which derive from these mechanisms: an upper class population, increasing in number but becoming a relative minority: a middle and lower class population which is now a majority. The first is relatively

TABLE 10.16 Relation between academic achievement and status of the chosen occupation, in terms of the cultural level of the family

Status of the chosen occupation	Low Academic achievement			Average Academic achievement			High Academic achievement		
	Low	Average	High	Low	Average	High	Low	Average	High
Low	27.5%	16%	8%	14.5%	8.5%	9%	11%	10.5%	8.5%
Average	45%	52.5%	28%	47.5%	47.5%	24.5%	15.5%	30.5%	20%
High	27.7%	31.5%	64%	38%	44%	66.5%	74%	59%	71.5%
N	40	212	25	55	391	45	27	144	35
(i)	14.5	76.5	19	11	79.5	9	13	70	17
			(100)			(100)			(100)

Cultural level of the family

Source: R. Boudon, F. Bourricaud et al., "Le choix professionnel des lycéens", *Convention D.G.R.S.T.*, July 1968, Mimeo.
(i) Distribution of pupils according to levels of achievement.

unselected. The second is over-selected. As a result, other things being equal, students from lower class background achieve better (Table 10.17).

TABLE 10.17 Degree passes, according to social background, sex and "situation" (age on entry to university and participation in paid employment)

| | Social background | | | | | |
| | Low | | Average | | High | |
Situation	Men	Women	Men	Women	Men	Women
Young, without	53%	39%	49%	43%	42%	39%
occupation	(57)	(145)	(156)	(390)	(219)	(911)
Mature, without	44%	26%	20%	21%	24%	15%
occupation	(34)	(70)	(50)	(98)	(82)	(192)
Young, with	18%	16%	11%	14%	20%	18%
occupation	(33)	(61)	(27)	(105)	(44)	(157)
Mature, with	13%	10%	13%	4%	11%	11%
occupation	(64)	(89)	(46)	(78)	(82)	(155)

Source: N. Bisseret, "Carrière scolaire d'une cohorte d'étudiants inscrits en 1962 à la faculté des Lettres de Paris: les filières d'orientation les facteurs de réussite", *Rapport Convention Ministère Education Nationale*, June 1968, mimeo.

It is possible to make some generalisations from these results which are derived from the Faculté des Lattres, Paris. In Orléans, first cycle failures (Sciences, Humanities, Law) are more common among students from upper class backgrounds even though they probably benefit from better material conditions. (Table 10.18).[11]

TABLE 10.18 Failures in terms of social background

| | Social background | | |
	Low	Average	High
Failed at least once	35%	36%	42%
	(84)	(157)	(89)

Source: C. Delage, *La naissance d'une université*, Orléans, 3rd cycle dissertation, typescript.

High rates of failure can therefore be seen among middle and lower class students because they are often forced either to undertake paid employment or to delay their entry into university[12] and upper class students because of the lack of "natural selection".

Failures are not only high, which fosters the tendency for students to limit their horizons to the next examination, but there is great uncertainty about occupational futures. A large proportion of students are undecided about their future occupation. However, in contrast to the finding among fourteen and fifteen-year-old secondary school pupils, it is students from the upper classes who are most undecided at the university level (Table 10.19).

TABLE 10.19 Occupational choice in terms of sex and social class (Paris)

| | Social background | | | | | |
| | Low | | Average | | High | |
	Men	Women	Men	Women	Men	Women
Choose teaching	69%	73%	55%	69%	48%	52%
No choice stated	26%	23%	39%	27%	42%	41%
Other occupations	5%	4%	6%	4%	10%	7%
N	153	283	217	536	308	1066

Source: N. Bisseret, "Carrière scolaire d'une cohorte d'étudiants inscrits en 1962 à la faculté des Lettres de Paris; les filières d'orientation et les facteurs de réussite", *Rapport Convention Ministère Education Nationale*, June 1968, mimeo.

The reversal can be explained quite easily: at the secondary school level, upper class pupils rely on occupational models which are either suggested or imposed by the family context. At university, they realise that their occupational horizon is restricted and provides too few possibilities to match their aspirations. This is why upper class students in the Faculté des Lettres are reluctant to become teachers because this would expose them to *social downgrading* in terms of their background. This also explains why many of them cannot or dare not tackle examinations (agrégation, doctorate) which would give access to the upper strata of the teaching profession.

For some, high risk of failure, of being trampled underfoot and of status degradation; for others, the problem of finding a job corresponding to four or five years of higher education. This is the situation especially of the university student in the humanities and sciences. Social mechanisms have been left to operate unchecked, thus causing a significant decline in the situation of the student in an increasingly affluent industrial society, whose ills the intelligentsia love to denounce, perhaps prematurely.

TABLE 10.20 Occupational choice in terms of sex and fathers'
occupation (Caen): percentage of students having made a choice

	Fathers' occupation		
	Manual	*Clerical*	*Professional*
Men	90 %(17)	80 %(23)	73 %(18)
Women	70 %(14)	73 %(14)	45 %(27)

Source: G. Desaunay, *Rapport d'enquête sur les étudiants de 1er cycle de
la faculté des Lettres de Caen (1966–67)*, typescript.

The fact that the same university system was maintained throughout a
time of growth and change in student numbers resulted in a complete
disruption of its harmony with the social system. Formerly, access to
university was the guarantee (subject to the *a posteriori* control of
examinations) of access to the elite, when it was not simply a
confirmation of the family's social standing. To a large extent, the family
took the responsibility for guidance. Today, the family's hold and
influence is becoming ineffective for a growing percentage of future
students, from the secondary stage onwards.

The school system therefore takes over the main responsibility for
guidance, using a series of eliminations. Their effect is to impose the
choice of entry to university without its ever having been discussed. The
formal (institutional) freedom of choice is transformed into a fate
decreed by blind mechanisms. Hence the opposition among students
towards what, in the attempt to identify a faceless enemy, they call "the
system".

A survey of 191 classics students in the Sorbonne shows that 75.9 per
cent (146) regard themselves as being destined for the teaching
profession. However, only 17 (11.6 per cent) of these 146 students
consider themselves to have been trained for the job of teaching.
Moreover, many of them think of this occupation as a refuge or
alternatively show without illusions that they see its main advantage as
being the amount of time it leaves available for non-work activities.[13]

This resigned attitude towards teaching comes more easily to students
from lower class social backgrounds than to others. The finding which
we have quoted for a range of students is confirmed at the level of
particular disciplines. Thus, a survey of the English section in the
Sorbonne (N = 56) shows that students from lower class backgrounds
nearly always chose teaching, whilst students from upper class backgrounds only choose this occupation in slightly more than one out of

every two cases. But even then, those who do not choose teaching are usually incapable of alighting on an exact choice or refer to occupations which they can vaguely describe when they try to specify their future. These are occupations which appear to be distance and difficult of access but which give an occupational form to their desire for escape: cultural representative, foreign newspaper correspondent, etc.

Among many upper class students there is confusion, but a refusal to accept social downgrading. Others are resigned and anxious. A feeling that things have developed to this point under their own momentum.

"I feel as though I've been going through a mill", states a student of classics. "I did 'A' because at the time it was the done thing for the best students to go on to do 'A'. Then I did 'A' and I did Greek. Since then I've been following a well-worn path . . . My parents didn't give me a lot of guidance. I think . . . I've simply been following a path. I've just been carried along."

When guidance is not automatic (the pathway) and is not pre-determined by the complex of parental and academic values, it is due to accidental and fortuitous circumstances.

"I came across this fellow, an army doctor actually, a really great guy who I thought a lot of, so I suddenly thought to myself . . . he really was a kind of model for me . . . simply this way of explaining people's behaviour, accounting for it, or at least understanding them, that seemed to me like a good definition of psychology" (Female psychology student).

In both cases (and both of these cases are typical), guidance comes from outside. Destiny takes the form of *fatality* in the first case and a *miracle* in the second. The "fatalistic" orientation seems to be typical of disciplines which are held in high regard socially (like classics for example); the "revelation" orientation being more typical of disciplines which have somewhat uncertain status and a less well defined image. For example, this is the case with psychology: especially among women psychology students (who considerably outnumber the men). Apparently, this discipline is often chosen because it is perceived as a "soft" (i.e. less academically and occupationally demanding) equivalent to medicine.

In reply to the question "If you had complete freedom of choice (regardless of previous studies, length of education, personal aptitude, family reactions, etc.) which activity or occupation would you be inclined towards?" only one-quarter of psychology students (Sorbonne, 1966) said that they would have chosen psychology – which means that three-quarters saw themselves as having chosen psychology for external reasons. Thirty per cent of first year students and 39 per cent of those in the final year would have chosen medicine. This suggests that disenchantment with psychology grows as the course progresses.

The difference between men and women can be explained in the following way. In the first place, the women students come from more privileged social backgrounds (52 per cent of women students and 38 per cent of women psychology students are from upper class backgrounds). This means that they have greater difficulty in accepting the "social downgrading" which psychology represents when compared with medicine. Secondly, they are much more interested than the men in therapeutic applications of psychology and show little enthusiasm for experimental psychology.

The considerable variation in the "motivation" and interests of psychology students according to the stage reached in the course is further confirmation of the fact that choices are often based on hazy impressions which may be borrowed from popular literature.

To summarise, one could say that entry to university is no longer directly related to "anticipatory socialisation", to use Merton's term. The risks of failure and mistaken choices have increased, not only because there is a whole new range of occupational models which have a content which lends itself to vague descriptions and ambiguity in terms of the occupational hierarchy, but also because the mass of students who cannot expect to receive guidance from their own circle has grown considerably in absolute as well as relative terms. Meanwhile, students from upper class backgrounds are everywhere becoming more and more exposed to competition from the "rising strata" and to social downgrading. This is reinforced by the fact that, not having been subject to such intense selection, they are generally less able students.

One factor which we have already mentioned needs to be underlined because it adds considerably to the problems of occupational choice: namely the increase in jobs and opportunities of a "semi-professional" kind. The adult education instructor, the psychologist, the sociologist and the consulting engineer do not have precise social images such as those which are associated with the school-teacher, the doctor or the engineer. The labels refer to activities whose content is obscure, often variable and usually only partly codified. The social status they can lay claim to is uncertain and variable. This explains why women psychology students, being generally uninformed about the nature of psychology at the beginning of their studies, prefer to use a familiar frame of reference, that of medicine. It also helps to explain the high rates of withdrawal that are to be seen in sociology.

250   *The Crisis in Sociology*

TABLE 10.21 Ideal choices of psychology students, according to sex and year of study

| | Women | | Men | |
	First year	Final year	First year	Final year
Would have chosen:				
Psychology	25 %	21 %	32 %	52 %
Psychiatry, psyche-analysis	13 %	12 %	11 %	13 %
Medicine	30 %	39 %	11 %	13 %
Artistic careers	11 %	10 %	21 %	4 %
N	202	67	28	23

Source: P. Oléron, "Opinions d'étudiants en psychologie sur leurs études et leur future profession", *Bulletin de Psychologie*, 255, xx, January 1967, pp. 6–7.

In general terms, the May–June disturbances seem to have been particularly acute in those sections involving unfamiliar disciplines with outlets mainly in semi-professionalised jobs.

The collapse of the mechanisms of anticipatory socialisation has therefore transformed the student condition into one of *social marginality*. Whereas up until about 1950 university entrance was a pledge of the student's future participation in the adult world, and a promise of social status, it is now a kind of social purgatory (especially in faculties of humanities and social sciences, but elsewhere too).

Moreover, this social purgatory often extends beyond the university to the stage when the ex-student enters one of the growing mass of semi-professional occupations. This explains why the May–June student movement created such a profound response among young cadres in research and development service departments in both public and private organisations and among public sector scientific workers.[14]

The marginality of the student condition largely explains the "murder of the father" and hostility towards the adult world. As far as one can tell, student radicalism cannot be explained in terms of a parent–child conflict within the family. On the contrary, various surveys show that more often than not the student who are most active politically come from liberal families. Therefore, hostility towards the adult world has its origins, not in the family but in the school and university system which makes the contemporary student a marginal figure in the wait for social recognition.

Again, this marginality is certainly greater in the humanities and sciences than in law or, above all, medicine. This is firstly because both law and medicine have been much less affected by the processes of democratisation, feminisation and the increase in numbers. Secondly, it is because the humanities and sciences have experienced more far-reaching changes in terms of their related professions. At one time, faculties of humanities and sciences were essentially pedagogical institutions. To a large extent they have now become multi-functional. This fact certainly goes a long way towards explaining the differences between levels of participation in university elections which have recently taken place in accordance with the "*loi d'orientation*".

III

Of course it is not altogether accurate to say that French university institutions remained unchanged between 1939 and 1968. Several reforms were carried out in different faculties during the last decade. The Fouchet reform, which was the most recent of these prior to the May–June 1968 events, was a deliberate attempt to alter the system of humanities and science faculties. All of these reforms had the aim of making higher education courses more *serious*. They sought to bring an end to dilettantism and replace it with professional and scientific training. In Martin Trow's terms, they were trying to substitute a "vocational culture" or "academic culture" (public authorities not having taken the trouble to distinguish between the two) for a "collegiate culture".

Prior to these reforms, the student was the sole arbiter of his choice of subjects. He could not even take a course or a series of practical sessions, which were few and far between anyway. The only requirement for sitting an examination was to be enrolled and to attend. The student had complete freedom in preparing for the examination. Some professors gained the reputation of admitting to the examinations only those students they knew from attendance at classes. But there were not many of them and they were known to the students, who showed their disapproval.

Another feature was that students could sit the examinations as often as they wished, and move from one discipline to another.

The reforms were directed against these aspects of "*akademische Freiheit*". For example, the Fouchet reform meant that students had to choose a discipline on entry to the university and stick with it on penalty of losing a year and starting the new chosen discipline from scratch.

Moreover, the number of examination attempts was strictly limited (two re-sits) at the level of the first cycle (first two years). Attendance at practical sessions was also made compulsory.

The outcome of these measures was not so much a movement from the "collegiate culture" to an "academico–professional" culture as a movement towards the fourth category in Trow's typology: "non-conformist" or "oppositional" culture.

For these reforms meant that students were suddenly subjected to a system of constraints and strict controls at the very time when it was becoming increasingly obvious that the social returns which they could except to receive from higher education were diminishing. The greater the investment, the less the return. What is more, the restriction of opportunities for reorientation came at a time when social guidance mechanisms had lost much of their effectiveness because of changes in the composition of the student population and the proliferation of occupational models.

In many disciplines the resulting system has a truly Kafkaesque absurdity. Take the case of sociology, for example. As we mentioned earlier, 400 students were enrolled in this discipline in the Faculté des Lettres in Paris alone. Because the reforms preserved intact the principle of unrestricted access to university, teachers had to resign themselves to noting the numbers and improvising the necessary reorganisation. Students, on the other hand, once registration was complete, were practically condemned to follow the remainder of their studies in higher education within this discipline unless they were prepared to accept a heavy penalty (loss of a year). In theory, attendance was still compulsory (a rule applied in the regions although not in Paris). Given the state of the job market in sociology a maximum of 1 out of every 10 students could expect to find a job corresponding to the time invested on completion of the course of study. Hence a large proportion of these students were condemned in advance either to withdrawal or failure, whilst the remainder were exposed to teaching which was automatically made less satisfactory by the numbers and the average level of the students involved.

IV

Summarising the reforms carried out in recent years, it could be said that the persistence of the institutional type of reform with its liberal orientation and cultural focus in the context of the changing social composition of the student population and the growth of numbers has led gradually to a new university system. This system is profoundly unstable, as the events of May–June 1968 showed. It has the following characteristics:

1. *Confusion of functions.* The social diversity of the student population and the diversity of their educational backgrounds means that there are fundamental differences in students' aspirations. Among psychology students who are all studying the same syllabus up to degree level one finds a range of professional aspirations from psychoanalyst to teacher and motivations which range from a disinterested search for greater knowledge of the self to scientific research in the context of the new professional occupations.

Formerly, language departments were mainly a source of secondary school teachers and, after a further process of selection, teachers in higher education. Today the English department in the Sorbonne alone numbers nearly 9000 students so that in all probability (it would be worth carrying out a survey of this) future university teachers are rubbing shoulders with students looking for instruction in a language which they think will be useful in a variety of ordinary occupations. Up to degree level they all follow a common curriculum. A series of interviews conducted among students of English reveals a typical set of motivations: some regard English as a straightforward language, while for others, contact with Anglo–American civilisation gives a feeling of openness towards the outside world. Students of English (84 per cent of whom are female) were often average achievers in secondary school (only 29 per cent of them gained a merit in the baccalaureat compared with 39 per cent among students of German, for example) who made their choice by a process of elimination and whose "vocation" was confirmed by a visit to Britain.

The result of this confusion of functions is that none of them are properly fulfilled. Training for research is very poorly organised, especially so in the humanities faculties; but so is instruction in basic techniques (like language instruction in the departments of languages). And although the main function of the faculties of humanities is to train future teachers, only a very small minority of those who have chosen this profession consider themselves to be well prepared for it.

2. *Localised explosion of numbers.* In the absence of a rational guidance system, the choice of discipline is largely determined by sex, previous educational achievement and social background. Consequently, those disciplines which recruit in the first place mainly among

females and secondly among lower levels of achievement are most liable to the explosion of numbers (hence the feminisation which has occurred, especially in the faculties of humanities and sciences). This is what has happened in English and psychology. Added that choices guided by fashion become all the more important when the influence of social background diminishes, it means that these phenomena of explosion are combined with erratic variations in numbers, like those which have occurred in sociology and psychology. This has serious consequences both for the organisation of teaching and for the harmonisation of studies and employment. It should also be stressed that democratisation and feminisation have entailed a much larger expansion in faculties of humanities and sciences than in faculties of law and medicine.

3. *Anomie in the student condition.*   If his choice is based on vague impressions, a process of elimination or accident, the student runs the risk of being disappointed by the content of his subject. Once the choice has been made, there is a considerable risk of failing the examinations. If the examination is passed there is no guarantee of social status or even a job. The individual finds that the outcome of his period of study is largely indeterminate.

Clearly, this anomic situation accounts in large measure for the student revolt. What is surprising about this revolt is not so much the existence and behaviour of the politicised minorities (which have always been present to a greater or lesser extent) as the speed and extent of the contagion. The explanation must lie mainly in the students' situation of anomie. The fact that many of them refused to sit their examinations can certainly be interpreted partly in terms of some students lack of preparation but the main reason must be that the social credit which an examination brings can be lightly dismissed.

Observational evidence, which has to suffice in the absence of more systematic surveys, seems to show that the students engaged in "opposition" are recruited in disproportional numbers from among students of upper class social backgrounds. Although an ecological analysis is particularly hazardous here, there does appear to be a relationship between the degree of anomie and the high level of social recruitment on the one hand and the strength of the "opposition" on the other. Thus there appears to be a relationship between the social composition of universities and the amount of disturbance which they have experienced. In May–June 1968, more was heard of Paris, Lyon, Aix, Bordeaux and Caen than Clermont, Dijon, Nancy, Besançon or Poitiers (Table 10.22). At the same time, Nanterre, whose students come mainly from western sector of Paris, gained a world-wide reputation.

TABLE 10.22 Social composition of French universities in 1960

	0/00 Liberal professions Senior management	0/00 Middle management White collar workers	0/00 Blue-collar and agricultural workers
Paris	391	260	22
Aix	287	341	33
Besançon	163	353	54
Bordeaux	252	325	32
Caen	247	333	36
Clermont	225	327	93
Di̧ ͻn	230	414	48
Grenoble	257	312	44
Lille	288	309	82
Lyon	295	283	49
Montpellier	188	264	64
Nancy	229	338	63
Poitiers	212	298	43
Rennes	250	352	46
Strasbourg	254	312	41
Toulouse	216	315	37

Source: Informations statistiques, Bulletin published by the Ministére de l'Education Nationale: No 32–33, October–November 1961, p. 274.

In the faculties of humanities and social sciences, sociology departments were generally notable for their effervescence. In fact they brought together two characteristics which favoured this: firstly, recruitment from upper social strata and secondly, high levels of anomie (failures, withdrawals, resits). In the Faculté des Lettres in Paris, 68 per cent of the sociology students come from upper class social backgrounds. This percentage is higher than in any other department (with the exception of art history). Similarly, sociology comes second in the list of failures and withdrawals. In short, sociology departments are those which contain the highest proportion of students who are exposed to social downgrading.

V

Obviously there is no simple solution to the problems posed by the May–June 1968 university crisis. In any case, it is not simply a French crisis.

However, the crisis was specially acute in France largely because its university system accumulated all the dysfunctions of other systems and carried them to their paroxysmal conclusion. In particular these dysfunctions arose because of the complete absence of any system of positive guidance and because of the lack of differentiation between institutions of higher education. The only significant distinction is between the Grandes Écoles (which recruit a smaller and smaller proportion of students) and the universities. The two features are interrelated because a system of guidance could scarcely develop without some degree of institutional differentiation. The outcome of this system was to place a major section of the student population in a situation of social marginality.

As a result, it would seem that the establishment of a system of guidance and a system of channels distinguished according to length, nature and functions and between which passages could be contrived, would make a substantial contribution both to the reduction of the social marginality of the student and to the rapid and comprehensive democratisation of higher education, at least until changes in secondary education can make a contribution of their own. As every study of social mobility shows, changes in education at the secondary level are not sufficient in themselves to affect more than one highly specific source of inequality. This can be demonstrated simply by comparing differences in levels of achievement in terms of social background. These are very important in the first form and especially prior to that but they gradually diminish and practically disappear by the fifth form. Since inequalities of social composition are much greater in the universities than in the fifth form of secondary school, this shows that the "cultural inheritance" which is currently so fashionable only provides a very partial explanation of the inequality of recruitment at the level of higher education.

VI

Although the university crisis has been more extensive and more acute in France than in other countries, we can show in conclusion how the sociological diagnosis which we have made can perhaps be used to explain what P. Coombs calls "the world educational crisis".[15]

In our view the basic element in this diagnosis lies in the transition from the ideal type of "bourgeois" university to that of the "middle class" university. In the first case, as we have seen, the university simply endorses the social standing of the family and occupational choice is made essentially on the basis of this standing. Thus the "bourgeois" university helps to consolidate a social system in which the mechanisms of guidance are essentially in the hands of the family. In the second case, the family's role in social selection and filtering tends to disappear. The result is that this function is increasingly taken on by the school system and especially the university system. Thus the university has an entirely new role: in a society in which social status is more and more completely determined by occupation, it becomes – or tends to become – the basic mechanism of social mobility, as much in decent as ascent.[16]

The transition from the first ideal type to the second is typical of the industrial societies. It can be seen in the American, British or German university systems as well as in the French system.

To the extent that it has become "middle class", the university is a source of anxiety for the individual: examinations are no longer a symbolic test which could never call into question a social position determined by other factors. On the contrary, they are becoming a basic mechanism for the distribution of individuals among the different levels of the social system. These profound changes in the function of the university including its examinations and the *control* which the university can exert over the destiny of individuals are perhaps the common denominator of the university crises which have occurred throughout the world in recent years.

However, the transition from the "bourgeois" university to the "middle class" university – a transition which is of course far from complete – has been made in different ways and in different contexts depending on the country. In the United States, a number of institutional mechanisms have been installed which will give the university system effective control over one basic function of the "middle class" university: that of guidance.[17] In France there has been greater institutional inertia: the institutions are still generally characteristic of the "bourgeois" university although the social system demands the introduction of a "middle class" university. This leads to the situation of *"anomie"* which we have attempted to describe, the effects of which are combined with those of the university system's *control* over individual destiny.

Notes

CHAPTER 1

1. *La vocation actuelle de la sociologie* (Paris: Presses Universitaires de France, 1950) p. 1.
2. The positivist dispute has occupied an important place in German sociology for a number of years. On this, see T. W. Adorno *et al.*, *Der Positivismusstreit in der deutschen Soziologie* (Berlin: Luchterhand, 1969); Eng. trans. *The Positivist Dispute in German Sociology* (Heinemann, 1976). This book brings together a number of contributions from Theodor Adorno and Jurgen Habermas on the side of the dialecticians and from Karl Popper and Hans Albert on the side of those whom the dialecticians call positivists.
3. See for example *Epistémologie sociologique* (Paris), *Quality and Quantity*, *European Journal of Methodology* (Bologna, in French and English), *Journal of Mathematical Sociology, Multivariate Methods, Theory and Decision* (Berlin, in English and French).
4. Cf. Fernand Braudel "Histoire et sociologie" in G. Gurvitch *Traité de sociologie* (Paris: Presses Universitaires de France, 1958) pp. 83–98.
5. Cf. Philip G. Altbach *Student Politics and Higher Education in the United States, a Select Bibliography* (St. Louis, Mo.: United Ministries in Higher Education, 1968).
6. Pierre Bourdieu, Jean-Claude Chamboredon, Jean-Claude Passeron, *Le métier de sociologue* (Paris: Mouton/Bordas, 1968).
7. Cf. for example Nicolas Ruwet, *Les grammaires generatives* (Paris: Plon, 1968).
8. The notion of "total social phenomenon" which has a very clear meaning in Marcel Mauss is not always so specific among those who use it like a battering ram or custard pie. Correctly interpreted, it shows the need for the sociologist to take care, in the language of systems theory, to construct models with an appropriate degree of complexity: he should thus avoid analysing a relationship in isolation when this is located within a set of relationships forming a system. Unfortunately, this notion is often taken to be equivalent to the familiar axiom that "everything is related to everything else"; in this way it helps to defend an epistemology of the "return to the concrete" which does the sociologist the favour of removing any need for genuinely scientific exertion.
9. Cf. for example, Raymond Aron "Une sociologie des relations internationales" *Revue Française de sociologie*, 4(1963), 3, pp. 307–20 and *Paix et guerre entre les nations* (Paris: Calmann Levy, 1962).
10. Cf. for example, Leo Goodman "On the statistical analysis of mobility tables", *American Journal of Sociology*, 70(1965), pp. 564–85.
11. See also "Methodological issues in the analysis of social mobility", in Neil Smelser and Seymour M. Lipset *Social Structure and Mobility in Economic Development* (Chicago: Aldine, 1966) pp. 55–97.

12. For a remarkably clear and concise presentation of the principal theories of stratification, see Jean Cazeneuve, "Les stratifications sociales" in *La Sociologie*, Les dictionnaires du savoir moderne (Paris: CAL, 1970) pp. 454–89.
13. *Social Mobility*, 1927 reprinted in *Social and Cultural Mobility* (Glencoe: The Free Press and London: Collier–Macmillan, 1964).
14. Cf. Pierre Birnbaum, *Sociologie de Tocqueville* (Paris: Presses Universitaires de France, 1970).
15. Cf. Chapter 7.
16. Cf. Chapter 2.
17. Philip Coombs *La crise mondiale de l'éducation* (Paris: Presses Universitaires de France, 1968).
18. Cf. for example Helmut Schelsky *Die skeptische Generation, Eine Soziologie der deutschen Jugend* (Düsseldorf–Köln: Eugen Diedrichs Verlag, 1957).
19. Cf. Paul Lazarsfeld "La sociologie" in *Tendances principales de la recherche dans les sciences sociales et humaines* (Paris/La Haye: Mouton/UNESCO, 1970).
20. Amitai Etzioni, *The Active Society* (London: Collier–Macmillan and New York, The Free Press, 1968).
21. However, for a critique of this movement, see Jean Padioleau.
22. See, for example, S. M. Lipset and P. Altbach (ed.) *Students and Politics* (Boston: Houghton–Mifflin, 1969); S. N. Eisenstadt, *From Generation to Generation* (London: Collier–Macmillan, 1956).
23. Gösta Carlsson, *Social Mobility and Class Structure* (Lund: Gleerup, 1969); David Glass, *Social Mobility in Britain* (London: Routledge and Kegan Paul, 1954); Natalie Rogoff, *Recent Trends in Occupational Mobility* (Glencoe: The Free Press, 1953); Kaare Svalastoga, *Prestige, Class and Mobility* (Copenhagen: Gyldendal, 1959).
24. Cf. for example, Carl-Gunnar Janson "Project metropolitan", *Acta sociologica*, 9 (1966), 1–2, pp. 110–15.
25. Cf. for example, Ludwig von Bertalanffy, "General system theory – A critical review" and A. D. Hall, R. E. Fagen "Definition of a system" in Walter Buckley (dir.) *Modern Systems Research* (Chicago: Aldine, 1968).
26. (Chicago: Lippincott, 3rd ed., 1959).
27. On this point, see Chapters 7 and 8.
28. Cf. for example, François Chazel, "Pouvoir et influence chez Parsons", *Revue française de sociologie*, 5(1954), 4, pp. 387–401.
29. Talcott Parsons "The Present Position and Prospects of Systematic Theory in Sociology" (1945); reprinted in *Essays in Sociological Theory* (Glencoe: The Free Press, 1940/1954).
30. Cf. for example, Etzioni, *The Active Society*, op. cit. and also the work of political sociologists such as David Easton or Karl Deutsch.
31. On this point cf. Chapter 7.
32. Three authors seem to have played a fundamental role in this rediscovery. They are respectively, in the case of Montesquieu, Raymond Aron (*Les étapes de la pensée sociologique*, Paris, Gallimard, 1967); in the case of Condorcet, the mathematician G. Th. Guilbaud ("Les théories de l'intérêt général et le problème logique de l'agrégation", *Economie appliquée*, 5[1952], 4, 501–584. Reproduced in *Eléments de théorie des jeux*, Paris, Dunod, 1968); in the case of Quételet, Paul Lazarsfeld, (*Philosophie des sciences sociales*, Paris, Gallimard, 1970).
33. Cf. Lazarsfeld, *La sociologie*, op. cit.
34. (Paris: Presses Universitaires de France, 1970).

35. Op. cit., p. 24.
36. This temptation is particularly evident in the work of Michel Crozier (*The World of the Office Worker*, Chicago, 1971) who does often excellent analyses of particular "organisations" using macrosociological propositions which are less convincing. See also F. Bourricaud's critical review of Michel Crozier's *La société bloquée* (Paris: Seuil, 1970) in "Michel Crozier et le syndrome de blocage", *Critique*, 285 (November 1970), pp. 960–78.
37. To the best of our knowledge, Daniel Bertaux is the first to have drawn attention to the unfortunate character of the concept "social mobility" and its possible epistemological consequences.
38. Cf. *Philosophie des sciences sociales* op. cit. and Chapter 5.
39. Cf. Chapter 5.
40. Cf. Chapter 4.
41. Cf. for example *The Nerves of Government: models of political communication and control* (Glencoe, Ill.: The Free Press, 1963).
42. Article "Epistemologie", in *Encyclopaedia Universalis*, Volume 6, pp. 370–73.
43. Cf. Chapter 7.
44. Ibid.
45. For a useful discussion of these distinctions, see for example Haroun Jamous "Technique, méthode, épistemologie, suggestions pour quelques définitions", *Epistemologie sociologique*, 6(1968), pp. 21–38.
46. S. Yasuda, "A methodological inquiry into social mobility", *American Sociological Review*, 29(1964), pp. 16–23.
47. Cf. for example Vittorio Capecchi "Methode de classification basée sur l'entropie", *Revue française de sociologie*, 5(1964), pp. 290–306.
48. Cf. Chapter 6 in H. and A. Blalock (eds.) *Methodology in Social Research*, McGraw Hill, New York and London (1968) "A new look at correlation analysis" pp. 199–235.

CHAPTER 2

1. First published in *Après-Demain*, No. 119, December 1968, pp. 8–10.

CHAPTER 3

1. *Theory and Decision*, 6 (Dordrecht-Holland, D. Reidel Publishing Company, 1975) pp. 381–406.
2. *Tendances principales de la recherche dans les sciences sociales et humaines* (Paris/La Haye: Mouton/UNESCO, 1970) Chapter 1, "La sociologie", by Paul Lazarsfeld.
3. (New York: The Free Press of Glencoe; London: Collier–Macmillan, 1964).
4. Hannah Arendt, *On Violence* (Allen Lane, The Penguin Press, 1969).
5. Nicos Poulantzas, *Pouvoir politique et classes sociales* (Paris: Maspero, 1971).
6. See Chapter 8 "The Notion of Function".
7. John Rawls, *A Theory of Justice* (Cambridge, Mass.: The Belknap Press of Harvard University Press, 1971).
8. *American Sociological Review*, April 1945, X, pp. 242–9. This paper has provoked extensive discussion among sociologists. See for a summary Melvin Tumin, *Social Stratification* (Englewood Cliffs, N. J.: Prentice Hall, 1967). Again it should be

stressed that my presentation of the three paradigms discussed in this text is *idealtypical*. Consequently it ignores important differences in the use made of the paradigms by various authors. Thus, beyond any doubt Parsons's use of the functional paradigm is much more sophisticated than Davis's and Moore's. It seems to me, however, that the notions of what I call individual and collective equilibrium are always present in Parsons's analyses.

9. George C. Homans, *Elementary Forms of Social Behaviour* (New York, Chicago, San Francisco and Atlanta: Harcourt, Brace and World, 1961).
10. See Anatol Rapoport and Melvin Guyer, "A Taxonomy of 2 × 2 Games", *General Systems*, XI, 1966, pp. 203–14.
11. See, e.g. Talcott Parsons, "A Revised Analytical Approach to the Theory of Social Stratifications", in R. Bendix and S. M. Lipset, *Class Status and Power* (Glencoe, Ill.: The Free Press, 1953).
12. See, for instance, Albert Mathiez, *La Révolution française* (A. Colin, 1963).
13. J. Galtung, "Violence, peace and peace research", *Journal of Peace Research* 3, 1969, pp. 167–91.
14. See, for instance, *Du contrat social*, Livre IV, Chapter 1, Oeuvres complètes de J. J. Rousseau (Paris: Pléiade, Gallimard) p. 438.
15. See, for instance, M. Castells, *La question urbaine* (Paris: Maspero, 1972); G. Kolko, *Wealth and Power in America* (New York: Praeger, 1962). The Miliband–Poulantzas controversy (see John Urry and John Wakeford (eds.), *Power in Britain* (London: Heinemann, 1973) is worth considering in respect with the present discussion: Miliband wants to identify concretely the *elites* which constitute the ruling class. For Poulantzas, the notion of "elite" is "ideological" does not belong to the "scientific concepts of Marxist theory"; classes are "objective structures" not reducible to "interpersonal relations", etc. etc. Thus, classes are not visible. Their existence is *deduced* from the existence of public evils redounding to the private benefit of some members. Needless to say, this way of reasoning is entirely tautologous.
16. H. L. Nieburg, *Political Violence* (New York: Saint Martin's Press, 1969).
17. *The Functions of Social Conflict*, op. cit.
18. Lewis C. Ord, *Industrial Frustration* (London: Mayflower Books Ltd., 1953) p. 133.
19. C. Wright Mills, *The Power Elite* (New York: Oxford University Press, 1959).
20. See for instance, John Goldthorpe, "Social Stratification in Industrial Societies" in R. Bendix and S. M. Lipset, *Class. Status and Power*, 2nd edn., (Glencoe, Ill.: The Free Press, 1966).
21. See, for instance, M. Castells, *La question urbaine* (Paris: Maspero, 1972).
22. See H. Marcuse, *One Dimensional Man. Studies in the Ideology of Advanced Society.* Traduction française (Paris: Editions de Minuit, 1968). Paul Goodman, *Growing up Absurd* (New York: Vintage Books, 1956).
23. Parsons, op. cit.
24. Kaare Svalastoga, *Prestige, Class and Society* (Copenhagen: Gyldendal, 1959).
25. *Education, Equality and Social Opportunity* (New York: Wiley, 1974).
26. Although I consider here purely economic variables, the concepts of costs, investments, etc. can be given a broader meaning. The concept of social status, a key notion in sociology, can be defined as a flow of social rewards (amount of prestige, power, income, etc.). Consequently it can be considered as a generalisation of the economic notion of benefit. In the same way, the *costs* of education can be described as including purely economic costs or social costs as well (social marginality for instance).

27. "Games, Justice and the General Will", *Mind* 74, 1965. Rousseau is, of course, not the only sociologist who uses what I call here the interaction paradigm. It can be found in Marx's *Capital*, in de Tocqueville's *'Ancien Régime*, in Pareto's *Treatise*. My contention is that it has been forgotten by many contemporary sociologists because of Durkheim's influence. In Durkheim's work human actions are systematically analysed as the product of social causes or "forces", never as the product of intentions.
28. Thomas Schelling, *The Strategy of Conflict* (London: Oxford University Press, 1960); Albert O. Hirschman, *Exit, Voice and Loyalty* (Cambridge, Mass.: Harvard University Press, 1970).

CHAPTER 4

1. Published in *Annales internationales de Criminologie*, 1964, pp. 1–16.
2. R. Daval et al., *Traité de psychologie sociale*, Volume I (Presses Universitaires de France, 1963).
3. A. Pizzorno, "Lecture actuelle de Durkheim", *European Journal of Sociology*, Vol. III, 1962, p. 2.
4. H. Hyman, *Survey Design and Analysis* (Glencoe, Ill.: The Free Press, 1955); H. Selvin, "Durkheim's *Suicide* and Problems of Empirical Social Research", *The American Journal of Sociology*, 63 (1958), pp. 607–19.
5. Cf. Chapter 9.
6. "Between 1828 and 1879, the proportion of recidivists out of every 100 prisoners or accused almost *doubled* and, between 1850 and 1879 it increased by more than a third, while in this latter period it averaged 32 per cent per year for France as a whole. This general average is far from being reached in the mountainous regions or rural areas, for example the Basse-Alpes, Corsica, the Ardèche, the Upper Loire and Ariège which had 20 per cent; and it is greatly exceeded by the densely-populated departments of the Nord, by Seine-Maritime, Seine-et-Oise and the Marne where it reaches 40 per cent and especially by the Seine, where it is 42 per cent." *La criminalité comparée*, 8th edn. (Paris: Felix Alcan, 1924) p. 82. The majority of the studies brought together in this volume, the first edition of which appeared in 1888, were published in the *Revue Philosophique*. See also Ibid., p. 97.
   There are a number of passages in the *Philosophie pénale* (4th edn., Paris, Storck) which show clearly how, according to Tarde, a causal analysis which tries to establish a general law nevertheless encounters the action of a process: cf. p. 307. "This supposed law (which links criminality with climate) does not apply in France, as can be seen from the splendid official maps by M. Yvernes which show the distribution of crimes of violence among our departments including Corsica and the Mediterranean littoral. What is most striking is the blackness of the areas surrounding the major cities in the Seine, the Bouches-du-Rhône, the Gironde, Loire-Inférieure, Nord, Seine-Inférieure and the Rhône. The larger the city, even in the northern region, that is the more human contacts are multiplied, the greater the proportion of murders among a given number of inhabitants." See also, Ibid., p. 343, the analysis of crime amongst immigrants.
7. *Les lois de l'imitation* (Paris: Alcan, 1890). The quotations used here are taken from the 2nd edn., 1895. See also *La philosophie pénale*, op. cit., "le crime", pp. 294–425.
8. On this, it would also be useful to refer to A. Davidovitch, "Remarques sur la

criminologie de G. Tarde", mimeo proceedings of the *Séminaire d'histoire de la sociologie empirique en France*, published under the direction of Paul Lazarsfeld and Bernard Lecuyer.

9. In *Essais et mélanges sociologiques* (Lyon, Storck and Paris: Masson, 1895) pp. 235–309.

10. "When a convicted prisoner in police detention wonders whether to appeal, he cannot decide on the basis of the example of other prisoners, since all he knows is that some of them appeal and some do not. He is also unaware of the statistics which would show him that appeal courts are more and more inclined to confirm the decisions made by the first judges. He is impelled only by the hope of a revised sentence; he is held back only by the fear of a confirmed sentence and his feelings will be swayed one way or the other (the reasons for hoping and fearing being the same in typical cases) according to whether he is naturally bold or timorous, or more prone to confidence or discouragement for physiological reasons. These are unchanging factors whose additional weight combines with the unchanging balance of the motives themselves to produce on average an identical effect, a practically stable number of appeals. This is what the statistics show with remarkable regularity. Since 1826, out of every hundred sentences there have always been about forty-six which prisoners have appealed against. But appeals lodged by the public prosecutor have been declining, from 43 per cent in 1831 to 22 per cent in recent years; the prosecuting magistrates are using one another as examples. And confirmed sentences are growing for a similar reason." *La criminalité comparée*, op. cit., p. 107; see also *Les lois de l'imitation*, op. cit., pp. 130–31.

11. *Compte général de la justice criminelle pendant l'année 1909*, Rapport préliminaire (Paris: Imprimerie Nationale, 1911).

12. See *Les lois de l'imitation*, op. cit.

13. *La criminalite comparée*, op. cit., pp. 67–8.

14. "Once set in motion, an idea or a need always tends to spread further of its own accord, following a true geometric progression. This is the ideal form which the graphic curve would assume if they were able to spread freely. But sooner or later, in the long run, each of these social forces is bound to reach a limit beyond which it cannot pass and thus temporarily arrives at a stable state whose meaning most statisticians seem to have appreciated. It is accidental rather than naturally determined. Stability here, as anywhere else, means equilibrium or the mutual checking of competing forces. I have no wish to deny the theoretical interest of this state, since these equilibria are so many equations." *Les lois de l'imitation*, p. 126. See also, Ibid., p. 22. "To illustrate the effect of the geometric progression of imitations, one could quote the statistics which refer to the consumption of coffee, tobacco, etc. from the time when they were first imported up to the period when the market became saturated." These references to the generality of the geometric progression clearly show that Tarde was aware of the importance of these processes, which we have defined in a simple way in the text, for the interpretation of time series.

15. "The proportion of indictments dismissed without sufficient cause is constantly decreasing; that of charges dismissed has fallen from 12 per cent to 4 per cent", *La criminalité comparée*, op. cit., p. 100, note 1; see also *Les délits impoursuivis*, op. cit., p. 216.

16. "Out of every hundred cases in petty sessions, the proportion of those tried in the first month after the offence has gradually increased from thirty-two to sixty-eight. . . .", *La criminalité comparée*, op. cit., p. 99; Ibid. "Between 1831 and 1835, two-fifths of

cases (brought to court) were committed to examination and only three-tenths of
them were classified as not liable to further proceedings; the first proportion fell from
41 per cent to 13 per cent while the latter rose from 31 per cent to 49 per cent."
17. *La criminalité comparée*, op. cit., pp. 99–100.
18. "In fact, this uniformity seems to me to be the distinctive characteristic by which
action can be translated statistically into social facts or an organic and vital cause like
the influence of age, sex or race, or into the action of a physical cause like climate or
the seasons, or finally into the action of a social cause so old and so deeply rooted,
notably the influence of marriage or certain religious sentiments, as to have passed as
it were into the bloodstream and reached long ago the full extent of its imitative
radiance." *La criminalité comparée*, op. cit., pp. 102–3.
19. *La criminalité comparée*, op. cit., pp. 106–7.
20. *Les lois de l'imitation*, p. 21. See also *Les lois sociales*, 3rd edn. (Paris: Alcan, 1902)
p. 10: "Indeed, it is not the relationship of cause and effect which is the sole element of
scientific knowledge." There is no need to stress the fundamental difference between
Tarde and Durkheim's *Rules*, for example, on this point.
21. F. Simiand, *Le salaire, l'évolution sociale et la monnaie* (Paris: Alcan, 1932) especially
pp. 5–25.
22. "The enumeration of actions of the most *similar* possible kind (a condition which is
hardly fulfilled in criminal statistics, for instance) and, where these are lacking, the
enumeration of objects like articles of commerce, also similar in kind, should always
tend towards and relate to this ultimate goal, or rather to these two goals: firstly, to
the registering of actions and objects, tracing the curve of successive increases,
standstills and decreases in each new idea or every old or new need, according to
whether they are dispersing or consolidating, whether they are homogeneous or
scattered; secondly, by careful comparison of the series obtained in this way and by
highlighting their concomitant variation, to identify the range of factors which in
various degrees help or hinder the imitative propagation of needs and ideas (to the
extent that they involve, as they invariably do, implicit propositions which more or
less mutually and comprehensively confirm or deny each other); not forgetting the
influence which can be exerted by sex, age, temperament, climate, seasons, or natural
causes whose effect ought to be measurable by physical or biological statistics." *Les
lois de l'imitation*, op. cit., pp. 120–1. There is obviously no need to emphasise either
the confused quality of this passage or the references to the language of Stuart Mill.
23. *Les lois de l'imitation*, op. cit., p. 115.
24. *Essais et mélanges sociologiques*, op. cit.
25. *Essais et mélanges sociologiques*, op. cit., pp. 269–70. *La philosophie pénale*, pp. 374–
5 ff.
26. "The growth or decline of religious faith, or the certainty attached to the threat of hell
and promise of heaven, is revealed in every country and at all times in comparative
figures for financial sacrifices made at the altar and by legacies and donations to the
clergy, taking account of course of the depreciation of precious metals and variations
in national wealth. With the help of these figures, figures for the population in two
successive periods, the total figure for public wealth in the same periods and other
numerical data, it would be a complex but not insoluble problem to determine the
precise fraction which would express the relationship between the two total
quantities of religious faith manifest at these two dates in the same nation." *Essais et
mélanges sociologiques*, op. cit., pp. 273–4. It is interesting to find Tarde proposing a
weighted index which seeks to measure a complex concept according to a strategy

which was not to develop in empirical research until very much later. See also: "At certain times in our century, the number of church attendances has remained steady whilst religious faith has experienced a decline . . . and it can happen that, when a government's prestige is under attack, the loyalty of its adherents is half-destroyed although their number has hardly decreased, as can be seen from ballots even on the eve of a sudden collapse. This is the illusory and non-rational basis behind the belief that electoral statistics can provide reassurance or discouragement." *Les lois de l'imitation*, p. 116. Here Tarde is proposing nothing less than the replacement of electoral sociography with a socialpsychological analysis of the mechanisms of voting decisions.

27. *Les lois de l'imitation*, op. cit., p. 115. On the social importance of "Ordinary statistics", see *La philosophie pénale*, op. cit., p. 279: "in some ways, social statistics is an awakening social sense, it is to societies what vision is to animals".

28. "It might seem quite natural to think that the amount of belief is proportional to the mathematical value of the reasons as I have just defined them. From this point of view, this calculation of *credibilities*, that is affirmations and denials, would be an algebraic logic of the kind dreamt of by our contemporary logicians, and the exact counterpart of this science would be nothing less than Bentham's utilitarian doctrine, this morality of *a* plus *b* which could be described as the calculus of positive and negative desirabilities. But the difficulty for the mathematicians, as for the utilitarians, consists in justifying this *obligation* which they impose upon me to choose or desire more or less or other than I either believe or desire." *Essais et mélanges sociologiques*, op. cit., p. 265.

29. "It is neither the actual increases or decreases in belief which determine the calculation in question (the calculation of probabilities) but rather those which would be if they were exactly proportional to the increases or decreases in what might be called the mathematical reasons for belief", Ibid.

30. Ibid.

31. See *La criminalité comparée*, p. 79; *Essais et mélanges sociologiques*, p. 265 and also pp. 236 ff.

32. ". . . it is only beyond a certain level of intensity that a growing desire becomes an act, or that a decreasing desire suddenly unveils and unleashes a contrary desire previously held in check." *Les lois de l'imitation*, pp. 115–16. See also *Essais et mélanges sociologiques*, p. 266: "In general, when belief verges on its maximum or on certainty, the rate of increase slows down markedly. In the sciences one can observe strong resistance to the definite statement of a theory which was nevertheless accepted as being *practically* proven when the facts it explained were only half as numerous. Every day one finds new facts which are favourable to the transformist or atomistic hypotheses but the faith of their adherents is far from being increased as much as it was by the discovery of much less conclusive facts. From simple indices, Newton was *practically* convinced of the law-like status of his conjecture. Since then, astronomical observations have multiplied the proofs of his theory a hundred times and the faith of the experts in it has been unable to grow a hundred times stronger." See also *Les lois de l'imitation*, p. 29.

33. *Essais et mélanges sociologiques*, p. 266.

34. See, for example, Daval *Traité de psychologie sociale*, Vol. I, Chapter III, "Les échelles d'attitude" (Paris: Presses Universitaires de France, 1963).

35. Although the formation of the concepts "belief" and "desire" is obviously related to the importance which he attributed to the processes of persuasion and decision-

making, Tarde did, in order to convince himself of their quantitative character, attempt to give them a status analogous to space-time in Kantian philosophy, that is a form *a priori* to internal feelings: "Firstly, at the basis of internal phenomena, whatever they may be, analysis pushed to the farthest limit comes up against these irreducible terms, belief, desire and their point of application, pure feeling, derived by abstraction and hypothesis from the mass of propositions and volitions with which it is associated; secondly, the first two terms are the innate and constitutive forms or forces of the subject, the moulds which receive the raw materials of sensation." *Essais et mélanges sociologiques*, p. 240. The analogy with Kantianism which Tarde frequently made, at least by way of Renouvier, is striking. But, in the end, Tarde had to recognise that this kind of metaphysical discussion was useless and that the importance of "belief" and "desire" derives principally from the importance for social psychology of the mechanisms of decision-making and persuasion: "I now recognise that I have possibly slightly exaggerated the role of *believing* and *desiring* in individual psychology, and I would no longer dare to claim with such assurance that these two aspects of the *self* are more or less the only susceptible ones. But I do nevertheless attribute them with ever-growing importance in social psychology," *Les lois de l'imitation*, p. 157n.

36. *Essais et mélanges sociologiques*, p. 260.
37. "It is obvious, I confess, that this method is quite impracticable", *Essais et mélanges sociologiques*, p. 261; "a psychological statistics, if it were practically possible. . . .", quoted in Chapter 4, note 27; yet "although it would be difficult to make, it is quite possible to imagine an approximate measure of even individual beliefs and desires if most people felt the need for it in addition to measurements of opinion and general attitudes", *Essais et mélanges sociologiques*, p. 266. See also *Les lois de l'imitation*, p. 148: "At the present time, statistics is no more than a kind of embryonic eye."
38. This wish has been fulfilled: several years after the above was written, Terry Clark published an excellent collection of selected pieces under the title *Gabriel Tarde, on Communication and social influence* (Chicago: The University of Chicago Press, 1969). A second wish remains to be expressed: that Tarde makes the return journey across the Atlantic.

CHAPTER 5

1. Introduction to Paul Lazarsfeld, *Philosophie des sciences sociales* (Paris: Gallimard, 1970), first published under the title "A propos d'un livre imaginaire". We have made no attempt to rid the article of those features which derive from its introductory character. We apologise to the reader for references to texts which will obviously not be found here.
2. On p. 279 of *Perspectives in American History*, Vol. II, 1968, pp. 270–337.
3. "Les relations entre proprietes individuelles et proprietes collectives" (with H. Menzel) in R. Boudon and P. Lazarsfeld, *L'analyse empirique de la causalité* (Paris: Mouton, 1967) pp. 41–51, especially p. 51.
4. In J. Charlesworth (ed.), *Mathematics and the Social Sciences* (Philadelphia: The American Academy of Political and Social Science, 1963) pp. 95–121.
5. (Glencoe: The Free Press, 1962).
6. Op. cit.

7. "An episode . . . ," op. cit., p. 282.
8. Ibid.
9. Ibid.
10. H. Blumer "Public opinion and public opinion polling", *American Sociological Review*, 13, 1948, pp. 542–54.
11. As Lazarsfeld is careful to point out, certain notions in the natural sciences, like magnetism, are not unlike the dispositional concepts of the human sciences.
12. *The Uses of Sociology*, published in association with H. Wilensky and W. Sewell (New York: Basic Books, 1967).
13. See for example Ernst Nagel, "Measurement", *Erkenntnis*, I, pp. 313–35.
14. "*The American Soldier*, an expository review", *Public Opinion Quarterly*, Vol. XIII, Autumn 1949.

CHAPTER 6

1. Paper delivered in 1968 to the Société de philosophie at Bordeaux and published in the *Revue philosophique*, Vol. 94, No. 3–4, 1969, pp. 303–18 with the title "Pour une philosophie des sciences sociales".
2. "What is dialectic?" in *Conjectures and Refutations* (London: Routledge & Kegan Paul, 1963).
3. "Typological methods in the natural and human sciences" in *Aspects of Scientific Explanation* (New York: The Free Press, 1965).
4. See Paul Lazarsfeld, "La philosophie de la science et la recherche sociale empirique", *Les Etudes philosophiques*, No. 4, 1964, October–December, reproduced in *Philosophie des sciences sociales* (Paris: Gallimard, 1970) pp. 480–93.
5. "Social Behaviour as Exchange", *American Journal of Sociology*, 62(1958) pp. 697–706.
6. *Models of Man* (New York: Wiley, 1957).
7. In *Gesammelte Aufsätze Wissenschaftslehre* (2. Auflage, Tübingen, Mohr, 1951).
8. Don Martindale, "Limits to the uses of mathematics in the study of sociology", in *Mathematics and the Social Sciences*, Philadelphia, American Academy of Political and Social Science, June 1963.
9. *Pensée formelle et sciences de l'homme* (Paris: Aubier, 1960).
10. *Elements de theorie et de methode sociologique* (Paris: Plon, 2nd edn., 1965).
11. Cf. Chapter 8.
12. Kingsley Davis, " The Myth of Functionalism as a Special Method in Sociology and Anthropology", *American Sociological Review*, 24 (1959) pp. 757–773; Carl Hempel, "The Logic of Functional Analysis" in *Aspects of Scientific Explanation* (Glencoe: The Free Press, 1965) pp. 297–330; Ernest Nagel, *Logic without Metaphysics* (Glencoe: The Free Press, 1960).
13. See Chapter 8.
14. Leslie White, "Definitions and Conceptions of Culture" in G. Direnzo, *Concepts, Theory and Explanation in the Behavioural Sciences* (New York: Random House, 1966).
15. Cf. R. Boudon, *Modèles et méthodes mathématiques dans les sciences humaines*, Unesco.

CHAPTER 7

1. This article was published in the *European Journal of Sociology*, XI (1970), pp. 201–51 with the title "Notes sur la notion de théorie dans les science sociales".
2. (Glencoe: The Free Press, 1949). The reference here is to pp. 85–101.
3. Ibid., pp. 96–7.
4. Howard Becker and Albin Boskoff *Modern Sociological Theory* (New York: The Dryden Press, 1957); Llewlyn Gross (ed.), *Symposium on Sociological Theory* (Evanston: Row, Peterson and Co., 1959); Talcott Parsons and Edward Shils (eds.) *Theories of Society* (Glencoe: The Free Press, 1961).
5. George Zipf, "The P^2P^1/D Hypotheses: on the intercity movement of persons", *American Sociological Review*, XI (1946), pp. 677–86; Thorsten Hägerstrand, "A Monte-Carlo Approach to Diffusion", *Archives européenes de sociologie*, VI (1965), pp. 43–57; Samuel Stouffer, "Intervening Opportunities: a theory relating mobility and distance", *American Sociological Review*, V (1940) pp. 845–67.
6. Perhaps this is a general law of scientific development. Mathematical biology borrowed a great deal from physics, at least in the beginning, as did economics. Sometimes the analogies are unfortunate (Descartes's machine–animals).
7. Op. cit.
8. See, for example, N. T. Bailey, *The Mathematical Theory of Epidemics* (London: Griffin, 1957).
9. Homans is not alone in this. In Parsons there is a much-debated attempt to reduce certain sociological concepts (power, influence, etc.) to economic concepts (exchange, money, etc.). On this point see, for example, F. Chazel, "Reflections sur la conception du pouvôir et de l'influence", *Revue française de sociologie*, V (1964) pp. 387–401.
10. See for example Martin Shubik, *Game Theory and Related Approaches to Social Behaviour* (New York: Wiley, 1964).
11. Cf. Pierre Auger, "Les modèles dans la science", *Diogene*, LII (1965) pp. 3–15.
12. Sometimes, certain theoretical paradigms which involve an artificial reality have been given the name of "models". Systematic study of this notion of "model" needs to be carried out but here we can do no more than signal its importance.
13. Merton, op. cit. pp. 50 ff.
14. Ibid., pp. 72ff.
15. A. R. Radcliffe-Brown, *The Andaman Islanders* (Glencoe: The Free Press, 1948).
16. We shall see later how it is possible to give a precise definition of the validity/truth distinction.
17. P. F. Lazarsfeld and A. H. Barton, "Some Functions of Qualitative Analysis in Social Research", *Frankfurter Beiträge zur Soziologie*, I (1955), pp. 321–61.
18. Talcott Parsons, "General Theory in Sociology" in R. Merton et al., *Sociology Today* (New York: Harper, 1959), pp. 3–38.
19. French translation by F. Bourricaud in *Eléments pour une sociologie de l'action* (Paris: Plon, 1955). Cf. T. Parsons, *Essays in Sociological Theory*, Revised Edn. (Glencoe: The Free Press, 1954) pp. 386–439.
20. T. Parsons *Essays* . . . op. cit. pp. 406–7.
21. In *Sociology Today*, the book we referred to earlier, Parsons attempts to give an account of why sociology, no less than other sciences, cannot be content with recording facts but must incorporate them instead within a more general language. In physics, this language has a mathematical form. What Parsons wished to create for

sociology was a language with a function like that of mathematics in physics. His discussion possibly helps to shed light on the vexed question of the existence, the possibility or the necessity of a general theory in sociology. Indeed, it demonstrates the importance of theory for the development of sociology. All the same, it is not clear why theoretical research should necessarily take the form of a *conceptual* paradigm, however general it may be. Parsons's later work, including his fascination for economic theory and cybernetics, reveals a movement away from paradigms of a conceptual kind towards formal and theoretical paradigms. Doubtless a whole variety of paradigms including these will contribute to the development of the "general theory" which Parsons has in mind.

22. On this subject, cf. Paul Lazarsfeld, "Concept Formation and Measurement in the Behavioural Sciences: some historical observations" in G. Direnzo, *Concepts, Theory and Explanation in the Behavioural Sciences* (New York: Random House, 1966). French translation in P. Lazarsfeld *Philosophie des sciences sociales* (Paris: Gallimard, 1970).

23. On this, see for example Hubert and Ann Blalock (eds.), *Methodology in Survey Research* (New York: McGraw Hill, 1968).

24. Cf. for example the chapters on linguistics in D. Luce et al., *Handbook of Mathematical Psychology* (New York: Wiley, 1963) and on generative grammars in N. Ruwet, *Introduction a la grammaire generative* (Paris: Plon, 1968).

25. Admittedly the notion of a "singular phenomenon" poses some rather tricky logical problems. To the extent that it is explained by subsumption beneath universal propositions, a phenomenon of this sort always presupposes a more or less implicit comparative analysis. Thus, deTocqueville accounts for the singular features of French society by constant reference to other societies, especially Anglo–Saxon societies.

26. Cf. A. Rapoport, "Mathematical Aspects of General System Analysis" in *Les sciences sociales, problèmes et orientations* (Paris/La Haye: Mouton/Unesco, 1968).

27. We have attempted a very small-scale analysis of this kind in our observations on the notion of function *Revue française de sociologie*, VIII (1967), pp. 198–206. Reproduced in this volume, Chapter 8.

28. (Vienna: Springer, 1935). Enlarged English edn.: *The Logic of Scientific Discovery* (New York: Hutchinson, 1959). See also *Conjectures and Refutations* (London: Routledge and Kegan Paul, 1963).

29. However, this observation too has its own limits. It is by no means certain that singular propositions *do* exist, even in history. Singular propositions actually need to be seen as steps in the historian's procedure for establishing more general propositions.

30. This observation is similarly valid only as a first approximation. If one looks at mathematics from a historical rather than a logical point of view, it is possible to find evidence of processes of confrontation between existing theories and counter-examples which entail an extension of the theoretical framework.

31. Parsons, *Essays*, op. cit. pp. 435–6. Some of these applications of the Parsonian theory of stratification are not Parsons's but our own.

32. Ibid., pp. 416–17.

33. Cf. R. Dahrendorf, *Demokratie und Gesellschaft in Deutschland* (Munich: Piper, 1967); A. Inkeles and P. Rossi, "National Comparisons of Occupational Prestige", *American Journal of Sociology*, LXVI (1956) pp. 329–39.

34. Alexis deTocqueville, *L'Ancien Régime et la Révolution* (Paris: Gallimard, 1952) pp.

229–32. English translation *The Ancien Regime and the French Revolution* (London: Collins/Fontana, 1966) pp. 160–63.

35. On this subject, cf. G. Homans, *The Nature of Social Science* (New York: Harcourt, Brace and World, 1967).

36. With this we re-encounter the famous opposition between *Erklären* and *Verstehen* (explanation and understanding). It should be noted however that "psychological" relationships can be verified empirically. Our reason for not using the conventional language at this point is in order to signal the *complementarity* of the elements which are normally opposed. This would appear to be the path of genuine progress in the social sciences.

37. See for example C. Cherry, *On Human Communication* (New York: Wiley, 1957), and R. Jakobson, *Essais de linguistique générale* (Paris: Minuit, 1963).

38. See for example, H. Selvin, "Aspects méthodologiques du suicide" in R. Boudon and P. Lazarsfeld, *L'analyse empirique de la causalité* (Paris: Monton, 1966) pp. 276–91.

39. Difficult, but not impossible. In principle the measurement techniques developed in the social sciences can be applied just as well to subjective value judgements about a scientific theory as to other types of attitude. With the anticipation of genius, G. Tarde envisaged an experimental epistemology in which one could measure the weight of conviction pertaining to scientific theories (cf. "La croyance et le désir" in *Essais et mélanges sociologiques* (Paris: Masson, 1895). See also V. Pareto *Traité de sociologie générale* (Geneva: Droz, 1968) pp. 64, § 60: "When a very large number of deductions from a hypothesis have been verified by experiment it becomes *extremely probable* that a further deduction will likewise be verified." (Our stress).

40. *Le suicide* (Paris: Presses Universitaires de France, 1960) pp. 174 ff.

41. *Les structures élémentaires de la parenté* (Paris: Presses Universitaires de la France, 1948).

42. This example is interesting for more than one reason. This *ad hoc* theory, which today seems to be inexcusably naive, was popular in its day. In retrospect, it allows us to assess the amount of risk involved in accepting a theory of this kind and shows that epistemologically, the criterion of refutability has no meaning except in combination with the notion of structural complexity associated with (q).

43. Obviously, by *positive* epistemology we are not referring to *positivist* epistemology. What we have in mind when using the term *positive* epistemology is an epistemology based on the positive and systematic analysis of scientific output rather than *a priori*, that is a discipline with an approach which is more reminiscent of science than philosophy.

44. This is a more detailed and systematic reiteration of a theme which we sketched out in an analysis of structuralism in *A quoi sert la notion de structure?* (Paris: Gallimard, 1968): English translation, *The Uses of Structuralism* (London: Heinemann, 1971).

45. This observation suggests a precise distinction between the two terms *validity* and *level of verification* applied to a theory.

46. See references in notes 24 and 48.

47. This is a very succint summary of a series of developments made by Chomsky and Miller. Cf. D. Luce, op. cit. Vol II, Chapter II, "Introduction to the formal analysis of natural languages".

48. Cf. N. Chomsky, "Explanation models in linguistics" in E. Nagel et al., *Logic, Methodology and Philosophy of Science* (Stanford: University Press, 1962) pp. 528–50.

49. In any case, this class of facts requires scientific *elaboration*, whilst that of Chomsky

and Miller is given by nature. This process of elaboration could itself be the object of an interesting epistemological enquiry.

50. Lazarsfeld is unjustifiably harsh towards Durkheim in *Concept formation* . . . , op. cit. It is true that Durkheim has a very traditional idea of the concept of *definition* and that, unlike Max Weber, he never conceived of a logical instrument to replace the logic of classes. But on a different level, he did appreciate the great importance for theorisation of a precise definition of the *class* of facts to be explained.

51. The literature on this subject is so abundant that we will simply mention one good modern reference: Blalock and Blalock, op. cit.

52. Selvin, op. cit.

53. *Les causes du suicide* (Paris: Alcan, 1930).

54. *The Social Structure* (Glencoe: The Free Press, 1965).

55. Ibid., p. 145.

56. S. M. Lipset, *Agrarian Socialism* (Berkeley, 1950). Quoted by Lazarsfeld and Barton, op. cit.

57. R. Boudon *Les méthodes en sociologie* (Paris: Presses Universitaires de France, 1969).

58. The case of the notion of system is significant in this respect. It is used by the natural sciences and by the social sciences. It first appeared in the form of a conceptual paradigm but was subsequently transformed into more complex paradigms (cybernetics, systems theory, for example). As far as the natural sciences are concerned, the *conceptual* phase of this paradigm belongs to the realm of history. For the human sciences, this conceptual phase is an integral part of their texture, as discussions of structuralism show.

CHAPTER 8

1. This article was published in the *Revue française de sociologie*, VIII, 1967, pp. 198–206, with the title "Remarques sur la notion de fonction".

2. C. Hempel in L. Gross (ed.), *Symposium on Sociological Theory* Evanston, Ill. 1959).

3. Kingsley Davis, "The Myth of Functionalism as a Special Method in Sociology and Anthropology", *American Sociological Review*, 24 (1959), pp. 757–73.

4. Karl Popper, *Logik der Forschung* (Vienna: Julius Springer, 1935). Enlarged English edn.: *The Logic of Scientific Discovery* (New York: Harper, 1959).

5. The reason why most formal systems embody the principle of non-contradiction is simply that, if they did not, it would be possible to show that any proposition could follow from any other proposition.

6. Note that when present day mathematicians describe a "self-evident" proof, they use the qualifier "trivial" precisely in order to avoid the ambiguity of the notion of evidence.

7. A. R. Radcliffe-Brown, "On the Concept of Function in Social Science", *American Anthropologist* 37, July–September 1935, p. 394.

8. Robert K. Merton *Social Theory and Social Structure* (Glencoe, Ill. The Free Press, 1949).

9. Radcliffe-Brown, op. cit., p. 397.

10. *Ibid.*

11. Talcott Parsons, *The Social system* (Glencoe, Ill.: The Free Press, 1951)p. 177.

12. *Ibid.*, p. 178.

13. *Ibid.*

14. Notice that the form of argumentation in this example is free from ambiguity. However, to the extent that the terms corresponding to the symbols A, B, $a, b \ldots, n$, $a', b', \ldots, m$ are inadequately explained and poorly defined in Parsons's account, it cannot be said that this is a truly rigorous argument.

15. The relativisation of the notion of function is less directly obvious in Merton than in Parsons. This has to do with the fact that, for the most part, Parsons's analyses are general, whilst those of Merton relate to particular examples. However, an example like Merton's analysis of the *functions* of the American political machine reveals a structure of argument which is similar to Parsons's. In formal terms, it would look like this (taking only a few of Merton's arguments):

   In a society which has visibly underprivileged classes and in which inequality is not accepted, there is a collective demand for the organisation of social welfare.

   In a society where the political power of parties depends on electoral strength, the parties will have an interest in meeting collective needs which are not satisfied by other structures.

   In a society which has the above features and where public authorities cannot meet a collective need, there is every chance that these needs will be satisfied by the parties' "political machine".

   This argument clearly involves showing that certain features of the society in question (in this case American society) imply the existence of certain social needs, whilst the nature of official political structures prevents them from satisfying these needs. And since the society in question is one where use is made of every need, it can be deduced that the political parties will effectively ensure this "exploitation" because they have a prime interest in doing so.

   It would be possible to reformulate the whole of Merton's reasoning in the same way. It would reveal that the notion of function could be avoided and that it actually breaks down into a sequence of propositions which constitute a hypothetico–deductive argument. This argument could be set out by a sociologist who had not the slightest knowledge of the existence of the word function.

16. Notice incidentally that structural–functional accounts which can actually be formalised are those which aim to show the *impossibility* of the co-occurrence of two elements within a social system. Thus the argument from Parsons which we used earlier for purposes of illustration can be summarised symbolically as follows:

$$A \rightarrow a, b, \ldots, n$$
$$B \rightarrow a', b', \ldots, m$$
$$a \rightarrow \bar{a}', \text{ etc.}$$

Hence: $A \rightarrow \overline{B}$

It is obviously much more difficult to conceive of an argument leading to the conclusion that $A \rightarrow B$. We cannot get involved here in a formal discussion of the difference between demonstrating the *impossibility* and demonstrating the *necessity* of the co-occurrence of certain elements within a system. Nevertheless, it does seem that contemporary structural–functionalism is vaguely aware of this asymmetry: like the example from Parsons, the majority of its proofs are negative (demonstrations of impossibility), whilst the proofs of classical functionalism are usually pseudo-demonstrations of necessity (non-formalisable demonstrations which·cannot avoid using the concept of function).

CHAPTER 9

1. This article was first published in the *Archivs européennes de sociologie*, IV, (1963) pp. 191–218 with the title "Quelques fonctions de la formalisation en sociologie".
2. P. Sorokin, *Tendances et deboires de la sociologie americaine* (Paris: Aubier, 1959).
3. Thurstone has paid some attention to the problem in his work on paired comparisons; see W. Torgerson, *Theory and Methods of Scaling* (New York: Wiley, 1958). The idea used here comes from M. G. Kendall, "Further contributions to the theory of paired comparisons", *Biometrics*, II (1955), p. 43. It is taken up by Claude Berge, *La theorie des graphes et ses applications* (Paris Dunod, 1958), pp. 128 ff.
4. To obtain the unit in the ith row and the jth column which is the product of two matrices, A and B, multiply the first unit of the ith row of A with the first unit of the jth column of B, the second unit of the ith row of A with the second unit of the jth column of B, and so on until the final unit and then add up these products.
5. $P^*(A_i)$ is obtained by finding the ratio $P^{(4)}(A_t)/(P^{(4)}(A_1) + P^{(4)}(A_2) + \ldots + P^{(4)}(A_1))$. As can be seen, the values of P^* are more or less identical if they are calculated from $P^{(3)}$, $P^{(4)}$, $P^{(5)}$. . . . This property, which means that, for certain matrices, the distribution of the marginal quantities remains unchanged when it is raised to increasingly higher powers has been used in very different contexts, not only in Markov learning processes, but also in the analysis of groups. See Paul Lazarsfeld and Robert K. Merton, "Friendship as social process: a substantive and methodological analysis" in Morroe Berger et al., *Freedom and Control in Modern Societies* (New York: Van Nostrand, 1954) pp. 16–66.
6. See Leon Festiger, "Matrix analysis of group structures" in P. Lazarsfeld and Morris Rosenberg, *The Language of Social Research* (Glencoe: The Free Press, 1955) pp. 357–68.
7. See Raymond Boudon, "Propriétés individuelles et propriétés collectives: un probléme d'analyse ècologique", *Revue française de sociologie*. IV,(1963) pp. 275–99.
8. The theorem which is expressed in the equation (2a. 4) is presented in a different form by W. Robinson in "Ecological correlation and the behaviour of individuals", *American Sociological Review*, XV (1950), pp. 351–357. See also P. Lazarsfeld, "The algebra of dichotomous systems" in H. Solomon *Studies in Item Analysis and Prediction* (Stanford: Stanford University Press, 1961).
9. Herbert Simon, *Models of Man* (New York: Wiley, 1957) Chapter VI: "A formal theory of interactions in social groups".
10. Ibid., Chapter VII: "Mechanisms involved in pressures toward uniformity in groups" and "Mechanisms involved in group-pressures on deviate members".
11. Richard McCleery, "Policy change in prison management"; Allan Barton and Bo Anderson, "Change in an organisational system: formalisation of a qualitative study" in A.Etzioni *Complex Organisations* (New York: Holt, Rinehart and Winston, 1961).
12. The model used here is derived from an analysis of secular criminological trends carried out in conjuction with A. Davidovitch.
13. In the case where S_1 and S_2 represent two stages in a system of occupational selection, the "valid" elements are the best suited; if S_1 is the court and S_2 the examining magistrate, the "valid" elements are cases which give grounds for prosecution; if S_1 is the public prosecutor and S_2 the bench, the "valid" elements correspond to conviction and "non-valid" elements to acquitals.
14. See for example S. Goldberg, *Introduction to difference equations* (New York: Wiley, 1958).

15. To clarify this notion, take a very simple model in which the value of a variable at t is proportional to its value at the previous moment in time: $V_t = aV_{t-1}$. Applying the equation for successive values of t one obtains: $V_1 = aV_0$; $V_2 = aV_1$; $= a^2V_0 \ldots$; $V_t = a^tV_0$. Bearing in mind the original value of V, the behaviour of the system through time depends on the *structural parameter* a: it is possible to identify typical values of a which correspond to types of system behaviour. If a is negative, for example, it is obvious that the system will be oscillatory; if it is positive, and less than 1, the system will tend towards stable equilibrium; if it is greater than 1, V will assume increasingly large values as time proceeds.

16. Although the "*verstehen*" approach developed by Dilthey, Rickert, etc. is no longer very fashionable, there are still many authors who, implicitly or explicitly, have the idea that social facts are by their very nature immediately graspable. It would be easy to cite a whole range of similar examples where *Verstehende Sociologie* could be caught unawares.

17. If we may be allowed to elaborate this point by quoting Levi-Strauss: "Following Rousseau, and quite conclusively in my view, Marx taught that the social sciences are no longer based on physical events using sense data: the aim is to construct a model, to study its properties and its different responses in the laboratory situation, in order to apply these observations to the interpretation of what occurs empirically, which may be very far from what is expected." *Tristes tropiques* (Paris: Plon, 1955) p. 49.

18. Cf. G. Gurvitch, "La conscience collective dans la sociologie de Durkheim", in *Essais de sociologie* (Paris: Sirey, 1939).

19. Cf. A. Vierkandt, *Gesellschaftslehre* (Stuttgart: 1923).

20. For example: "(. . .) a being, psychic if you will, but constituting a psychic individuality of a new sort." *Régles de la methode sociologique* (Paris: Presses Universitaires de France, 1950) p. 103; English edn. (trans.), *The Rules of Sociological Method* (New York: The Free Press, 1964) p. 103.

21. The reflections which follow are inspired by the work of James A. Davis. See especially: "The effects of group composition; a technique of analysis", *American Sociological Review*, XXVI (1961).

22. *De la division du travail social* (Paris: Alcan, 1893) p. 84.

CHAPTER 10

1. This article was first published in *Annales*, Vol. 24, No. 3, May–June 1969 with the title "La crise universitaire française: Essai de diagnostic sociologique".

2. R. Poignant, *L'enseignement dans les pays du Marché Commun* (Institut Pedagogique National, 1965), p. 232.

3. N. Bisseret, "La 'naissance' et le diplôme: le processus de sélection au début des études universitaires", *Revue Française de Sociologie*, Vol. 9, 1968, numero spécial, pp. 185–207 and "Carrière scolaire d'une cohorte d'étudiants inscrits en 1962 à la faculté des Lettres de Paris: les filières d'orientation et les facteurs de réussite" *Rapport Convention Ministère Education Nationale*, June 1968, mimeo.

4. C. Delage, *La naissance d'une université, Orléans*, 3rd cycle dissertation, typescript.

5. Kath, Ochler, Reichwein, *Studienweg und Studienerfolg*, Institut für Bildungsforschung, Max Planck Gesellschaft, Heft 6 (Berlin, 1966).

6. M. Vermot-Gauchy, *L'éducation nationale dans la France de demain* (Paris: S.E.D.E.I.S., 1965).

7. P. Oléron, "Opinions d'étudiants en psychologie sur leurs études et leur future profession", *Bulletin de Psychologie*, 255, XX 6–7, January 1967, pp. 329–345 and P. Oléron, M. Moulinou, "Données statistiques sur un échantillon d'étudiants en psychologie," *Bulletin de Psychologie*, 263, XXI, October 1967, pp. 1–4.

8. See, for example, *Quelle université, quelle société?* (Paris: Seuil, 1968): a collection of articles published by students in May and June 1968.

9. See, for example, P. Bourdieu and J. Passeron, *Les Héritiers* (Paris: Seuil, 1965).

10. A. Girard and P. Clerc, "Nouvelles données sur l'orientation scolaire au moment d'entrée en sixième", *Population*, October–December 1964, No. 5, pp. 820–64; A. Sauvy and A. Girard, "Les diverses classes sociales devant l'enseignement", *Population*, March–April 1965, No. 2, pp. 205–32.

11. As a result, a system of selective recruitment combined with a system of bursaries would make a *direct* and significant contribution to the democratisation of university education. In this context it is worth noting that the English universities, in which democratisation (measured by the proportion of sons and daughters of working class parents who reach higher education) is more advanced than in other western European countries, use the selective system and are the only ones to do so. Whilst they may convey the stereotype of the class-based university, this is largely because of the difference between the social composition of "Oxbridge" and the "redbrick" universities. It may even be the case that this factor also contributes to democratisation. For instance, the superiority of lower class students seems to be appreciably greater in Orléans than Paris and social recruitment is lower in Orléans than in Paris. However, the contextual influence of social composition on differential achievement in terms of social background remains a hypothesis requiring systematic confirmation.

12. N. Bisseret, "Carrière scolaire d'une cohorte d'étudiants inscrits en 1962 à la faculté des Lettres de Paris: les filières d'orientation et les facteurs de réussite", *Rapport Convention Ministère Education Nationale*, June 1968, mimeo.

13. This finding and those which follow are taken from reports written by post-graduate students at the Sorbonne (Mmes Faugeron, Netter, Valetas, M. Mazloum).

14. A. Touraine (*Le mouvement de mai ou le communisme utopique*, Paris, Seuil, 1969) maintains that the May movement is a social movement analogous to the nineteenth century labour movement. The "programmed" society gives rise to class conflicts of a new kind in which the technicians, the "professionals", etc. are opposed to the technocrats. I see a difficulty in this argument, namely that many technicians and "professionals" were untouched by the May movement. Further, it could be shown quite easily that in a great many cases, conflicts and strikes took the classical form of wage claims instead of pre-figuring new types of social movement. On the other hand, it is true that the technical and "professional" occupations are taking up an increasingly large proportion of those jobs which are semi-integrated into the employing organisations (research officers etc.). From one point of view, my conclusion would be similar to Touraine's, for it is true that the "programmed" societies seem to create new forms of alienation. But this kind of alienation looks much more like Durkheimian anomie than Marxian alienation. From another point of view, it is hard to believe that the data support the idea that the students were revolting against the future "technicians" or "professionals" which society was forcing them to becoming. It seems to be much simpler and more true to the evidence to interpret it as a revolt against the semi-professionalisation and social marginalisation which many students and cadres are exposed to, rather than as a

revolt against the programmed society. Compared with explanation in terms of alienation, the explanation in terms of anomie also has the advantage of giving an account of the "psychodramatic" character of the revolt.

15. P. Coombs, *La Crise mondiale de l'éducation* (Paris: Presses Universitaires de France, 1968).

16. These observations echo both P. Sorokin's (Social Mobility (1927) in *Social and Cultural Mobility*, London, Macmillan, 1959) theory of mobility and H. Schelsky's (*Schule und Erziehung in der industriellen Gesellschaft*, Würzburg, Werkbund Verlag, 1957) analysis.

17. See B. R. Clark, "The 'cooling-out' function in higher education" in A. H. Halsey et al., *Education, Economy and Society* (London: Macmillan, 1961) pp. 513–23.

Name Index

277

Subject Index